PRAISE FOR *LUDICROUS*

"*Ludicrous* is a revealing look at Tesla's tumultuous history from the internet's leading Tesla skeptic."

—TIMOTHY LEE, reporter at Ars Technica

"Ed Niedermeyer's deep dive into Tesla reveals the complex, fascinating, and often frustrating world of a company that has achieved great heights and is at risk of an even bigger fall. This isn't a book for the faint of heart. It lays bare all of Tesla—including the flaws and scar tissue—giving an unadulterated view of an enigmatic company and its rise from unknown upstart to a high-profile global automaker."

—KIRSTEN KOROSEC, senior reporter at TechCrunch

"The Tesla book we need, but don't deserve."

—ALEX ROY, founder of the Human Driving Association and author of *The Driver: My Dangerous Pursuit of Speed and Truth in the Outlaw Racing World*

"Tesla's public coming out party in 2016 roughly corresponded to the beginning of my own automotive journalism career and like Ed, I've written way too many words about the company and its problematic CEO, Elon Musk. It's a tough company to cover in part because of aggressive fan base that has developed into a cult of personality around Musk himself. Tesla has probably done more to improve the public vehicle electrification than any other company. Unfortunately, while the erratic and troubled CEO has many fascinating ideas from reusable rockets to hyperloops to ludicrously quick electric sedans and SUVs, his refusal to cede control to competent people that can execute has caused the company endless headaches. Ed has taken on the challenge of chronicling a company that prefers to only be discussed by its fans in an even-handed way that covers what went right and what failed. It's a fascinating read, especially for those that have only read the superficial coverage in most of the media or the bickering on twitter."

—SAM ABUELSAMID, principal mobility research analyst at Navigant Research

LUDICROUS

LUDICROUS

THE UNVARNISHED STORY OF **TESLA** MOTORS

EDWARD NIEDERMEYER

BenBella Books, Inc.
Dallas, TX

Copyright © 2019 by Edward Niedermeyer

BenBella Books, Inc
10440 N. Central Expressway, Suite 800
Dallas, TX 75231
www.benbellabooks.com
Send feedback to feedback@benbellabooks.com

Printed in the United States of America
10 9 8 7 6 5 4 3 2 1

Library of Congress Cataloging-in-Publication Control Number: 2019009578
ISBN 9781948836128 (trade cloth)
ISBN 9781948836326 (ebook)

Editing by Claire Schulz
Copyediting by Scott Calamar
Proofreading by Greg Teague and Cape Cod Compositors, Inc.
Indexing by WordCo Indexing Services, Inc.
Text design by Aaron Edmiston
Text composition by Katie Hollister
Cover design by Kara Klontz
Cover photo by Alessio Lin on Unsplash
Author photo by Sharad Vegda
Printed by Lake Book Manufacturing
Distributed to the trade by Two Rivers Distribution, an Ingram brand
www.tworiversdistribution.com

Special discounts for bulk sales (minimum of 25 copies) are available.
Please contact bulkorders@benbellabooks.com

For Andrea

CONTENTS

NOTE TO READERS

Writing this book has been the greatest challenge of my professional career. Tesla's story not only sprawls across a broad variety of complex subjects, it's also permeated with nuance that tends to get lost in the polarized public debates it inspires.

To say that this story had a few twists and turns in the years since I started working on this book would be a wild understatement. To the company's fans, Tesla has always appeared on the brink of total domination, while to its skeptics, it has always been on the edge of complete collapse. Each new development, positive and negative, tends to send perceptions and expectations soaring or sinking and can easily appear to reshape the narrative arc of Tesla's history.

The auto industry is one of the most complex and challenging businesses possible; new entrants face particularly steep obstacles. That worldview has always informed my coverage of all automakers, not just Tesla. But, perhaps misunderstanding my cautious perspective, Tesla fans have often categorized me as a "hater" and characterized my work as an attempt to destroy the company they love. Almost as soon as I began seriously writing about Tesla, I received heated attacks, first from its fans and investors, and later (just as I was starting to work on this book) from the company itself.

I usually avoid injecting myself into my writing because I want my work to stand or fall on its merits alone (and also partly because I don't believe I am particularly interesting). But because the majority of these attacks focus on my perceived motivations rather than the substance of my reporting and analysis, I feel that I have little choice but to explain how I came to my perspective on this story. In hopes of limiting this distracting speculation about my motivations, I will share my personal experiences at times in this book.

Tesla's ruthlessly personal approach to public relations, and the similarly aggressive fan culture it has inspired, also explains why there are essentially no named sources in this book. Hundreds of hours of interviews with then current and former Tesla employees, executives, directors, and partners went into this book, and almost every one asked for some form of anonymity out of fear of retribution by the company. Numerous anecdotes and data points have been left out at their request, lest they betray a source's identity.

As frustrating as it is not to be able to share some of these richly illustrative (and often wildly entertaining) stories or show how well-informed these sources are, I can't blame any of them for speaking only on the condition of anonymity. Having seen so many actual and potential Tesla whistleblowers smeared, sued, and intimidated, I believe their fears are reasonable. Under the circumstances, the fact that any of them risked their personal and professional well-being to share their stories with me at all speaks to their courage and conviction. I owe them all the deepest thanks, and I only wish they could receive the credit they so richly deserve.

INTRODUCTION

When I started studying and writing about the auto industry in 2008, I had no idea that cars and mobility were on the precipice of fundamental change. I was simply a kid who had left college at the wrong time and couldn't even get work waiting tables, thanks to the fact that the economy was crashing down around me. My dad, a lifelong car guy, spent his spare time writing for an automotive blog called *The Truth About Cars* (*TTAC*) that had made its name predicting the downfall of the Detroit automakers, and when the opportunity was offered, I agreed to start freelancing there.

Within months of diving into the woestruck auto industry, I realized that I had lucked into one of the most fascinating and underappreciated subjects in modern life. Cars, it turned out, are more than just the expensive consumer goods I had always thought them to be; they are a cornerstone of our material culture that touches almost every aspect of society. From aesthetics and engineering to history, politics, economics, the environment, trade, and urban development, the auto industry was a lens through which I could explore a wealth of complex topics and ideas.

That year was also the perfect time to learn about the hidden forces that govern the auto industry. The entire sector was in the process of blowing up as the one-two punch of an economic downturn and soaring gas prices collided with the industry's structural issues and individual automakers' cultural and strategic problems. Diagnosing the ills that had led up to the bankruptcy and bailout of GM and Chrysler, and analyzing their subsequent public open-heart surgeries, was an object lesson in the brutal realities of a uniquely capital-intensive yet low-margin business. The allure of cars themselves is what typically brings people into the auto industry's orbit, but in my case it was the complex system of people and ideas that make and define cars that sucked me in.

I threw myself into a process of intense self-education, reading everything I could find about cars and the auto business and synthesizing what I learned into blog posts. In my first year on the job, I became *TTAC*'s managing editor, in my second year I became its editor-in-chief, and by the start of my third year, I had been asked to contribute an op-ed to the *New York Times*. The subject that I never would have picked as a lifelong obsession was turning into a career that I never could have planned.

Over the course of the last eleven years, I've been lucky enough to share my ongoing self-education with the readers of the *Wall Street Journal*, Bloomberg View, The Daily Beast, *Automotive News*, and others. Having started my career by casting a critical eye on the bailout of GM and Chrysler, I've always gravitated toward perspectives that cut against the grain of conventional wisdom and reveal the hidden stories that must be dug out and dragged into the light.

Compared to the intense debates and bitter animosity that surrounded the collapse and bailout of Detroit, which was both my and *TTAC*'s main focus at the time, my earliest exposures to Tesla seemed downright tame. With the entire auto industry in flames, a tiny California startup that converted imported British sports cars to electric drive was hardly worth getting worked up over. With the benefit of hindsight, however, it is possible to see that even in 2008, perspectives on the company were already beginning to diverge.

At a time when a whole crop of electric car startups were peddling either vaporware or glorified Chinese golf carts, Tesla distinguished itself from the crowd by attacking the high end of the market with an electric sports car. Reports of the Tesla Roadster's face-melting

acceleration and popularity with green-conscious California celebrities suggested that this was one electric vehicle (EV) startup that at
least had the potential to be something more than a flash in the pan.
At the same time, the company's situation was fraught: It was burning
through cash, critical components needed reengineering, its founders
were starting to feud, and the funding it would need to survive was dry-
ing out as the downturn took hold. Just like Tesla today, the Tesla of
2008 was a volatile mix of enormous long-term potential with intense
short-term challenges.

As Tesla began to actually deliver a trickle of cars during 2008, which
was more than most EV startups could claim at the time, *TTAC* began to
document the company's struggles in a brief series of blog posts labeled
the "Tesla Death Watch." Though it would later gain far more attention,
the Tesla series was barely an afterthought to the GM, Chrysler, and
Ford Death Watches that had built the *TTAC* brand in the years before
I arrived. We hadn't added a Tesla Death Watch to our coverage out
of any special animosity—in fact, when I took over the site in 2009,
I discontinued all of the Death Watch series because I was concerned
the inflammatory name might make readers think we were rooting for
the subject companies to fail rather than documenting the challenging
nature of the industry. The Tesla Death Watch was simply an interesting
story that illustrated just how brutally tough it was for new automakers
to survive, as well as a refreshing break from the Detroit Death Watches.

After less than a year of sporadic Tesla coverage—during which
we missed several opportunities to dig into stories that were a *lot* more
interesting than we realized at the time—*TTAC*'s founder canceled the
Tesla Death Watch on the occasion of Tesla's one-hundredth Roadster
delivery. Over the next five years, I watched with bemusement and a little surprise as Tesla clawed its way through controversy and adversity to
become a full-blown automotive phenomenon. Though I was inclined
to be skeptical of the company's runaway ambitions, I developed a deep
admiration for its ability to survive in a business in which the odds are
stacked against newcomers.

No matter what it overcame, Tesla's success always seemed to be built on shaky ground. Its branding, design, engineering, and rapid prototyping capabilities were second to none, but the dreary fundamentals of manufacturing and finance that I had learned during the dark days of 2008 were almost always lacking. These unsexy factors, which most of the public seemed completely unaware of, could be overlooked by a small premium brand. But they would be fundamental for the company to pursue any mass-market aspirations.

A surprise invitation to Tesla's headquarters near Stanford University in 2014 gave me my first real glimpse behind the curtain. The office's open floor plan was unlike anything I had seen at an automaker, with PR people seated next to engineering work spaces covered in electrical and mechanical components, and the CEO's desk indistinguishable from the others. It was a vibrant and unpretentious environment, whose layout and youthful staff spoke to the flat structure and creative collaboration of a software startup. Compared to the aging, hermetically sealed executive suite at the top of Ford's "glass house" headquarters, or GM's imposing C-Suite offices high above downtown Detroit, Tesla's headquarters were as different as a Model S was from an F-150.

But as alluring as the idea of a Silicon Valley startup automaker was, I had learned the hard way that the freshest and most intellectually appealing approaches to the car business are often the most troubled when it came to fundamentals. Earlier in my career, I had become fascinated by an Israeli startup called Project Better Place, which had the most daring and unique strategy I had ever heard. It would sell electric cars without batteries, making them cost-competitive with internal combustion out of the gate, and charge owners for a mileage plan that allowed them to use the company's network of battery swap stations. Using this cell phone–inspired business plan, Better Place promised to solve the two biggest problems with electric cars: cost and charge time.

I was so excited by the potential of this brilliant idea that I was completely blindsided when, in 2013, Better Place suddenly collapsed into bankruptcy. Not only did this experience teach me that smart ideas can blind you to massive execution problems, but it also set up the experience that would fundamentally shift my perception of Tesla: my impromptu investigation of its battery-swap station (see chapter 9). What I encountered at a truck stop halfway between San Francisco and Los Angeles in 2015 convinced me that potentially massive gaps existed between Tesla's carefully cultivated image and reality—yet the company was capable of saying and doing whatever it thought it needed to maintain its reputation.

Finding myself suddenly disillusioned about Tesla, even as its popularity was hitting new highs, I began digging into the company's past and present. The more I questioned and deeper I dug, the more I found evidence that the company's popular image was a consciously constructed facade that concealed underlying dysfunction. But as I developed more sources among current and former employees, I also found genuine heroism: without deeply talented people doing brilliant work under brutally tough circumstances, Tesla would never have become the phenomenon that it did.

As I began to collect and tell these stories, on my blog and at various outlets, the idea for this book began to take shape. (My writing also started generating an increasing number of heated comments and impassioned emails from Tesla fans defending the company.) Then, in the summer of 2016, after I reported that Tesla had been making owners sign nondisclosure agreements in return for "goodwill repairs" to defective vehicles (see chapter 12), the story broke into the national news and Tesla itself decided to strike back.

In an official company blog post, Tesla accused me of "fabricating" the story and misleading the national media, insinuating that I had done so for financial reasons. The relationship between an investigative reporter and his or her subject is seldom warm, but there's usually a fundamental understanding that both sides are just doing their jobs. Tesla's blog post, and the ensuing flood of abuse filling my email and social media, sent a clear message: I was an enemy of the company.

Between the series of troubling tactics that I had uncovered and the extremely personal assault that followed, my original vision for this book solidified: It would unmask the "real Tesla," showing the cynicism and dysfunction that lay beneath the company's calculated facade of high-tech enviro-altruism. In the months of research and interviews that followed, I found no shortage of stories and data points that validated this vision. But as I dug ever deeper into Tesla's history and spoke with sources who had dedicated years of their lives to the company, I also began to realize that the antagonism between Tesla and myself threatened to get in the way of the full story.

As time put some distance between me and my confrontation with the company, I began seeing more of the nuance in the story. Customers would complain about hilariously inept quality or service problems one minute, and then extoll the company as the future of the car business the next. The sources I spoke to would tell me eye-opening stories about the company's ugly culture and profound dysfunction but then wax eloquent about how working there had been the most inspiring and motivating experience of their careers. A deeper understanding of the history of electric cars in the United States began to show me more clearly why so many people were so adamantly passionate about Tesla and so convinced of its inevitable success. The blossoming and rapid evolution of the mobility technology sector provided a sophisticated context for Tesla's assault on the auto industry.

Unlike some other recent tales of high-tech hubris, there's no way to wrap up the Tesla story in a neat package with a bow on top. It's a necessarily sprawling and complex saga, with heroic villains and villainous heroes, and my telling of it may well disappoint the company's committed fans and its dedicated skeptics alike. But that same complexity can also teach us a number of important lessons about technology, economics, the auto industry, mobility, society, and the way each of us sees and understands the world.

After all, Tesla is but one part of a larger story that is every bit as complex and uncertain as this one company's future. For all the enthusiasm that electric cars inspire, both among consumers and increasingly inside the industry, their single-digit market share tells us the long-awaited electric car revolution is still in its very early days. Though massive investments in electric vehicles are already being made, technologies like smartphone-based ride hailing and car sharing, autonomous drive, and micromobility suggest that there are even more socially and environmentally friendly opportunities than simply turning gas cars into electric cars.

We are still in the very earliest stages of a potentially massive transformation of mobility, and the vagaries of technological progress, government policy, and consumer acceptance could lead us to wildly different outcomes. Whether Tesla will continue to lead that transformation or be left behind still remains very much to be seen. But its successes and challenges in the early stages of this change have already inspired many of the new players now hoping to reinvent mobility and also left important warning signs for them.

In this highly dynamic and unpredictable moment, only one thing *is* certain: The coming decades will be the most fascinating time to pay attention to cars and mobility in a century. And the story of Tesla Motors—with all its twists and turns—is a perfect introduction to the forces that will shape the future of how we get around.

CHAPTER 1

THE SURVIVOR

This isn't a Silicon Valley versus Detroit story.
Elon Musk, January 15, 2009

"You did it!"

The words rang out over the roar of the crowd, inspiring fresh waves of jubilation.

"Whooo!"

Elon Musk hesitated, letting out a brief laugh as he took in the wild cheers. Arms spread, the CEO of Tesla Motors acknowledged the crowd with a bob of his head. "So," he said, trying to return to his prepared remarks before being cut off by the same ecstatic outburst, shouted even louder this time.

"YOU DID IT!"

"Thank you," Musk responded, breaking into a chuckle. It was the first sentence he had been able to form since announcing that Tesla had received 115,000 preorders for the Model 3 he had revealed just seconds before. "That's a lot, yeah," he said, grinning. The crowd roared again as Musk beamed down at them from the stage.

As far as most observers were concerned, Musk *had* done it. All day, images of fans lining up at Tesla stores around the world to preorder a car they hadn't even seen yet flooded the internet. By the end of the next day, the number of preorders would double to more than 230,000, and headlines would hail the tidal wave of demand as "the auto industry's first iPhone moment." Within a week, Tesla would announce that it had received 325,000 preorders for Model 3, representing more than $10 billion in potential sales, and its reservation count would eventually top a staggering 450,000. Across a century of automotive history, there had never been anything quite like Model 3 mania.

Of course, there had also never been an automaker quite like Tesla. At a time when cars seemed to be slouching toward technological maturity and commodification, Musk had positioned his electric automaker as the vanguard of an automotive revolution and reignited the long-dormant public passion for cars. Each new model Tesla introduced was more than a mere improvement on the last: it was a speedy, sexy step toward a cleaner, safer, *better* future.

Now, with the $35,000 Model 3 poised to deliver on Musk's decade-old promise to make a truly affordable electric car, a piece of that future was within reach of anyone who could afford a $1,000 refundable deposit. Surrounded by gleaming Model 3 prototypes and awash in the crowd's admiration, Musk had never looked more like the smiling prophet of a seismic shift in the $4 trillion car business.

The belief that Tesla had already reached the end of its heroic journey—that Musk had truly "done it"—was understandable. Thirteen years earlier, when Tesla was first incorporated, even its founders could hardly have believed that their startup would some day begin taking deposits for an affordable electric car. The company had repeatedly overcome extraordinary odds, and it had never seemed so close to fulfilling its revolutionary promise.

But even as the shouts of triumph echoed into silence and the crowd dispersed to await delivery of the Model 3, an awkward question remained: Had Tesla *really* "done it"? Years of hard work, huge challenges, and massive missteps still lay between Tesla and its dream of an affordable, mass-produced Model 3. For all the obstacles Tesla had already surmounted, it was stepping into the unknown to an extent that even its visionary CEO didn't yet fully appreciate.

Today, after years of relentless struggle, the Model 3 exists, and at the time of this writing, it is being produced at a rate of more than five thousand units per week. Yet it's taken about $4.5 billion in fresh capital (enough for at least two new factories) to reach that production volume, which is only slightly over half the 500,000 units per year rate Tesla said it would hit by the end of 2018. By the first quarter of 2019, demand for all but the cheapest versions had been exhausted in North America, which is Tesla's largest market, and deliveries were down by more than thirty percent from the previous quarter.

The company has always been hugely successful at tapping into the public's aspirations, yet challenges have dogged it every step of the way and kept it from delivering on its most important promises. For more than fifteen years Tesla's expertly crafted popular perception kept it afloat in the face of setbacks, but with the Model 3 it has reached the point where the gritty realities of the car business can no longer be ignored. There's a disconnect between the perception that Tesla has effectively achieved its mission of creating a truly affordable mass-market electric car and the reality of the company today. This disjuncture has been a defining characteristic of the company nearly from day one.

When I started writing about the auto industry in 2008, the first thing that struck me was that this was a business that nobody should want to be in. Companies have to spend billions of dollars to develop new products, knowing that they'll be released into market conditions that are four years away or more; then, they must sell them into a brutally competitive marketplace that operates on a massive, globe-spanning scale. It's arguably one of the hardest ways to make a buck. When things go well, an automaker might generate reasonable (but hardly exciting) returns. But when things go badly, the losses quickly become staggering—as America's automakers were just then in the process of proving.

To survive this meat grinder, existing players were consolidating in order to spread their massive capital expenditures over as many cars as possible. Sergio Marchionne, who masterminded one of the biggest consolidations of the period by merging a bailed-out Chrysler with the Italian automaker Fiat, loudly pronounced that an automaker needed to produce on the order of five million units per year just to survive over the long term. The top three automakers, GM, Toyota, and Volkswagen, each sell a little under twice that number of vehicles most years.

This industry of leviathans was suffering billions of dollars in losses. Yet despite that, the period around 2008 also witnessed a bizarre phenomenon: new startup companies trying to break into the punishing business of making and selling cars. Soaring gas prices had caught the truck- and SUV-dependent Detroit automakers flat-footed and were inspiring a new generation of entrepreneurs to launch fledgling "green car" companies for the coming era of "Peak Oil." Whether or not these new players fully understood how tough the car business could be, their boundless optimism and often wildly experimental ideas presented a sharp contrast to the homogenized, commodified mainline auto industry.

Though the explosion of new ideas and companies in the automotive world was a hint at the "mobility technology" revolution we see unfolding today, it was still firmly anchored in the privately owned car paradigm (with the exception of car-sharing pioneers like Zipcar). Some of these new green car startups, like ZAP, Miles, and Coda, imported cheap electric vehicles from China. Some, like Aptera, designed aerodynamic and hyperefficient vehicles that looked like they rolled out of an episode of *The Jetsons*. Companies like Brammo and Zero got into electric motorcycles; a Norwegian startup called Think Global developed a lightweight plastic-bodied electric commuter, TH!NK; and Israeli startup Project Better Place launched an ambitious battery-swap network that promised to make EVs as cheap and fast-refueling as gas cars.

This wasn't the first time that electric cars had loomed large in the public imagination. Since the fuel crises of the 1970s, battery-powered electric cars had been held up as the answer to fossil-fuel dependence and pollution. They were seen as a kind of automotive cure-all that would sustain America's car-crazy culture while doing away with its worst attributes. Actually, electric cars had outsold crude gas-powered cars at the dawn of the auto industry, and for many Americans it was just a matter of time before they rose again, like the return of King Arthur, to deliver us from the woes of internal combustion.

Even in the 1990s, electric cars had inspired a sense of anticipation and inevitability, especially when the California Air Resources Board (CARB) determined that electric vehicles were both technologically viable and capable of cutting the growing local emissions coming from the state's booming vehicle fleet. CARB has historically been the most aggressive regulator of auto tailpipe emissions in the United States. It sets its standards high enough to drive regulation at the federal level (and consistently frustrate mainstream automakers), and its Zero Emission Vehicle (ZEV) mandate has been hugely influential. This mandate seeks to incentivize the development, production, and sale of ZEVs by requiring that a certain percentage of each automaker's California sales be made up of vehicles with no tailpipe emissions. CARB enforces this mandate with a credit system, in which ZEV sales earn the automaker credits that must offset the debits created by non-ZEV sales.

Eight other states have adopted CARB's ZEV mandate, but none has the market size—and therefore, the impact—that California does. Thus, one state's mandate nudged the major automakers to start developing pure electric cars. Among these companies was General Motors, which introduced a small but affluent segment of the market to the joys of electric drive. Afraid of being shut out of the biggest car market in the United States, other automakers joined a technological arms race that convinced much of the public that a fundamental shift in the industry was at hand.

Originally conceived and engineered by a group of California engineers who would go on to develop some of Tesla's early technology, the Impact concept car was a pure expression of forward-thinking engineering. Its slippery aerodynamics and use of lightweight materials allowed it to squeeze eighty to one hundred miles of range and peppy acceleration out of lead-acid batteries—even after GM's engineers reworked it into a more market-friendly car, renamed the EV1 (a move that alienated its visionary engineer, Alan Cocconi). Still, the EV1's high cost and low volume, as well as GM's internal ambivalence toward it, doomed it to unprofitability. Lobbying and lawsuits eventually delayed and watered down CARB's requirements for ZEV sales, and as financial woes consumed GM in 2003, the EV1 program was cut.

When GM canceled the EV1 and crushed the remaining vehicles after their leases ran out, angry erstwhile owners protested with a mock funeral for the electric car. From their perspective, the EV1 had proven that electric cars could be viable, but the industry's subsequent lobbying against the ZEV mandate showed that the automakers simply didn't want to manufacture them. Filmmaker Chris Paine captured their anger in *Who Killed the Electric Car?*, a documentary highlighting the EV1's adoring celebrity fans and exploring the possible culprits for its failure. The film was released in 2006, and its conspiratorial passion helped popularize the blossoming field of green car startups.

The logic forwarded in *Who Killed the Electric Car?* was intoxicating—electric-drive technology was mature, and battery-powered cars were viable and popular, but a conspiracy composed of automakers and oil companies was holding back their utopian promise. This belief had revolutionary implications: Electric cars needed political support to take on their entrenched enemies, but once the opposition was overcome, they would be rapidly and enthusiastically adopted by the public and turn the companies who made and sold them into industry leaders. It also strongly suggested that these new leaders would have to come from outside the established auto industry players, whose investments in internal-combustion engine technology made them the enemies of this inevitable revolution.

By 2010, however, gas prices declined nearly as precipitously as they had risen. The American automakers roared back as truck and SUV sales rebounded, and nearly all of the new green car startups were either bankrupt or circling the drain. The dream of a new environmentally friendly auto industry turned out to be a mirage—electric cars were no more appealing when gas was cheap than Detroit's gas-guzzlers had been when gas prices were high. One of the fundamental challenges of the auto industry, the need to develop vehicles for market conditions years into the future, claimed many of these optimistic new startups. The intense capital requirements, regulatory obstacles, and brutal competition did in most of the rest. But of all the companies that emerged during this tumultuous period, one hung on in spite of all the headwinds, surviving the "green car winter" and emerging as a serious force in the industry: Tesla Motors.

Tesla had always stood out among its green car contemporaries: Founded by proven high-tech entrepreneurs, it tapped into Silicon Valley's burgeoning venture capital scene and pursued the high end of the market. The typical electric vehicle of the time was an overpriced and design-compromised commuter car, either converted from a cheap internal combustion vehicle or little more than a golf cart, which appealed only to the most hard-core environmentalists. By parting with the flock and building a fast, beautiful electric sports car, Tesla attracted customers who were less price sensitive, more forgiving of quality problems, and constantly on the lookout for a car that helps them stand out.

Tesla's first car, the Roadster, offered more range than any electric vehicle on the market, sleek, handsome styling, and acceleration rivaling the best sports cars. Its six-figure price tag was eye watering, but you simply couldn't get a better or more desirable electric car for any price. Despite running into nearly every possible roadblock along the way (as we'll explore in the coming chapters), it came to market in 2008 with a healthy waiting list packed with celebrities and the financial and political elite. It also didn't hurt that its arrival coincided with the first successful private rocket launches by its sister company SpaceX, which dramatically raised the profile of the founder and key figure at both companies, Elon Musk.

Prior to 2008, Tesla had received only a smattering of public attention outside the blogs and forums dedicated to electric and other green cars. Over the course of that year, with Roadsters finally reaching owners and SpaceX finally reaching orbit, Tesla's profile began taking off. Not all the attention was good. The Roadster had launched with a transmission that would require replacement. Tesla was burning through cash, Musk had to take over as the company's fourth CEO in two years, and his personal life was becoming a staple of Silicon Valley gossip blogs. Yet somehow, Musk would manage to raise more funding at the height of the financial crisis, and over the course of several dizzying years, a combination of good luck and sheer hustle kept the company afloat.

By 2013, a decade after it was founded, Tesla's Model S had made it the most successful American automotive startup since the Chrysler Corporation, which had been founded some ninety years before. The perception that Tesla was on its way to establishing itself as a dominant force in the auto industry was becoming increasingly commonplace, as the company's base of hard-core fans grew bigger and ever more emboldened thanks to their investments in Tesla stock. The company even managed to straddle the growing ideological divide in America, appealing to both libertarian techies and left-leaning environmentalists in equal measure.

Here, finally, was the champion that electric car fans had been waiting decades for: Having survived major technical, financial, and organizational challenges, Tesla was selling cars as fast as it could make them, it was backed by two of the most respected automakers in the world, and its high-flying stock and ubiquitous media coverage made it the envy of the industry. And for all its accomplishments, the company's future seemed to have no limits, thanks to a string of announcements promising bold innovations to come.

Tesla's triumph seemed to be the long-awaited return of the king and the fulfillment of prophecies passed down for decades. It also tapped into the most popular new ideology in American life. As the internet, social media, and smartphones gave birth to some of the most profitable and powerful companies in history, many people believed that software-centric startups would bring about inevitable "disruption" in every traditional business. Having already established Tesla as the auto industry's champion of the environment, Musk increasingly positioned the company as the cutting edge of Silicon Valley's conquest of the auto industry.

Thus, by 2013, Musk turned Tesla into one of the most powerful brands of the twenty-first century. Between the planet-saving mission and the disruptive potential to dominate the trillion-dollar auto industry, nearly everyone had a reason to support Tesla, and there was always a positive way to frame news about the company. Headlines lauded the company's world-saving mission as well as its cars' extraordinary features, such as the super quick zero-to-sixty acceleration option that Musk nicknamed "Ludicrous Mode." And at a time when heroic public figures were an increasingly rare commodity, Musk's centrality to Tesla's capitalistic, technological, and environmental ambitions (to say nothing of his numerous other techno-utopian causes, including SpaceX, Hyperloop, The Boring Company, Neuralink . . . and, of course, the company whose success provided the funding for all of them, PayPal) made both him and his car company even more appealing.

As Tesla's brand solidified and its stock took off, Musk poured gas on the fire. Starting in 2013, he embarked on a hype campaign that continually ratcheted up Tesla's ambitions and set him apart from anyone else in the public sphere. His wild-eyed production targets, seemingly impossible technological promises, goofy sense of humor, and relentless pursuit of media coverage quickly turned into a runaway train. Musk and Tesla were entering a kind of "Ludicrous Mode" of hype, supercharging the company's image and stock price in a never-ending spiral of ambition and expectation that increasingly seemed impossible to fulfill—or even control.

Surfing these powerful cultural and technological trends, the popular perception of Tesla was overwhelmingly positive—but it quickly outran the reality on the ground. When you stopped to assess Tesla as an automaker, things simply didn't add up: The company wasn't making money, its operations were chaotic, its supplier relations were unstable, turnover was high, its manufacturing quality was poor, and its increasingly implausible promises were eroding its credibility. Though its software-style culture had helped it create deeply appealing cars and a powerful brand that pushed the entire industry forward, when it came to the core challenges that determine the fates of large manufacturing companies, Tesla was not only not leading, it was miles behind. To live up to its ambition of selling affordable, mass-market electric cars, Tesla would have to find a way to balance its well-known strengths with these very different and often-overlooked challenges. These challenges have persisted even in the present day.

First, at its heart, Tesla is driven by innovation and design, like so many Silicon Valley startups. But the automotive business is, at its core, a low-margin, manufacturing-based industry. From the start, Tesla rejected the values that are needed to succeed in this sort of enterprise, and it shows no signs of changing, even now. A disciplined, process-driven culture, not more creativity and innovation, is the key to overcoming this challenge.

Next, though it knows how to fund raise and has even earned modest quarterly profits, Tesla has never figured out how to overcome the most fundamental challenge in the modern auto industry: earning a sustainable return on invested capital. As we'll see, Elon Musk's original vision for the company—starting with a more expensive car, using the money from that car to build a cheaper one, and continuing to make ever cheaper cars—has yet to materialize. To date, the critical factor in Tesla's survival has been its ability to raise ever more cash from venture capitalists, the government, and Wall Street.

Lastly, the idealistic mission that is central to Tesla's appeal has transformed over time into the belief that its noble ends justify any means, including making statements that either aren't true or are unlikely to come true. From the outside, Tesla's escalating hubris has become increasingly evident in its missed deadlines, abandoned goals, and increasingly implausible promises. Inside Tesla, it is reflected in the cultural dysfunction that prevents the company's own experts from countering Musk's whims with their experience and expertise.

These contradictions between Tesla's popular image and its reality are all the more unfortunate given how much Tesla has done to bring increasing public attention and interest to the auto industry. For too long, cars have been understood and appreciated only on the most superficial levels, with little to no attention paid to where they come from, the forces that shape them, and the ways in which they in turn shape the broader world. Tesla has not only reinvigorated cars themselves, it has made the auto industry more relevant than it's been in decades. But it has done so in ways that reinforce its own mythology rather than providing a deeper understanding. Meanwhile, as we will see, Tesla itself is being left behind by the very "mobility technology" revolution that it once spearheaded.

Tesla's unique positioning makes it the perfect case study for this unique historical moment for cars and mobility. The company is on the cutting edge of changes that are already transforming century-old ideas about the automobile. It is pointing the way to the future of cleaner, smarter cars and generating a level of public interest in the auto industry we haven't seen in decades. At the same time, the shortcomings of the startup-style culture that makes Tesla's vehicles and brand so appealing also highlight the importance of the "boring" traditional auto industry cultural values that have been refined by decades of competition.

The triumphs and failures of Tesla's blue-sky attempt at creating a high-tech automaker hold critical lessons for the future. They show the areas in which startups can contribute to the design and development of innovative new vehicles, while also pointing out which tasks are best left to the less creative but more disciplined and regimented traditional automotive companies. Tesla's experience proves that the anticipated conflict over the future of mobility—between startups and established companies, disruptors and incumbents, Silicon Valley and Detroit—needs to be a convergence instead. The companies that dominate mobility technology will need to weld the best parts of Tesla's fast-moving, creative culture to the methodical pace, disciplined focus, and operational excellence required to develop, validate, and manufacture modern vehicles.

No matter what happens, Tesla will be remembered as a historically significant company in one of the most pivotal periods of automotive history. Simply by making such desirable high-end electric vehicles, it has created a market where none existed, helped jar the established automakers out of complacency, and fulfilled its mission of accelerating the transition to electric drivetrains. No history of the great transition from the first century of the automobile to the world of mobility technology that awaits is complete without reference to Tesla.

The lessons about the auto industry and the future of mobility are what make this topic worth discussing. I've spent a decade studying and writing about the auto industry and mobility technology. A good portion of those years have been spent sifting through documents, following online Tesla communities, and verifying sources, in an attempt to differentiate the truth from myths and lies that Tesla has spun. I would love to see the company succeed, and for Tesla to find a better balance between the freewheeling innovation it does so well and the areas where it has struggled.

That's why it's worth understanding the good, the bad, and the ugly of this one-of-a-kind company. Sustainable transportation may not depend on Tesla's survival, as the company's PR department has claimed, but nobody else has had as big an effect on cars in recent memory . . . or revealed as much about the perceptions and reality of automobiles in the twenty-first century. The fact that its story is as dramatic as any great historical epic is just the icing on the cake.

CHAPTER 2

THE TOP SECRET MASTER PLAN

We say the things we believe, even when those things are delusional.
Elon Musk, May 31, 2016

The story of the company called Tesla Motors opens in 2003, when the firm was incorporated by Martin Eberhard and Marc Tarpenning. But the mythology that would make Tesla one of the most valuable and best-known car companies in the world didn't enter the public consciousness until three years later, when Tesla's chairman and chief financier Elon Musk wrote a post on the company blog.

The post, titled "The Secret Tesla Motors Master Plan (just between you and me)," was published on August 2, 2006, just as the first wave of media coverage presented the electric car startup to the public. In it, Musk introduced himself as a central figure in the company, marking his first step toward his eventual domination of Tesla and its image. He began:

Background: My day job is running a space transportation company called SpaceX, but on the side I am the chairman of Tesla Motors and help formulate the business and product strategy with Martin and the rest of the team. I have also been Tesla Motor's primary funding source from when the company was just three people and a business plan.

In what would become his signature rambling style, Musk went on to explain the advantages of electric cars and address some of the main criticisms leveled against the technology. Musk's nerdy digressions into "well-to-wheel efficiency" calculations and criticisms of hybrids were largely a rehash of an earlier white paper authored by Eberhard and Tarpenning. But the terse formula that concluded the post would be remembered as Musk's key contribution to Tesla's strategy and become the cornerstone of its image:

Build sports car
Use that money to build an affordable car
Use that money to build an even more affordable car
While doing above, also provide zero emission electric power
*   generation options*
Don't tell anyone

If Musk conceived this strategy prior to 2006, he wasn't the only Tesla founder to do so. Eberhard and Tarpenning's initial business plan, written well before Musk joined the company as its chairman, called for the same top-down approach. Ultimately the strategy was defined by the technology: because lithium-ion batteries were still relatively new and incredibly expensive, Tesla had little choice but to start with a high-end electric sports car and move down-market as battery technology matured.

This was also the classic Silicon Valley game plan for marketing new technologies, and Eberhard and Tarpenning were a classic Silicon Valley "hardware-software" team. Eberhard, a tall, bearded engineer whose charismatic charm barely conceals a smoldering intensity, had cut his teeth designing computer terminals at Wyse computers. Tarpenning, the more laid-back and humorous of the two men, had made a name for himself developing software and firmware at companies like Seagate and Packet Design.

Together they had founded NuvoMedia, where they leveraged improvements in lithium-ion batteries into one of the first commercially available e-readers. (The product segment they established would become a cornerstone of Amazon.com's broader transition from physical products like books toward software-based products that can be delivered online, like e-books, music, and films.) Their ability to integrate hardware and software into compelling new technology products was renowned in the high-tech sector, and after selling NuvoMedia in 2000, they began looking for new opportunities to pursue their passion.

Recently divorced and newly wealthy, Eberhard had wanted to buy a sports car but he couldn't, as he put it to Business Insider's Drake Baer, bring himself to buy something that got eighteen miles per gallon. Torn between his love of fast cars and his growing awareness of the environmental and social costs of fossil-fuel dependence, he began studying the "well-to-wheel" efficiency of every possible form of energy. His research showed not only that electric cars held the promise of both high performance and incredible efficiency, but also that every electric car company since World War II had tried to build an affordable vehicle that could compete with internal combustion offerings and failed. Through this combination of personal desire and research into technological opportunities, the idea of building a high-end electric sports car using lithium-ion batteries began to take shape.

Eberhard eventually discovered a small Los Angeles–based firm called AC Propulsion that was offering a lead-acid battery-powered kit car called the tzero that could accelerate from zero to sixty miles per hour in about four seconds. AC was a tiny operation, but it boasted more electric-drive know-how than most major automakers at the time; cofounder Alan Cocconi had single-handedly designed much of the drivetrain electronics for the GM Impact/EV1. But Cocconi was always more engineer than businessman, and consequently AC was always more of a cult hero for Southern California's nascent EV conversion scene than a serious effort to commercialize its breakthrough electric-drive technology.

Finding AC loaded with talent but in dire financial straits, Eberhard offered the company $500,000 to build him the latest version of the tzero, which had dropped its lead-acid battery pack for an array of small cylindrical lithium-ion battery cells. The crude, ugly yellow sports car that resulted had blistering acceleration and an astonishingly long range for an electric car. AC declined to join Eberhard's new electric sports car company, possibly due to Cocconi's bitter experience with the EV1 program (see chapter 1). Still, their tzero would become Tesla's proof of concept and the basis of its drivetrain technology.

While Eberhard was mapping out the technical specifications of an electric sports car, Tarpenning began researching the commercial opportunities for a premium electric car that would offer the environmental image of a Toyota Prius with the performance of a Porsche. Tarpenning's research found that buyers of the earliest green cars tended to be wealthy enough to afford almost any car they wanted, as was evidenced by the Priuses sharing driveways with high-end sports and luxury cars around Silicon Valley. Having identified both a technological and commercial opportunity, Eberhard and Tarpenning incorporated Tesla Motors in 2003, fatefully naming it after the brilliant electrical engineer who never reaped the financial rewards of his breakthrough inventions.

According to Elon Musk, electric cars were what had first brought him to Silicon Valley. While obtaining bachelor's degrees in physics and business from Wharton, Musk claims to have become fascinated with the opportunity to power cars with ultracapacitors. After graduating, he moved to California and began working on the energy storage technology at a firm called Pinnacle Research.

Musk had grown up immersed in technology. Born in South Africa to an affluent family (his father, Errol, owned a 50 percent stake in a Zambian emerald mine), Musk escaped what he calls a difficult childhood by throwing himself into books and computer programming. Even as a world-famous billionaire, he retains an air of awkwardness from his solitary childhood, umming and erring through product announcements and quarterly earnings calls. But beneath his sometimes uncomfortable social presence, Musk has deep reserves of self-confidence, having sold his first computer game at age twelve and living on his own since seventeen, when he left South Africa to avoid mandatory military service.

His interest in ultracapacitors and eye for opportunity quickly led him to Stanford, where he was accepted to a graduate program in material sciences engineering. But Musk never actually enrolled, instead choosing to found his first startup. As he saw it, the internet revolution was too great an opportunity to pass up, and he could always return to his passion, hopefully with funds from his internet businesses.

Yet after successfully selling two startups (Zip2, which created online listings for local businesses, and X.com, an "online bank" that eventually merged with Confinity to become PayPal) and walking away from the internet boom with tens of millions of dollars, Musk's first major move was to start a rocket company called SpaceX, with which he hoped to someday colonize Mars. His only large automotive investment prior to Tesla was in purchasing a McLaren F1, a V12 hypercar that was among the fastest and most expensive cars in the world. "It's a million-dollar car," his first wife, Justine, told a CNN documentary crew on hand to film the delivery in 1999. "It's decadent . . . my fear is that we lose a sense of appreciation and perspective."

What Musk hadn't lost was a sense of ambition. "I'd like to be on the cover of *Rolling Stone*," he said as footage of him driving his new car rolled. "That'd be cool."

Musk's apparently dormant passion for electric cars seems to have been reignited in 2003 after meeting the man who would become his quiet but consistent ally at Tesla. JB Straubel had been fascinated with electric vehicles since he brought home and fixed a golf cart at age thirteen, and had gone on to work with Stanford's developing solar car program while studying physics there. After a stint at Rosen Motors, a startup that had been struggling to commercialize an exotic flywheel-hybrid car drivetrain since 1993, Straubel realized that improvements in lithium-ion cells were the key to his electric car dream and began developing and pitching an electric car powered by thousands of cheap cylindrical 18650 cells used in laptop computers. Despite his connections at Stanford and deep hands-on experience with electric cars, which included converting an old Porsche into one of the quickest electric vehicles in the world, he failed to generate interest and funding for his electric car concept.

More than a decade later, Musk would say that his first meeting with Straubel "was really what ultimately led to Tesla as it is today." The meeting had been arranged by Straubel's former boss Harold Rosen, with the intention of pitching Musk on an electric aircraft concept, but Musk was far more interested in discussing electric cars. Afterward, Straubel emailed Musk to provide more information about his electric car project and put him in touch with AC Propulsion. "They will be supplying the battery for the long-range car based on developments for the Li-ion tzero battery," he wrote. "It is essentially ~10,000 small cells of the same type in a laptop computer . . . if you have the time, you should really ask them to give you a ride in the tzero."

Like Eberhard, Musk needed only one test drive in the tzero to know he had found what he was looking for. Musk was blown away by the electric sports car's performance and almost immediately offered to fund a commercial version of the car. At the time, AC Propulsion had world-class expertise in the nuts and bolts of electric drive, but its leadership was focused on converting more modest existing automobiles to battery power. They were all too aware of the challenges Tesla would later face while trying to convert a high-end performance car to electric power. When Musk suggested that AC convert a Noble M12 to battery power for him, the company's CEO, Tom Gage, replied, "AC Propulsion shares your view that the top end of the market is a good place to sell electric vehicles . . . The Noble might make a good EV platform, but the difference between a battery, 240 liters, 700 lbs and a gas tank, 60 liters, 120 lbs, means that major modifications are inevitable. Given our commitments, that sort of one-off vehicle project is not feasible for us at this time."

Gage tried to steer Musk toward an investment in his plans to convert the tiny Scion xB to electric power, a venture Musk had no interest in. But Gage also mentioned that AC was working with two other startups that wanted to commercialize an electric sports car. "Would you be interested in participating with one of those companies?" he asked. Musk was indeed interested.

At the time, Tesla Motors was little more than Eberhard, Tarpenning, their technical specifications, a business plan, and a small office space. Eberhard and Tarpenning had pitched several venture capital firms, even bringing a tzero to Sand Hill Road near Stanford to convince Silicon Valley's money men to take a chance on their company, but they had obtained only token support. Most high-tech investors were still focused on opportunities in the digital frontier that the information technology revolution had opened up, and they couldn't get comfortable backing such an unusual play, especially in the notoriously challenging and low-margin car business.

From the moment Musk's interest in electric vehicles was brought to Eberhard's attention, his potential as a backer for Tesla was immediately obvious. Though his fortune had been made online, Musk's attention had clearly turned away from computers and connectivity and toward opportunities to apply high technology to the physical world. His decision to follow up his success at PayPal with a rocket company was highly unconventional, and though SpaceX was still young, it was already building and testing its first rocket, the Falcon One. At a time when Silicon Valley was transitioning from the dot-com bust to a new social-media boom, Musk's focus on new opportunities in high-tech hardware set him apart. His interest in commercializing electric cars, particularly the tzero, made him the perfect match for Eberhard's plucky startup.

Eberhard and the third member of the nascent Tesla Motors Team, Ian Wright, flew to Los Angeles and pitched Musk on the company's Series A (initial) funding round. With those funds, it hoped to develop a proof-of-concept prototype of its electric sports car. By Monday, Musk had committed to back the project on the condition that the transaction would be closed in less than two weeks. By providing $6.5 million of Tesla's $7 million seed money, Musk had become the firm's chairman and largest shareholder. In a matter of days, Musk had turned Tesla into a fully funded startup and put himself in control of its future.

In addition to funding, Musk introduced Straubel to the Tesla team. After a meeting at the startup's provisional headquarters in Menlo Park, Straubel agreed to incorporate his new electric car project into the company and was hired as its chief technology officer. Straubel in turn brought in several talented people he had met at Stanford and around Silicon Valley, adding to the team; Eberhard had previously talked a small but deeply talented group of engineers into joining the company while giving them exhilarating rides in his yellow tzero. The growing company moved from its tiny office space in Menlo Park to a workshop in San Carlos, and began converting a Lotus Elise into its first development prototype. By January 2005, eighteen Tesla employees had hacked together the company's first car.

It had been a whirlwind year. In January 2004, Tesla had been incorporated for just six months and consisted of three men, a small office, and a business plan in search of funding. In February 2004, Musk had told Tom Gage that if AC Propulsion was not interested in commercializing the tzero, he would "figure out the best choice of a high performance base car and electric powertrain and go in that direction." By the end of March, he had been approached by Tesla with plans to do just that, and by the end of April he had funded the startup's Series A. Less than nine months later, he was driving the first Tesla ever made. Though the company was still a long way from earning back Musk's investment, his dream of an electric sports car had become a reality in an astonishingly short amount of time.

Just eighteen months after producing its first development prototype, Tesla would launch the Roadster. Eberhard and Musk told the assembled media and prospective customers that a $100,000 deposit now would secure one of the first production Roadsters, with deliveries to begin by the middle of the next year. Blown away by the car's stunning looks and ferocious acceleration, customer orders and glowing media coverage started to pour in. The fragile prototypes only barely survived a full day of demonstration rides, disappearing behind a curtain between rides to have gallons of ice water discretely pumped through the battery. Still, Tesla's first major public event had been a smashing success (more on this in chapter 4).

But with Tesla's first taste of mainstream success came its first internal conflict. CEO Eberhard had been the focus of attention at the launch event, and his practiced explanations of the car's unique advantages were widely quoted in subsequent media reports. Musk had spoken at the event and been available for questions from the press, but his less-polished pronouncements received far less play than Eberhard's. Those reports that did mention him referred to him simply as the firm's financier. Musk was furious.

Musk's resentment at the lack of public recognition for his role at Tesla had been building for some time, and he had hoped that the launch event would result in a new appreciation for his contributions. The day before the event, he had sent an email (since published at Business Insider) to Tesla's de facto PR man, Mike Harrigan, saying that "the portrayal of my role to date has been incredibly insulting" and insisting that "we need to make a serious effort to correct this perception."

When this correction did not materialize in coverage of the launch event, Musk went ballistic. The *New York Times*'s coverage of the company particularly irked Musk, failing to make mention of him in its first two stories after the launch event and even mistakenly referring to Eberhard as "chairman," which was Musk's title. In an email to Eberhard and Harrigan, Musk professed himself "incredibly insulted and embarrassed" at the *Times*'s coverage and threatened to fire the company's PR firm "if anything like this happens again."

Musk and Eberhard had been at odds before the development and design of the Roadster, but as engineers they could always find enough common ground to work through disagreements. "It was always very collegial," Eberhard later told Business Insider's Drake Baer. "We would work through our opinions and come to a conclusion." But when Musk's discontent about his lack of publicity curdled into conflict with Eberhard, something changed. As Eberhard remembers it, "that was the first time where it was this emotional."

The conflict was the beginning of the end for Musk and Eberhard's relationship, which would soon lead to Eberhard's dismissal as CEO, a war of words in the media, and ultimately lawsuits and an out-of-court settlement. Though later phases of the conflict would focus on disagreements over technical and business decisions, it was rooted in Musk's desire for public recognition as a visionary electric car pioneer.

A few weeks after the launch event, Musk took matters into his own hands, publishing his "secret master plan" on the company's official blog. "I am the chairman of Tesla Motors and help formulate the business and product strategy with Martin and the rest of the team," he wrote, before laying out the company's long-term road map. In what would become a signature maneuver, Musk had cut the media out of the equation entirely and presented Tesla and its mission directly to the public in his own words. By publishing Tesla's master plan under his name alone, Musk laid the foundation of a mythology that would steadily erase Eberhard and Tarpenning's roles in the company's founding and establish himself as its guiding visionary.

At the time, grand strategy had little bearing on anything Tesla was actually doing, and few of the company's employees even believed the company would survive long enough to realize it. Letting Musk take credit for the company's vision seemed like an easy way to mollify their publicity-hungry investor, and with nobody else stepping up to match Musk's financial contributions, they had little choice but to keep him happy. Even in the wake of his first real clash with Musk, Eberhard couldn't have foreseen the long-term consequence of what at the time seemed like a minor blog post. As Eberhard's influence at Tesla waned and Musk began to assert more control, the company's use of publicity-grabbing announcements and events became a fundamental part of its culture.

A decade later, at the 2016 Tesla shareholders' meeting, Musk and Straubel would go on to lay out a version of the company's history that barely referenced the work Eberhard, Tarpenning, and Wright had put into the company before the two joined it. Musk did ask for a round of applause for AC Propulsion, which he said "never got enough credit," but failed to mention that Martin Eberhard had both proposed and inspired the lithium-ion-powered version of the tzero that was effectively Tesla's proof of concept. Even after ten years in which his public stature had grown to eclipse any of his fellow cofounders', Musk apparently still felt that Eberhard had received enough credit.

Had Tesla's business strategy been the key to their success as a company, Musk's actions might have been remembered as a scurrilous attempt to take credit for Eberhard and Tarpenning's strategy. Instead, Musk's desire for recognition as the visionary genius behind the most influential automaker of the twenty-first century became the company's defining characteristic. Over the years to come, Musk's legend would drive Tesla to heights that its original founders could have only hoped for. Though Musk's focus on publicity would help make Tesla a household name, its first victim was the company's lead founder—an early hint that this tendency could spell trouble for the company.

CHAPTER 3

THE ACCIDENTAL AUTOMAKER

Wish it wasn't so hard to be less stupid over time . . .
Elon Musk, August 25, 2018

"We had no idea what we were doing," Elon Musk told the crowd at Tesla's 2016 shareholder meeting, as he mimed cluelessness. "Like . . . how the hell do you build a car?" He shrugged dramatically, laughing. "No idea!"

His shareholders laughed along. They could afford to. Tesla's shares had jumped as reservations for the Model 3 poured in, and the company seemed on top of the world. The fact that Musk could admit that he had been utterly clueless about the car business over a decade before simply proved how far both he and Tesla had come. Surely the tough lessons Musk and company had learned along the way made the Model 3's triumph that much more inevitable.

Musk's admission that Tesla had been founded without a full understanding of the auto industry goes a long way toward explaining why its immense popularity is often overtaken by skepticism. After all, the auto industry has been a fundamentally tragic story for decades, particularly for small, plucky upstarts. The last major American automotive startup prior to Tesla was the Chrysler Corporation; founded in 1925, the company had to be bailed out twice by the US government before being merged with Fiat in 2009. In the nearly eighty years between Chrysler's founding and Tesla's, hundreds of automakers had gone bankrupt (Wikipedia's list of defunct American automakers alone lists over a thousand), incinerating billions of dollars along the way. Founding a startup car company in 2003 required either a total lack of familiarity with this history and unchecked optimism . . . or a high level of arrogance.

At least Tesla had come by its confidence honestly. Its founders knew more about lithium-ion batteries than most and had realized that they represented a new opportunity to create long-range electric cars. They had also noticed that the auto industry was ignoring the groundswell of enthusiasm unleashed by electric cars like GM's EV1, rightly concluding that the automakers had little interest in fostering that enthusiasm. As members of California's environmentally conscious tech elite, Tesla's founders were far more in touch with the technological and market opportunity for high-end electric vehicles than anyone in Detroit, and they had every reason to believe that the established automakers would completely miss it.

In fact, automakers like GM had built small-volume electric cars like the EV1 in order to comply with California's Zero Emission Vehicle (ZEV) mandate and had lost huge amounts of money on each one they sold or (more typically) leased. The cost to develop a new car easily exceeds a billion dollars even when manufacturers don't use an entirely new drivetrain technology, and the margins on new cars are small and under constant competitive pressure. Taking the electric car market seriously would require huge new development costs, a new supply chain, and a public charging network. Even if the resulting electric car were priced at cost or at a small loss, it would be thousands of dollars more expensive than an equivalent gas car and offer a far more limited range between charges. In the absence of hard evidence showing that they could sell enough electric cars to cover the massive fixed cost of developing them, the business model was a nonstarter.

As Musk laughed at his own cluelessness a decade later, seemingly safe in the knowledge that Tesla had become a multibillion-dollar company, this brutal economic reality had not changed. None of the electric cars launched since Tesla was founded—least of all any of Tesla's—has generated enough profit to pay off all of its development and factory investment costs. Tesla may have done more to change perceptions about electric cars than anyone else, but it has done so by burning billions of dollars without demonstrating the ability to turn a sustainable profit. Though Tesla's immense popularity took the entire auto industry by surprise, its inability to deliver returns to its investors has been entirely predictable since day one.

But great arrogance or absolute ignorance of the auto industry's crushing economics does not adequately explain how Tesla's founders were lured into this mess. These were brilliant, experienced businessmen who were not in the habit of staking millions of dollars and years of their lives on a startup oblivious to the challenges of the business they were entering. The actual problem was that they knew just enough about the car business to get themselves into trouble.

———————

Eberhard's original presentation to prospective Tesla investors shows that he was well aware of the auto industry's staggering barriers to entry. "Tesla will build high-performance electric sports cars," the executive summary of his presentation begins. "This sounds impossible—both the idea of building cars in the first place, and further, the idea of building a high performance electric car." But, argued Eberhard, two recent developments now made the impossible possible: new battery technology made electric cars "very attractive," and "the international business climate makes it now possible to build a 'fab-less' car company—a car company without a factory." By avoiding the staggering fixed costs associated with building and tooling a car factory, Tesla could turn the economics of the car business upside down.

This belief was rooted in a real auto industry trend that been developing for some time. As car companies battled to limit the high cost of developing cars that could keep pace with the competition, they pushed more and more development and design work on to their suppliers. Automakers themselves no longer developed or manufactured the increasingly commodified components that made up their cars, from suspensions to interior assemblies and even transmissions. Car brands that had at one time prided themselves in their superior starters, headlights, and spark plugs now focused entirely on integrating components purchased from suppliers, assembling them into finished vehicles and marketing them.

To industry outsiders like the early Tesla team, this development seemed to create a massive opportunity. The giant automakers had given up huge sections of the value chain to partners who could in theory supply the same components to anyone else, making it possible for new automakers to create a car from the same components used in the world's best-selling vehicles. For the first time in a century, the auto industry's notorious barriers to entry seemed to be falling, clearing the way for new players to replace the century-old companies at the end of an increasingly outsourced supply chain.

This decentralization had even reached a point where suppliers and small automakers were building entire cars for the majors. A few years before Tesla was founded, General Motors had contracted the storied but struggling British sports car company Lotus to build it a version of its lightweight Elise roadster, which it sold in Europe as the Opel Speedster. The relationship gave GM a world-class sports car for a fraction of the cost of developing one itself, and it kept Lotus's low-volume factories running even as demand for the Elise slowed. It seemed like a win-win relationship . . . unless you looked closely enough to realize that both Opel and Lotus were bleeding cash.

To Eberhard and Tarpenning, who, in their initial feasibility study, had identified the Elise as the most promising basis for the Tesla Roadster purely on its technical merits, everything seemed to be coming together. The Elise was light enough to carry a big battery without becoming an ill-handling mess, and it had already been through the crash tests required for US market approval. Lotus's engineering arm could be hired to take care of all the "car stuff" and help Tesla select the components it needed from existing suppliers. Once the car was developed, Tesla had only to build electric drivetrains based on AC Propulsion technology, ship them to Lotus's factory, and the rest would be taken care of there. Just like GM, Tesla would be able to sell a world-class sports car without having to spend billions of dollars developing a vehicle from the ground up or building its own factory. It almost looked easy.

This pleasant illusion evaporated almost as soon as Tesla began cobbling together its first driveable prototype out of a yellow Elise and the drivetrain from an AC Propulsion tzero. With its compact four-cylinder engine mounted in a small bay behind the driver instead of under a spacious hood, the Elise didn't provide enough room for the more than six thousand battery cells that made up Tesla's battery pack. The Elise's wheelbase would have to be stretched several inches to accommodate the massive battery and cooling system, meaning Tesla would have to license the Elise's aluminum chassis and then reengineer it.

From this one, seemingly innocuous decision, the Roadster began to transform from the simple Elise conversion Eberhard had initially envisioned into something far more complex. Pandora's box had been opened, and out of it spilled countless challenges that Tesla was ill-equipped to tackle. Tesla contracted Lotus's engineering arm for some of the work and hired away engineers to lead their own side of the design, bringing much-needed automotive expertise to the increasingly ambitious project.

The Lotus brand had been built on perfectly poised and balanced cars that were a pleasure to drive, and it would not sully that legacy by just adding a couple of inches to the Elise's wheelbase, throwing a battery in it, and hoping it would drive OK. Accommodating the size and weight of Tesla's battery in a car that Lotus would not be ashamed of building would require extensive modifications to the Elise's underpinnings.

Lotus's boffins laid out a laundry list of modifications that would be necessary to turn the Elise into an electric roadster that would still handle like a Lotus. The chassis would have to be redesigned to be larger and stiffer, the battery compartment would have to be reinforced to serve as part of the vehicle's structure, and a new rear subframe with modified suspension would have to be engineered. With such a complete reengineering already on the table, Musk pushed to lower the Elise's high door for easier ingress and egress, either out of concern for his wife (as he later told his biographer, Ashlee Vance) or for taller customers like himself and Eberhard (according to interviews at the time). By the time the Elise had been transformed into the Tesla Roadster, the resulting car shared only 7 percent of its parts with the original.

As the reengineering of the Elise chassis evolved and the project began to surpass anything resembling a simple conversion, the pressure to add more unique touches mounted. If the point of the Roadster was always to convince the world that electric cars could be truly desirable, performance alone wasn't enough. Tesla would have to make the car look and feel worthy of its six-figure price point, a goal that dragged Tesla ever deeper into the auto industry it had hoped to avoid.

One of the most important ways to achieve that was through the car's styling, and Tesla's top leaders invested considerable time and effort in the design process. After rejecting a number of proposals that he felt overemphasized the fact that Roadster was an electric car, Eberhard enlisted his old friend Bill Moggridge, a legendary designer who had cofounded the renowned consultancy IDEO, to help create a truly classic design.

Moggridge guided Eberhard through the range of aesthetic possibilities, from retro to futuristic, masculine to feminine. After multiple rounds of proposals, Eberhard invited the core Tesla team to help decide on the final concept. Musk would later insist that his input had resulted in a design that incorporated styling from his two favorite cars, the Porsche 911 and the McLaren F1, but according to the journalist Drake Baer, he was the only leading figure at Tesla not invited to Eberhard's final design bake-off.

Musk was only sporadically involved in the Roadster's development, dropping in every few weeks before returning to his "day job" at SpaceX, but his impact on the Roadster was undeniable. More than anyone else in the company's leadership, Musk was bent on making Tesla's first car as lustworthy as possible, regardless of the cost. He would later take credit for decisions that would both define the Roadster's appeal and bloat its development cost and schedule. In addition to the lowered door sills, Musk insisted on designing custom headlights instead of using off-the-shelf units, retooling seats for better comfort than Lotus's stock models offered, creating unique electronic door handles, and swathing the entire car in high-tech carbon fiber reinforced plastic (CFRP).

At the time, Musk wasn't involved with the day-to-day operations at Tesla, so he may not have even fully realized how much money each of these changes would cost. Without auto industry experience, the fact that redesigning a door could be more expensive than redesigning an engine comes across as hyperbole. And unlike a "real" car company, which tracks costs religiously at every stage in development, nobody at Tesla appeared to have a full handle on the company's expenses. Tesla had grown to more than fifty employees but still had no chief financial officer and no central enterprise management software capable of satisfying the needs of a growing company.

Eberhard resisted many of Musk's cost-inflating proposals, ratcheting up the tension between the two men, but at the end of the day it was mostly Musk's money to spend. Without Musk's funding, and that of his deep-pocketed friends in Silicon Valley, the business simply wouldn't exist.

By 2006, the company that Eberhard first envisioned had transformed entirely. Gone were the plans for a simple converted Elise with minimal development costs, replaced with what one Tesla insider called "elegance creep." Tesla had become a part of the auto industry it had hoped to bypass and was burning cash at a rate that its initial business plan had never foreseen. A Series C round of funding in May 2006 brought in an additional $40 million in capital, two times what it had raised in its first two rounds, and it would have to continue to raise similar amounts every year thereafter.

Ultimately, as we will see, Tesla would struggle to get the costs of making and selling a car under control—and it would pay a high price for its first lesson in the economics of the car business.

CHAPTER 4

THE STARTUP TRAP

*Raising venture capital is the easiest thing a
startup founder is ever going to do.*
Marc Andreessen

By 2006, Silicon Valley had fully shaken off its post-dot-com-bubble hangover and was entering a new golden age. The "Web 2.0" wave had already made companies like Skype, Pandora, and Yelp into household names, Facebook and Twitter were just starting their rise to ubiquity, and Apple was putting the final touches on the world's first smartphone.

The venture capitalist Paul Graham captured the mood in a speech he gave that year called "How to Be Silicon Valley." Between deriding the stifling effects of bureaucracy and celebrating the valley's "rich people and nerds," Graham argued, "a place that tolerates oddness in the search for the new is exactly what you want in a startup hub, because economically that's what startups are. Most good startup ideas seem a little crazy; if they were obviously good ideas, someone would have done them already."

As it so happened, this was precisely the figure Tesla cut when it broke out of "stealth mode" in 2006. Even by Silicon Valley standards, a startup that made cars seemed a bit crazy, but then nobody knew what might happen when nerds got into the auto business. The Roadster was obviously fast, it looked good, it was an environmental statement, and celebrities loved it. In the absence of anything resembling a precedent for what Tesla was doing, plenty of people in the valley were willing to give it the benefit of the doubt.

Further, the Detroit automakers were just beginning to enter another downturn of their own making, helping the pro-Tesla sentiment along. The industry's latest truck and SUV binge had given way to market saturation, slowing sales, and overproduction, which were in turn causing growing losses and job cuts. Though the worst—2008's "carmageddon"—was still ahead, America's increasingly ambivalent attitude toward its once-mighty automakers fueled the hope that Silicon Valley's startup ethos might make for a more innovative, environmentally friendly, and ultimately successful car company.

The Roadster did prove that a high-tech startup could identify new opportunities that the established automakers were largely ignoring, develop new intellectual property, and design a cutting-edge car. To most of the public, who relate to cars entirely as consumer goods, that was enough to make Silicon Valley's first automotive startup look like a potential world-beater. But behind the scenes, Tesla was proving that high-tech startup culture was an extremely poor match for the kinds of work that actually determine success and failure in the car business.

The worlds of car making and Silicon Valley startups couldn't be more different. Successful automakers are giant, process-driven bureaucracies that rely on rigidly systematized cultures to manage a continent-spanning ballet of manufacturing operations, supply chains, service infrastructure, and regulatory compliance. Their fundamental challenge is not so much designing the most innovative or desirable cars possible, but rather, designing vehicles that can be built at massive scale and at high levels of quality. Maximizing consistency and minimizing waste are the name of the game, and planning, structure, and regimentation are the keys to success, as we'll see in chapter 5.

Tesla, like most high-tech startups, was organized around the opposite principles: Rather than carefully planning and structuring itself into a giant, perfectly coordinated human machine, it sought to maximize each employee's creative and entrepreneurial potential by minimizing structure and control. With minimal structure and vague yet ambitious goals, Tesla's talented engineers were able to find the work that best suited their skills and pursue innovative solutions. It was a freewheeling engineer's paradise with minimal cost controls and a constantly changing timeline.

The advantages of this startup philosophy came to the fore as Tesla's plan to install AC Propulsion drivetrains into Lotus's modified Elise chassis gave way to a far more ambitious R&D effort. The need for an improved drivetrain became clear as soon as Tesla began testing its first engineering test vehicle, or "mule." AC's drivetrain, made up of an inverter, motor, and engine controller, provided the performance Tesla was looking for, but as development moved forward, problems were emerging. AC's analog circuitry was unreliable and poorly documented, frustrating Tesla's attempts to diagnose and fix problems as they emerged.

As Tarpenning explained in Charles Morris's history of the company, there was another, even bigger problem with AC's hardware:

> AC Propulsion had produced 60 drivetrains or something like that, all hand-crafted. Each motor was matched with each inverter and they were all hand-tuned. This is not manufacturing, this is high-end hobbyist. It's like when you buy an audio system from one of these places that makes a hundred stereos a year. We paid them a bunch of money to license [their motor] and we realized they couldn't manufacture it.

To anyone in the auto industry (or any manufacturing business), this is a common and well-understood problem: small custom shops can design components to deliver high levels of performance for any application, but these unique components are typically manufactured using slow, inefficient techniques and often require extensive calibration. If Tesla was ever going to build hundreds of Roadsters, much of the AC hardware was going to have to be redesigned with production in mind.

This process started with the development of a digital motor controller, which began life as a diagnostic tool. But just as Lotus's minor chassis modifications were expanding into a comprehensive redevelopment project, small improvements were turning into far more sweeping changes. Engineers were in hog heaven, free to pursue blue-sky solutions to new challenges and push their abilities into new technological spaces. As Tesla moved toward its ultimate goal of producing and selling cars to customers, however, their experimentation was wreaking havoc on the production timeline.

Eberhard's original plan for Tesla had assumed that the company would be able to start production in 2006, build five hundred cars in 2007, and be profitable by 2008. By late 2005, with the project spiraling out of control and cash running low, it was becoming clear that the plan would have to change. To raise the money it needed to bring the Roadster to market, Tesla would have to show investors that it was for real.

Just as Eberhard had used his tzero to recruit talent to the company, Musk now used the company's first two prototypes to raise Tesla's $40 million Series C round of funding. Unlike the first mule, the prototypes actually looked something like the sports car that Tesla would eventually produce, and its silent, neck-snapping acceleration helped land several big-name Silicon Valley venture capital outfits. Even when the car failed to work properly, as it did when an early version of Tesla's new digital motor controller limited the vehicle to ten miles per hour during a demonstration for Musk's friends and Google's founders Sergey Brin and Larry Page, the money came in anyway.

With its funds replenished, Tesla broke out of stealth mode and began to collect customer deposits to demonstrate that its rapidly growing R&D operation could support an actual business. That first launch event was held at an airplane hangar in Santa Monica, with a guest list made up of media and celebrities including Arnold Schwarzenegger, Ed Begley Jr., and Michael Eisner. The affair drew massive media attention (and would precipitate the rift between Musk and Eberhard mentioned in the first chapter). Within two weeks, Tesla had sold all one hundred of its limited-edition "Signature" Roadsters. In the months that followed, its tiny public relations and marketing operation would hold more private events and demonstrations for Hollywood celebrities and the Silicon Valley elite, and the orders began stacking up. The company promised that the cars would cost between $85,000 for a base version and $92,000 for a "Signature" and be ready for delivery by 2007.

This public commitment dramatically ramped up the pressure on Tesla's freewheeling innovation effort, forcing it to focus on solving the car's persistent problems while hitting its delivery timeline and cost estimates. And with each customer demonstration and endurance test, more and more problems materialized. Making a car that performed well and looked good was just the start: the new technology Tesla was developing also had to be safe, consistently reliable, and easy to use.

By late 2006, these competing goals were turning Tesla into a pressure cooker. Its public profile was soaring, technical challenges were multiplying, and cash was being incinerated at a shocking rate. Perhaps most troubling, the relationship between Musk and Eberhard was eroding. While Eberhard was managing the increasingly chaotic day-to-day work of pushing toward production, Musk was ratcheting up the pressure by simultaneously championing the Roadster's "elegance creep" and demanding tighter controls on its cost and timeline. By October he was pushing Eberhard to either "sacrifice a six month first mover advantage in a market that is like the Internet circa 1992 (but slower moving) or focus every bit of energy on getting our product right."

In November, Eberhard emailed Musk to explain that there was still much more to be done. "We have a tremendous number of difficult problems to solve just to get the car into production," he wrote. "Everything from serious cost problems to supplier problems (transmission, air conditioning, etc.) to our own design immaturity to Lotus's stability. I stay up at night worrying about simply getting the car into production sometime in 2007."

Tesla now had more than one hundred employees, making it larger than any startup Eberhard had managed. He was trying to implement an enterprise software system to track the rapidly inflating costs, but the company's complexity and lack of coordination—not to mention its lack of a CFO—was making the task incredibly difficult. By January 2007, he and Musk agreed to bring in a new CEO with more financial and management experience to push the Roadster into production.

The initial agreement was jointly made and mutually beneficial. Musk needed to convince potential investors in Tesla's next funding round that costs were under control and the production schedule was on track. Eberhard, meanwhile, wanted to throw himself into the company's next project: a cheaper electric sedan code-named Whitestar, which would increase Tesla's sales volume and make investments in sales and service more palatable.

Eberhard had started hinting at Whitestar almost as soon as Tesla had come out of stealth mode in 2006, but he said little more than it would be the more affordable sedan referenced in Musk's master plan and was scheduled for 2008. By September, Eberhard revealed in a presentation to CARB that Tesla had completed technical specifications, a feasibility study, and "preliminary vehicle architecture," and that the company was looking for a factory site to start production in 2009. With the chances of the Roadster making any money already slim, the prospect of the higher-volume, more mainstream Whitestar had been fundamental to Tesla's Series D funding pitch.

The arrangement should have worked well: a new CEO could take the Roadster over the finish line more efficiently, while Eberhard could keep doing the development work he enjoyed on the Whitestar that was crucial to selling investors on the company's future. But as the scope of Tesla's ambitions kept expanding, the startup was also entering a fundraising treadmill that would require significant new investments every year. Over time this dynamic, which required always having a next big thing, would start to take on a life of its own.

Tesla closed its $40 million Series D funding round in May 2007, but the money had come with fresh strings attached. In the prospectus for the investment, Eberhard had told Tesla's new investors that the Roadster would be in production by September and that it would cost just $65,000 to produce after the first twenty-five units . . . but the money people wanted to double-check his numbers.

One of Tesla's new investors, Valor Equity Partners, sent an auditor to dig through the chaos. What he found was gut-wrenching. The car Tesla hoped to produce by the end of the year and sell at a starting price of $85,000 would cost as much as $200,000 to produce. "Even in full production, they would have been like $170,000 or something insane," Musk later told biographer Ashlee Vance. "Of course it didn't much matter because about a third of the cars didn't flat-out fucking work."

By the time these facts surfaced, Tesla had already found a replacement for Eberhard: former Flextronics CEO Michael Marks. But with Musk and Eberhard's relationship eroding rapidly under the pressure of the situation, the board met without Eberhard and voted to bring in Marks as Tesla's new CEO. Eberhard was stunned at having been left out of the discussion, but when he convened a new meeting, he voluntarily stepped down to become the firm's president of technology.

On the day he took over as CEO, Marks emailed Musk asking to speak with him. "Lots of issues at this company, as you know," he wrote, "but some are a lot scarier and pressing than I thought."

The next day, Musk emailed his fellow board members to tell them that they had not been informed about all the issues. But his email also pointed back to the battle over publicity that had precipitated their split the year before. "Martin seems to be focused on his public image and position within Tesla, rather than solving these critical problems," he wrote. "If you should speak with Martin, please urge him to spend all his energy on making sure that the Roadster works and arrives on time. He doesn't seem to understand that the best way to maximize his reputation and position within the company is to help get this right." By November, Eberhard would be completely estranged from the company, having been paid by Musk to resign from his board seat.

With Eberhard sidelined, Marks began bearing down on the tasks needed to begin production of the Roadster. Tesla's first top executive with extensive manufacturing and supply chain experience, Marks began shutting down all the side projects that had proliferated in Tesla's engineering playground. Shuttered were an electrified Smart car project that Straubel and Musk had been experimenting with, Eberhard's plans for a New Mexico factory to build the new Whitestar sedan, and plans to produce batteries for other companies at Tesla's Thailand factory. But even with the renewed focus that Marks brought, a six-month delay was inevitable, and Musk began to work the media, promising that deliveries would begin in 2008 while teasing the longer-term prospect of the affordable Whitestar.

Marks forced the company to work long hours without distraction from side projects, but still, chaos reigned. Tesla had abandoned its plan to build battery packs in Thailand and was having to painstakingly produce its own packs by hand in California. And the CFRP body panels Musk had insisted on wouldn't hold their paint, forcing Tesla to seek a new supplier and retool at a cost of $5 million.

The major technical problem remaining was the Roadster's transmission, which had been required to achieve both the acceleration and top speed specifications that Tesla had promised its customers. The original transmission supplier, Magna Powertrain, had initially suggested a single speed rather than the "very challenging" dual-clutch two speed Tesla was asking it to design. When the Magna transmission didn't prove reliable enough, Tesla transferred the work to a second supplier, prompting Magna to sue for breach of contract. After working with three different vendors, Tesla still couldn't get a multigear transmission to hold up to the drivetrain's instant torque without destroying itself or performing with unacceptable harshness.

With the clock ticking, the first five hundred Roadsters would have to be built—and delivered—with a transmission that didn't work. Once again, Tesla's deep reserve of engineering talent (and some incredible luck) would turn the challenge into an opportunity to improve its technology. Stuck with a single-speed transmission, Straubel and his team would have to completely redesign the remaining AC Propulsion technology to develop enough power to make the transmission meet the promised specifications.

As it turned out, Moore's Law came to Tesla's rescue: a new, more efficient version of the insulated-gate bipolar transistor (IGBT) that Tesla used to synthesize waveforms in its power electronics module (PEM) had just come out, enabling 33 percent higher power throughput without overheating. Using these new IGBTs, Tesla was able to make just a few changes to its drivetrain and dramatically increase the horsepower and torque output. The new drivetrain and other improvements would deliver the specs Tesla had originally promised, but only after the company wasted millions trying to source a multigear unit and missed its goal for the start of production.

By the time the first Roadsters started coming off the line at Lotus's plant in Hethel, England, they were already obsolete. The earliest units would be delivered with a two-speed transmission locked to a single speed, and each car needed to be completely retrofitted with the new "Roadster 1.4"-spec motor, cooling system, PEM, and single-speed transmission after delivery. The midproduction upgrade and retrofit would cost the company any shot at profitability and force Musk to ask customers to pay more for cars they had already been charged for.

Musk did what he could to limit the damage. In late 2007, Marks, who had been serving as interim CEO, was replaced with Ze'ev Drori, a veteran of two successful hardware startups. As Musk began to raise the company's 2008 Series E round, the two took to the media to present a unified front. But Musk's ouster of Eberhard had badly shaken morale among the company's employees, many of whom had known Eberhard for years and worked directly with him throughout the Roadster program. Core team members began to quit, and as Tesla began to tighten its belt, others were fired.

Tensions ratcheted up in January 2008 when Eberhard launched his pointedly titled (and since deleted) Tesla Founders Blog. Despite promising that "the purpose of this blog is not to criticize Tesla" in his first post, the second post described what he called the "stealth bloodbath" at Tesla, complete with a collection of quotes from "anonymous employees and newly-former employees," like:

> I came to Tesla with a great deal of optimism to work for a company with a noble purpose that had a real chance to make a difference in the world. That sense of mission and hope generated incredible energy and determination to overcome the many challenges of producing a great EV. This energy has been drained by the cold, irrational bloodletting that has been going on there. Everyone understands necessary, rational cost management actions in startups, but this was neither necessary nor rational.

Within two weeks, Eberhard had taken down the post "at the strong request of Tesla's management," but the damage was done. The media had caught wind of Tesla's turmoil, and coverage would only get tougher as the company limped into what would become one of the toughest years in its history.

Tesla's internal turmoil and the Roadster's chaotic development, which continued even after deliveries began, were the predictable result of a startup approach to car making. Having failed to properly study the cost of developing and producing the Roadster up front and neglecting to track costs along the way, Tesla had fallen behind and been forced to raise money as it blundered along.

This had put Tesla on the Silicon Valley hamster wheel, requiring it to raise tens of millions of dollars every year; it had to diversify into new projects that would keep investors on board even when the Roadster proved to have been a money pit. In 2008 alone, the company had to build Roadster 1.0s, upgrade delivered cars to 1.5 spec, convert production to 1.5 spec, develop further improvements that would become Roadster 2.0 spec, and try to create the cheaper Whitestar sedan from the ground up. Such were the challenges that Tesla would skip the 2009 model year altogether. New investments intended to fix old problems gave rise to new promises—which, in turn, would need more cash.

As the costs piled up, Musk had become so deeply invested in Tesla that he could no longer afford to simply walk away. To keep the company rolling forward, Musk focused more and more on the Whitestar with investors and the media. He dangled the next car as an opportunity for Tesla to learn from its mistakes, take another step closer to popularizing electric cars, and become a serious automaker.

This pattern would become a defining characteristic of Tesla's culture: The company would be stuck having to hype ever-bigger new ambitions to raise the money needed to deliver on earlier endeavors that had bogged down in execution. "We never had the time or money to do things right the first time, but we always found the time and money to do things twice," recalled one former employee I spoke to, echoing a sentiment that I would hear again and again.

At a time when the mythology surrounding the high-tech sector and startups was beginning to blossom into a major force in American cultural life, Tesla's high-speed agility and constant cash raising helped their popular image more than it hurt. But even as Tesla played into fantasies of high-tech startup culture disrupting the car business, its ability to raise cash derailed Musk's master plan to fund each future generation of products with profits from the current product.

Had Tesla remained committed to Musk's plan, it might have developed the operational discipline that automakers must embrace to survive in such a capital-intensive, low-margin business (as we'll find in the next chapter). Instead, Tesla's mission creep led to repeated fundraising that eventually seemed to convince its leaders that the company's real product was its sense of future promise that it could monetize first with venture capital and later with stock and debt sales. Once caught in the startup trap, Tesla's incentives shifted away from lean execution and toward generating the kind of hype and anticipation that would keep fresh investment flowing.

Though the auto industry has always been fueled by dreams, it is fundamentally a business that lives and dies on execution. By definition, every manufacturing business must produce real results. But to raise the cash it would need to survive, Tesla appeared to focus mainly on producing grand visions for investors—producing cars seemed secondary.

As generating hype for upcoming funding rounds became ever more fundamental to Tesla's survival, the gap between perceptions of the company and the underlying reality grew. For many fans and investors, the perceptions became the reality. For the company, the perceptions were the products keeping the lights on. As this feedback loop built on itself, the company and its supporters steadily built a new reality for themselves that would eventually become almost entirely unmoored from that which the rest of the world occupied.

CHAPTER 5

MAKING CARS IS HARD

When the mess gets sorted out, I'd like to have a conversation
with whoever's in charge at the time—the car czar or whoever—
and say, "I'd like to run your plants, if you don't mind."
Elon Musk, June 15, 2009

Today, Tesla's factory in Fremont, California, looms over the surrounding business parks and subdivisions, its massive white profile framed by the brown hills that form the eastern boundary of Silicon Valley. In this epicenter of a new economy specializing in miniature microchips and ephemeral software, the plant—previously occupied by General Motors and New United Motor Manufacturing, Inc.—stands out as industrial-age atavism, the lone surviving dinosaur in a world of tiny, nimble startups. Its sheer size and the undisguised functionalism of its design are a stark reminder that, no matter how often or insistently Tesla claims it is a "technology company" rather than a traditional automaker, the core of its business is still old-fashioned manufacturing.

From the very beginning, Tesla's relationship to manufacturing has been deeply ambivalent. Remember, the company's original business plan was funded on the assumption that it could be a "fab-less" car company, focusing on electric drivetrain technology and sexy design while leaving the metal bending to suppliers and contractors. This belief quickly proved to be misguided, and Tesla eventually embraced the opposite extreme, insourcing the production of components like seats that every other automaker contracts to suppliers. Still, the company's uneasy relationship with manufacturing remained embedded in its corporate DNA.

Operating and identifying as a software-style Silicon Valley startup had given Tesla a unique skill set, one of its great strengths as a company. Brilliant and creative individuals were unleashed on complex challenges, working long hours with minimal oversight and more often than not delivering ingenious, outside-the-box solutions. This kind of dynamic, individualistic culture facilitates incredible achievements in design, research and development, and prototyping, which explains Tesla's undeniable prowess in these areas.

The reason no other auto company had embraced software startup values is that cars and software are very different products with different challenges. In software, design is everything; once a software product exists it costs almost nothing to make additional copies of it. Once you've sold enough copies to pay back the "fixed cost" of designing and developing a software product, each additional copy has very little incremental "variable cost" and thus enjoys incredibly high profit margins. Because the quality of a program's design determines the demand for it, software companies embody the cultural values that foster great design.

Cars also have high fixed costs, which go into the design and development of the vehicles as well as the factory and tooling needed to build them. But unlike software, which can be quickly and cheaply copied, each additional car has a significant variable cost for the materials and labor needed to manufacture it. No matter how good a vehicle's design is, every example must be built efficiently and at high quality to ensure its profitability.

Though consumers often think of "quality" in terms of design decisions—materials, features, functionality, and feel—in the industrial context, quality simply means the consistency of execution. Perfect quality means that each unit produced is exactly like every other, and that there are no variations across production runs of hundreds of thousands or even millions of examples. Sweating the tiniest details of such immensely complex collections of parts is brutally tough, especially when the standard for quality is so high that an inconsistency in one out of ten vehicles produced would cause a major automaker to stop production until they determined the source of the problems. Single-digit defective parts per million produced is a standard goal for most major automakers.

Whereas the building blocks of software are abstractions—ones and zeroes that exist in computer memory—every part of a car is made in the imperfection of the real world. From raw materials to components to modules to final assembly, each step in the massive automotive supply chains that stretch around the world introduces an opportunity to deviate from design specifications. By the time final assembly takes place, all the barely perceptible imperfections that were accumulated along the way can combine to create significant defects called "tolerance stack ups."

Even if every component is still within spec, every complex task that goes into assembly is another opportunity for tiny deviations that could end up as a misaligned body panel or a mysterious rattle in a dashboard. As standardized as auto production is, even tiny imperfections can mean that parts must be finessed together or judiciously discarded at the discretion of experienced production workers. And unlike software, which can be patched at any time, cars need to be built right the first time, every time to realize the efficiencies of standardized production.

So it is no coincidence that the car companies that emphasize creativity and passion are the luxury and sports car makers who build tiny volumes of vehicles that are bought more as artwork than a mobility tool. Outside of this rarified group, the core function of companies making the other 99.9 percent of all cars is to build those cars well. Though design and emotion still matter to all car companies, the core challenge they face is ensuring that every car that comes off their assembly line is built efficiently and as close to its specification as possible.

As the technology analyst Horace Dediu points out, all the most important innovations in the history of the car industry have been focused on this fundamental production challenge. The first major production innovation, Henry Ford's moving assembly line, gave birth to both the industrial age and the first truly global automaker. Though the Model T had undeniable design advantages, its utter dominance of the early car market was a product of Ford's manufacturing breakthrough, which continuously lowered the price of the car and thus expanded its market.

Even after the Model T had become hopelessly outdated and rival companies started eating into its once-dominant market share, Ford's formula of standardized parts, vertical integration, and economies of scale continued to define the car business for nearly a half century. Eventually, this too was surpassed by the Toyota Production System, or TPS. TPS grew out of the teachings of W. Edwards Deming and others and has now become the foundation on which every automaker's culture is built.

Starting with the concept of statistical process control, Deming developed a scientific approach to management that conceptualized companies as machinelike systems that could be optimized for ever-greater quality and efficiency. Like an engineer improving the design of an engine, Deming showed that by measuring and mapping a company's workflows, managers could identify and improve poor quality and waste. As this philosophy evolved, it increasingly focused on aligning every human component of the corporate machine with the goal of continuous improvement the only way possible: through culture.

Toyota understood the importance of industrial culture to manufacturing before it even built its first car. Unable to develop a power source that would improve on steam, founder Sakichi Toyoda became obsessed with the interaction of humans and machines, inventing a wooden hand loom that allowed an operator to efficiently produce high-quality fabric with just one hand. Over the following thirty years, he developed and evolved power spinning machines and looms that were not just faster and more efficient, but also safer and easier to operate.

After Toyota expanded into automobiles, an employee named Taiichi Ohno was put in charge of a machining shop. Ohno began combining Deming's ideas with concepts that had made Toyoda's looms so effective, like a system that would automatically shut off a machine when a defect was detected. Recognizing that employees understood their work processes better than anyone, he recruited them to not only help design a production system but also to forge cultural principles that would align the entire company around continuous, systematic improvement.

By the 1980s, Toyota's cultural innovations had made its quality so good that it quickly became one of the biggest and most successful automakers in the world. It doubled its production from about three million units per year in 1980 to about six million units per year in 2000, and it reached more than ten million units per year by 2015. This unmatched growth was not the product of superior styling or performance, but the consistent reliability and quality of its cars. This modern miracle proved conclusively that most car buyers value reliable utility above sexy looks or exciting performance, and that culture rather than technological innovation was the key to this consistent quality.

Today, every major automaker has embraced the fundamentals of the Toyota Production System—and so have businesses in every kind of manufacturing and beyond. Part of this success stems from the fact that TPS is values based rather than prescriptive, making it easily adaptable to almost any business undertaking. But it remains most effective—indeed, necessary—in the massive and complex business of making cars, where every step in global supply chains is an opportunity for defects and inefficiencies to work into the system.

One of the best known and most fundamental principles of lean manufacturing culture is *kaizen*, or continuous improvement. This goes in hand with another core value, long-term perspective. Both of these principles are part of Toyota's managerial approach, called the Toyota Way. Not only are these principles the best method to improve performance in a business as large and complex as an automaker, they are also the only way to build a successful culture. Put differently, a culture founded on the principles of kaizen will not simply try to improve its performance metrics over the long term, it will also seek to continuously improve its ability to continuously improve.

For this reason, any automaker with mass-market aspirations like those outlined in Musk's master plan must build its culture on the proven values of lean manufacturing long before it reaches mass-production volume. In fact, this is the great untapped value of Musk's strategy of starting with high-end, low-volume cars and working toward mass production: it should allow a startup to continuously improve its manufacturing capabilities and culture during the easier small-volume stages so that successful values are fully inculcated by the time it reaches the ultimate challenge of high-volume manufacturing.

But rather than embracing a process-oriented *kaizen* manufacturing culture, Tesla saw itself first and foremost as a Silicon Valley technology startup. According to longtime VP of Powertrain Technology Jim Dunlay, the company built its culture on values like "scrappiness, hiring the best people in the world, allowing people to exercise their judgment in the face of uncertainty, and leading by example." As a result, its earliest hires were predominantly talented young engineers from top schools, generally with little or no manufacturing or operational experience.

A member of Tesla's Roadster production team, let's call him Frank, was surprised to find that he was one of the few who did have prior auto manufacturing experience when he started building cars at the company's Menlo Park facility. Stranger still, his colleagues didn't show much interest in developing the TPS culture he had learned at his previous assembly line job. The brilliant young engineers tasked with building Tesla's Roadsters were eager to throw themselves into finding creative solutions to problems, but they were far less interested in adopting Frank's deliberate, process-driven approach.

There was plenty of scope for creative solutions, as the Lotus "gliders" (partially built cars without drivetrains) coming off cargo planes at the San Francisco airport often required considerable work before Tesla could even start turning them into Roadsters. Like most companies that build tiny numbers of unique and exhilarating cars by hand, Lotus had never been famous for its quality. The build quality of a contemporary Lotus Evora was described by Pulitzer Prize–winning auto critic Dan Neil as "miserable." Because Tesla's manufacturing process started with diagnosis and repair of Lotus's inconsistent gliders, it was harder to standardize into consistent procedures.

The engineers on the team seemed to expect this kind of dynamic and creative workflow out of a Silicon Valley startup, even one that manufactured cars. The whole point of hiring brilliant engineers was to throw their talent at problems as they popped up, and they enjoyed and took pride in the intellectual challenge of coming up with creative hacks and fixes. But continuous improvement can't rely on talent to create one-off fixes; defects need to be traced to their source so a permanent solution can be put into place. Every defect is a symptom of a flaw in the production system, and thus the solution must be a systemic one. Quality isn't a question of continuously improving your ability to fix individual defects, but rather steadily drumming *the causes of defects* out of the production system over time.

Because of his background, Frank believed he had been brought in to inculcate a culture dedicated to continuous, systemic quality improvement and his colleagues initially embraced his focus on quality. But as pressure to deliver cars mounted, the emphasis on speed—which would go on to distinguish Tesla's manufacturing philosophy from the Toyota approach, in the eyes of many analysts—won out. The engineers increasingly seemed to think Frank's fixation on finding the source of seemingly tiny problems was a waste of time better spent getting the car out the door.

This culture clash was exacerbated by the startup-style expectation that workers would dedicate six to seven twelve-hour days per week to the job, making production more of an endless sprint than the deliberate marathon pace encouraged by kaizen and the TPS's long-term perspective. Long hours would become one of Tesla's enduring cultural characteristics over the ensuing decade, with Musk extolling eighty-hour work weeks, and workers reporting twelve- to sixteen-hour shifts and six-day work weeks, employees sleeping in the factory, and an exhaustion- and Red Bull–fueled "Tesla stare."

It didn't take long for the culture clash to boil over. After he had identified one too many defects, a colleague took the production team's frustrations with Frank up the ladder. As Frank remembers it, "Elon Musk came out and said, 'We're not building Toyotas.'" The message was clear: unlike other car companies, Tesla was not focused on consistent quality. Before long, Frank would be fired. Payback, most likely, for giving a crap about quality and being vocal about it.

It's hard to imagine that a company with this attitude could thrive as Tesla has, but Musk knew his high-end clientele and he was ultimately right. The lower the price of a car, the more the owner is likely to rely on it and thus the more important quality is. At the high end of the market, factors like performance, styling, and brand prestige are the main concern, and customers are a lot less demanding of quality and reliability. Luxury and premium car brands like Ferrari and Land Rover are infamously unreliable relative to the rest of the market, but they are bought for performance and status rather than utility.

When a Roadster did break down, it was an opportunity to highlight the company's mobile "Ranger" repair service that would come to wherever the car was and fix the problem. This approach took the customer's focus off the problem and onto Tesla's white-glove service, which went well beyond what most other car companies offered.

Besides, anyone who owned a six-figure Tesla likely also had a multitude of other cars that they could take if the Tesla was broken, so the consequences of failure were typically low.

And when early customers were less than entirely forgiving after being genuinely inconvenienced by Tesla's poor quality, Musk was quick to leverage his own celebrity and Tesla's high-tech image to shut them down. When an interviewer from *Esquire* tried to find out if George Clooney "was susceptible to Hollywood cliché" by asking where his Tesla was, the actor gave a less than glowing review of his ownership experience:

> *I had a Tesla. I was one of the first cats with a Tesla. I think I was, like, number five on the list. But I'm telling you, I've been on the side of the road a while in that thing. And I said to them, "Look, guys, why am I always stuck on the side of the fucking road? Make it work, one way or another."*

Musk struck back, sardonically tweeting, "In other news, George Clooney reports that his iPhone 1 had a bug back in '07." It was a brilliant comeback, tweaking the Hollywood big shot while comparing Tesla's products to a high-tech device that was groundbreaking, deeply desirable, and more prone to malfunctions than most cars. These two tactics—excusing Tesla's quality problems by portraying it as cutting-edge technology and attacking anyone who dared complain—would become Tesla's go-to response to anyone who was surprised to find that its cars didn't match the rest of the industry's high-quality standard.

Had Musk never planned to move down-market with each subsequent car, eventually ending up in the mass market, its lack of a quality-focused manufacturing culture might never have been a major problem. Indeed, because the two vehicles that followed the Roadster ended up selling for six figures on average, Tesla has muddled along for a decade and a half without being forced to reboot its manufacturing culture. Since Tesla's brand reflected the prestige of both cutting-edge Silicon Valley high technology and Hollywood celebrity, its affluent customer base has been infinitely forgiving of its quality shortcomings.

Frank's story didn't become truly significant until almost a decade after he left Tesla, when the company's ambition to build the affordable, mass-market Model 3 turned into a year of "production hell." Suddenly higher volumes, tighter margins, and customers who rely on the quality of their cars meant that Tesla needed the efficiency and quality that Frank had tried to build into Tesla's manufacturing culture. All of the issues and attitudes that had troubled him during the Roadster days were pouring out into Tesla's media coverage and financial results, having become more impactful and deeply entrenched over the intervening years.

Musk had made a choice: Tesla's focus was not efficiently manufacturing reliable appliances but designing exciting cars that pushed the cutting edge of automotive technology. The company's prowess as an R&D and prototyping outfit would continue to develop, making it one of the top operations in these areas in the auto business and a playground for talented engineers. But the startup-style culture that made it so good at these intense bursts of creative development, not to mention fundraising and publicity, would ultimately trade off with the principles of successful manufacturing culture on which modern car companies are built.

These kinds of cultural choices determine the fates of automakers again and again. The Detroit automakers chose V8 power and tailfin fashion over efficiency and quality in the first half of the twentieth century, printing record profits until the Japanese invasion turned the US market toward more pragmatic values. Even after it was clear that Detroit's golden age had collapsed into malaise, it took decades (and in some cases, bankruptcy) for its humbled titans to fully embrace the cultural values that would start to bring them back into competitive shape.

The great miscalculation of Tesla's cultural choice is that its plan all along was to enter the affordable mainstream, where operational efficiency and high levels of quality are mandatory. Having battled for more than a decade against impossible odds, Tesla arrived at the brink of mainstream success without the ability or desire to truly embrace the role of a major automobile manufacturer. Somewhere along the way, Tesla had decided to be a startup forever.

CHAPTER 6

BAILOUT

Working at Tesla back then was like being Kurtz in
Apocalypse Now. *Don't worry about the methods or if they're*
unsound. Just get the job done. It comes from Elon.
Dave Lyons, in Ashlee Vance's Elon Musk

"We need to get the company to cash flow–positive in six to nine months or we're screwed." Musk was grim faced, the signs of profound stress evident in every expression and mannerism. "It's really pedal to the metal here," he said. "Each month that passes literally costs us tens of millions of dollars. We need to appreciate that." He stared, eyes wild with helpless frustration, at the silent conference room.

It was December 2008, and having sold just over one hundred Roadsters, Tesla was on the brink of oblivion. Filmmaker Chris Paine captured the grim moment at Tesla's headquarters in the documentary *Revenge of the Electric Car*—the company's cubicles emptied by layoffs, and its fourth CEO in five years calling for more heads. "It's not OK to be unhappy and part of this company," Musk said to his stone-faced lieutenants.

The year had been full of highs for Musk. Tesla had finally produced and delivered its first cars, kicking off an orgy of acclaim in the media. Sleek Roadsters zipped silently around the world's most exclusive neighborhoods, advertising the taste and environmental sensitivity of their owners as well as the brilliant potential of the company that made them. Musk was everywhere talking about the company's next car, the long-awaited affordable Whitestar, which promised to complete the company's transformation from a conversion project to a real car company.

But the soaring highs had also been accompanied by stunning lows. Tesla's first run of cars had been shipped with "interim" transmissions that couldn't meet the promised acceleration specifications, and the cars were plagued with problems. The company was bleeding cash as it tried to keep its customers' cars running, update the design for future production, retrofit cars it had already sold with the updated drivetrain, lower costs, and develop the Whitestar. Meanwhile, the global economy was collapsing into recession, threatening to cut Tesla off from the cash it needed to survive.

The last quarter of 2008 would be a pivotal one for Tesla, and it would prove that Musk was willing to go to any lengths to keep his struggling automaker afloat. Musk dipped into customer Roadster deposits to pay for operating expenses, leading to the departure of Tesla's VP of marketing, Darryl Siry. Even Musk's brother and fellow Tesla board member Kimbal Musk was worried about the lengths to which he was going to save the company, telling Ashlee Vance, "he definitely took risks that seemed like they could have landed him in jail for using someone else's money."

That October, Musk fired Drori, replaced him as CEO, and slashed a quarter of the company's jobs. Tesla had just $9 million in its bank accounts, and with credit markets drying up, Musk would have to dig deep to secure the company's next fundraising round. After a plan to raise $100 million over the summer failed, Musk told the *New York Times* that Tesla would raise just $20–$30 million from the company's existing investors.

Just a week later, it appeared that Tesla was out of the woods, when it put out a press release titled "Tesla Receives $40 Million Financing Commitment." The release stated that Tesla's board had "approved $40 million in convertible debt financing, based on commitments from almost all current major investors," and Reuters reported that the funding was "secured." But according to Vance's book, which was released years later, Tesla did not in fact close the funding round until nearly two months after it sent out the press release. Paperwork for the round was supposed to have been finalized on the third, but due to hesitation on the part of VantagePoint Capital Partners, the negotiations dragged on.

According to Vance, Musk switched the round from equity to debt in response to VantagePoint's hesitation on December 3, casting even more doubt on the announcement of a convertible debt deal at least a month earlier. Musk also liquidated assets and borrowed cash from SpaceX, taking personal loans for living expenses, to scrape together the $20 million he was asking his investors to match. After SpaceX received a surprise NASA contract to supply the International Space Station on December 23, and Musk threatened to fund the entire Tesla round himself, investors finally swallowed hard and wrote checks. On Christmas Eve 2008, just days before Tesla was about to bounce its payroll, the deal went through and the company received its stay of execution. Musk ultimately put in $12 million of the $40 million round.

This desperate maneuver would become a key part of the Musk mythology, emphasizing the profound personal sacrifice and risks he was willing to endure to keep Tesla afloat. If Musk realized that saying Tesla had funding nearly two months before it actually did might be problematic, it didn't stop him from repeating the Christmas Eve story in a *60 Minutes* interview and at a Q&A session at Sorbonne University in Paris. (A decade later, a similar preannouncement of "secured" funding that was anything but would lead to Musk settling fraud charges with the SEC.)

As dramatic as Musk's efforts had been, they only prevented an immediate bankruptcy. A broader bailout was already in the works, instigated by Eberhard more than a year before.

In mid-2007, just months before being ousted as CEO, Eberhard had testified at a Senate Finance Committee hearing on advanced technology vehicles. Though Tesla still had yet to deliver a single Roadster, Eberhard talked up the $50,000 Whitestar sedan that Tesla was planning on building at a factory in New Mexico, saying, "Tesla intends to become a major car company." He also suggested that the US had a strategic interest in establishing a domestic battery manufacturing sector, saying, "Tesla is not in the business of making cells, though I have thought about it a lot. If no one else steps up to the plate and if I can figure out how to finance such a venture, I might take a swing at it. Now if you are looking to invest about $500M, please let me know . . ."

Shortly thereafter, Congress had passed the Energy Independence and Security Act, which established a $25 billion loan program to support the manufacture of advanced technology vehicles. Before Eberhard's ouster, Tesla had applied to the still-unfunded program seeking $350 million to develop and produce the Whitestar and another $100 million to develop a battery production facility that could supply other automakers. Eberhard's half-billion-dollar figure had not been merely pulled out of thin air.

At the time, Tesla had obtained a contract to supply battery packs to another startup called Think Global, which was developing an electric city car. Other automakers had also approached Tesla to explore the possibility of buying its battery packs, and Eberhard had assigned his old friend and board member Bernard Tse to establish a new division for this business called "Tesla Energy Group." One of the interested parties was the German automaker Daimler, which was interested in the possibility of an electric version of its Smart city car, and Tesla had set about building a prototype. But when Eberhard was ousted and Marks took over with a mandate to focus the company on Roadster production, Tesla Energy Group was shuttered. By the time Musk took over as CEO in late 2008, Think Global had moved on to a new battery supplier, and another customer had to be found to revive the Tesla Energy Group business.

According to Musk's 2016 shareholder meeting history, he approached Daimler about supplying the drivetrain for the firm's electric Smart in October 2008, and Straubel produced a prototype by the following January, just in time to demonstrate it to a delegation of visiting Daimler executives. Vance's version is that Tesla's booth at the Detroit Auto Show in January 2009 led to a short-notice visit "about a month" thereafter (although curiously, he also mentions Michael Marks discovering a Smart project when he took over in 2007). A third version, published in *Wired* in 2010, says that Musk pitched Daimler in September 2007 and was turned down, but he got an email two months later saying a Daimler delegation would be in town in six weeks.

Whatever the timeline really was, all the accounts agree that Daimler was so impressed by their test drive of Tesla's hastily made hot-rod electric Smart—which was apparently powerful enough to pull a wheelie in a small parking lot—that it ordered 1,000 battery packs and chargers with which to convert Smarts to electric drive. Not only had Tesla revived the battery supply business that was part of its DOE loan application, it had a customer ready to buy more battery packs than it had built to date. The Daimler deal was a massive boost to Tesla's legitimacy: in a matter of weeks Tesla went from near bankruptcy to a partnership with the world's oldest automaker. Musk would later call Daimler's investment "a lifesaver," saying that "without that investment, Tesla would have been . . . game over."

But Tesla had to do more than revive its battery business to qualify for the DOE loan. It needed to prove that the Whitestar was real, it needed a factory to retool, and most important, it needed to prove that it could be "financially viable." The loan program required applicants to show that they would not need additional support to reach profitability; given Tesla's abysmal financial performance, this would not be easy.

To clear this formidable obstacle, Musk had to take extreme measures. He increased the base price of model year (MY) 2009 and later Roadsters from $92,000 to $109,000 (the original base price was $85,000), but those wouldn't be built until the middle of 2009 (as MY2010, since Tesla ended up skipping MY2009 entirely). In the meantime, Tesla still had to improve profitability on the MY2008 Roadsters that were about to be built. Since customers had already deposited between $35,000 and $50,000 to lock in the $92,000 base price for these 2008s, Tesla had only a few options, none of them good.

Early in January 2009, rumors began to surface online to the effect that Tesla would be raising prices on all its Roadsters, including the MY2008 vehicles whose price had been "locked in." In one of the first emails to customers about the changes, Musk held up a recent charity auction result as evidence that "owning a Roadster can be a smart investment," talked about how Roadster customers would be funding the more affordable Model S, laid out a series of new options, and then at the end revealed that "we have removed a couple of items from the list of standard features." It was clearly an effort to slip the news past customers, and it predictably fueled confusion and suspicion.

As angry customers registered their shock, Musk wrote another email explaining both the problem and his solution far more directly. Summarizing the company's struggles to wrangle the Roadster's runaway costs, Musk wrote that the variable cost of the car would be between $90,000 and $100,000—though he estimated the price would be at or below $80,000 by the summer. Musk continued:

> *Obviously, this still creates a serious problem for Tesla in the first half of 2009, given the $92k to $98k price of most cars delivered over this time period. The board and I did not want to do a retroactive increase of the base vehicle price, as that would create*

an unavoidable hardship for customers. Instead, apart from a $1k destination charge increase to match our true cost of logistics, we only raised the price of the optional elements and provided new options and a new model (Roadster Sport) to help improve the average margin per car.

In reality, customers suddenly were being asked to either accept an additional $1,000 "destination charge" and reduced standard options or pony up $6,700 to $9,350 more for previously included options. Among the no-longer-base options was a 240-volt charger that could charge a Roadster in eight hours, leaving base version buyers with a 120-volt charger that would take upward of thirty hours to fully charge. But at least Musk was now being honest about the reason for the increase, concluding the email with the real story:

There is one additional point that relates to the government loans that Tesla is seeking for the Model S program, a much more affordable sedan that we are trying to bring to market as soon as possible. A key requirement is that any company applying be able to show that it is viable without the loans. If we allow ourselves to lose money on the cars we are shipping today, we place those loans at risk. Mass market electric cars have been my goal from the beginning of Tesla. I don't want and I don't think the vast majority of Tesla customers want us to do anything to jeopardize that objective.

Musk followed up on this email with a series of town hall meetings at Tesla's California facilities, in which he explained the necessity of these moves. The meetings ranged from civil to heated, in some cases becoming downright confrontational. Musk tried to diffuse the tension by playing up the obstacles Tesla had overcome, telling deposit holders at one meeting, "I can't understate the degree of grief that I've personally gone through . . . to make this work. When I say it was like eating glass, I mean a glass sandwich every bloody day."

Ultimately, there were relatively few cancellations, as most reservation holders were easily able to afford the increase and had been aware of the risks going in, but there was real anger, which didn't help public perceptions of the company. After one meeting, Musk told the filmmaker Paine, "There seemed to be a little bit of anger from some people in the room who felt that we'd kind of done a bait and switch . . . and that's sort of a little bit true that there was a bit of a bait and switch. That's kind of what happened."

To help manage the blowback, Musk turned again to the "funding secured" tactic he would use repeatedly to get Tesla through dire moments in its history. In a February 11, 2009, email to customers, Musk again echoed his earlier assertion that "it seems owning a Roadster can be a good investment" and made an astonishing claim:

> Regarding funding, I am excited to report that the Department of Energy informed Tesla last week that they expect to disburse funds from our $350M Model S loan application within four to five months. The Obama administration has thankfully made it a top priority to move quickly on the Advanced Technology Vehicles Manufacturing loan program, as this will both generate high quality jobs in the near term and lay the groundwork for a better environment in the future.
>
> This will keep us on track for production to start in 2011. As a gesture of gratitude for their early support, Roadster owners will receive a $10,000 discount off the price of the Model S Signature series and automatically be first in line for the sedan.

Four months later, the DOE did announce that Tesla was among the companies that had received "conditional commitments" through the loan program, but the actual loan agreement (let alone the disbursement that Musk claimed was imminent) wouldn't be signed for nearly another year. After Musk's announcement, both a Tesla spokesperson and the Department of Energy confirmed that it "has made no final decisions on specific applications," but Musk's claim made more waves than the subsequent corrections. (Tesla also changed the wording from "they expect to disburse" to "they may disburse" when it posted the email to its blog.)

In fact, Freedom of Information Act (FOIA) requests of Tesla's applications to the program reveal that its December 2, 2008, application had been rejected due to insufficient data to verify efficiency claims and environmental regulation compliance. Tesla's successful application to the loan program wouldn't be filed until May 4, 2009, months after Musk's claim about imminent disbursement.

The gambit paid off: In August 2009, Tesla proudly announced that July had been its first-ever profitable month, with $1 million in profit on $20 million revenue. In the company's official press release, Musk claimed that improved quality, reduced costs, and strong demand for the Roadster had been responsible for the milestone result. But with 109 Roadsters delivered in the month, the company's per-car revenue was over $180,000 even though its price was only $109,000, suggesting that the profit would not have been possible on the strength of the Roadster alone.

It wasn't clear how exactly Tesla had pulled off its first profit until the following January when the company filed paperwork to go public, revealing that it had earned more than $7.5 million over the first three quarters of 2009 from sales of ZEV credits alone. In fact, 85 percent of Tesla's 2009 gross margin (which only includes the parts and labor to produce cars) came from ZEV credits, and in 2008 its negative gross margin would have been four times worse without the credits.

But no matter how it was earned, one million dollars was not much of a return on the more than $200 million that had been invested in Tesla. Musk warned investors not to get used to profitability, telling Bloomberg that Tesla "will soon plunge into the red . . . when it ramps up production and fills out a dealer network." But the point had been made to DOE's loan officers: Tesla could be financially viable, if only for a single month.

This would not be the last time Tesla would use ZEV credits to push it over the line to a quarterly profit at a crucial moment. In fact, Tesla seemed to be waking up to the opportunities that the ZEV program opened for it as the singular EV-only automaker. In 2010, former VP of marketing Darryl Siry reported in *Wired* that during the IPO roadshow, "a Tesla finance vice president told analysts they could assume every Tesla Model S sold would generate approximately $5,000 in ZEV credit profit."

In the meantime, Tesla had been hustling to convince the government and the public that its Whitestar sedan was more than just vaporware. The cost of developing, tooling, and producing the "more affordable" sedan accounted for $350 million of the $465 million in loans that Tesla had applied for, making it the company's top priority. But because Tesla had cut jobs and expenditures to the bone during 2008, including the Detroit-area office it had opened in 2007 to build up its automotive know-how, little development work had actually been done. Just as it had done with the Roadster, Tesla was going to have to reveal the car it was staking its future on in the form of a fragile, hand-built prototype.

On March 26, 2009, Musk drove a sleek, fastback, silver-gray sedan out from behind a black curtain and into a raucous party of fans, customers, and supporters. "You're looking at what will become the world's first mass-manufactured electric car," Musk told the crowd. Noting that some had doubted Tesla's ability to bring the Roadster to market, he added, "people should have complete confidence that, y'know, this car is going to come to market. I think we can do it in about two years."

Only from behind the curtain was it clear that the car was in fact a long way from completion. Just like the Roadster, the prototype was essentially a conversion: according to Vance, Tesla had bought a Mercedes CLS, converted it to electric drive using a modified Roadster drivetrain, and added new body panels (some of which were held on with magnets). At the reveal event, Paine's cameras disclosed that

Tesla had set up a massive external cooling system that pumped ice water through the battery while workers scrambled to prep the car for its debut. During a test ride in the prototype that evening, the product specialist had to admit that the car's large central screen had frozen up and needed to be rebooted. Once again, Tesla had done just enough to create the perception that the car was real and was relying on Musk's bluster and showmanship to deliver the cash needed to turn that perception into reality.

The sedan was the more affordable "Whitestar" that Tesla had been promising since 2006, now called the Model S. It would accelerate from zero to sixty in no more than six seconds and be offered with 160, 230, or 300 miles of range per charge. Most important, the Model S would cost just $57,400 to start, or less than $50,000 including the $7,500 federal tax credit for electric cars. Tesla was making good on its master-plan promise to dramatically reduce the price of its second car even as it raised prices for the Roadster. Musk emphasized the car's affordability in Tesla's official press release, saying:

> Model S costs half as much as a Roadster, and it's a better value than much cheaper cars. The ownership cost of Model S, if you were to lease and then account for the much lower cost of electricity vs. gasoline at a likely future cost of $4 per gallon, is similar to a gasoline car with a sticker price of about $35,000. I'm positive this car will be the preferred choice of savvy consumers.

Once again, customers who were willing to believe Musk were asked to put down deposits: a limited-edition "Signature" run could be reserved for $40,000, and a standard Model S could be secured for $5,000 down. With controversy over Tesla's decision to spend Roadster deposits swirling around the media and online forums, Musk backed customer deposits, saying he would pay them back personally. Still, deposits came in relatively slowly and did not exceed a few million dollars. Though the media response to the Model S was uniformly positive,

Tesla's recent near-death experience tempered the public optimism, leading to tentative headlines like "The Tesla Model S Won't Be Real Unless Elon Musk Has a Few Hundred Million to Spare."

Of course neither Musk nor Tesla had that kind of money "to spare," but piece by piece they were getting closer. After the Model S reveal, Daimler bought 9 percent of Tesla's equity for $50 million, deepening the relationship and valuing the startup at $550 million. The German automaker also agreed to support development of the Model S, and it would explore other opportunities to deploy Tesla's batteries in electric versions of its cars. Not only did the investment provide more cash than Tesla would typically raise in its annual funding rounds, it guaranteed future battery supply business and gave the Model S program access to Daimler's massive parts bin.

This last point was especially critical, given the high cost of developing high-quality interior switchgear (stalks, switches, knobs, and the like) for low-volume vehicles. Unbeknownst to the public, Tesla revealed in its DOE loan application that it had also entered into a strategic agreement with Ford that allowed Tesla to use more than three hundred components from the CD3 (C/D-class midsize) platform that underpinned vehicles like the Ford Fusion. By using borrowed control stalks, steering columns, window switches, pedals, and much more, the Model S was able to save millions of dollars in development and tooling costs that had been paid for by Ford, Daimler, and their suppliers. Tesla was already standing on the shoulders of the giants it would later be said to be "disrupting," and even more help from established automakers was still to come.

But there was one more thing that Tesla needed: a factory that could build at least 20,000 Model S sedans every year. Eberhard had initially favored building a new plant near Albuquerque, New Mexico, but that idea had been dropped when he left the company. Drori had pursued a factory closer to home, in San Jose, California, but that dream had also died when the financial crisis made it obvious that the necessary $250 million in funding would not be forthcoming. As 2009 dragged on, Musk pursued a third option, negotiating a deal to build a new plant in the Southern California town of Downey. By the end of the year, the DOE had confirmed that Tesla would indeed receive the $465 million loan it had requested, and the mayor of Downey told the media that negotiations to secure the new Tesla plant were "99.9 percent done."

Once again, however, fate had a surprise in store for Tesla that would prove to be its biggest and least-expected windfall yet. Toyota, one of the biggest and most successful automakers in the business, had been beset by challenges since the global downturn. Brand-new plants, planned years before when sales were booming, were sitting unused. The company was embroiled in a highly public scandal involving alleged "sudden unintended acceleration" in its vehicles, and its top managers were being excoriated in congressional hearings. Toyota's new CEO, Akio Toyoda, the grandson of the company's founder, was deeply worried that "big company disease" was eroding the automaker's competitive edge and was determined to shake up its deeply conservative culture.

In Tesla, Toyoda saw the antithesis of his company's slow-moving, risk-averse bureaucracy: a young, nimble, innovative automaker forged in Silicon Valley's startup culture. By partnering with Tesla, as Daimler had, Toyoda saw an opportunity to expose his top employees to an "enterprise culture" that he hoped would reinvigorate Toyota. Best of all, Toyota had a factory that it was happy to be rid of: the NUMMI plant in Fremont, California. GM had walked away from NUMMI during its bailout/bankruptcy, and with other, more modern US assembly plants lying idle, Toyota was happy to offer it to Tesla.

Tesla leaped on the opportunity immediately, in May 2010. Toyota would buy $50 million worth of Tesla's stock at the IPO price, it would sell Tesla the NUMMI plant for a mere $42 million, and the two firms would jointly develop an electric vehicle based on one of Toyota's existing vehicles. Toyota would also help Tesla source parts for the Model S and provide engineering and manufacturing support during its development and production. As mentioned in the previous chapter, Toyota's success was built on its Toyota Production System and cultural principles known as the Toyota Way, which had revolutionized how the entire industry built cars. The combination of Tesla's innovative engineering and Toyota's industry-leading manufacturing and supply-chain expertise seemed like a match made in car-making heaven.

Along with auto industry legitimacy came access to major supplier relations. Starting in 2010, the battery cell maker Panasonic invested $30 million in Tesla, and the two firms began to partner on the next generation of EV batteries. Over time, the Panasonic partnership would become Tesla's most important and most enduring supplier relationship, culminating in a 2014 commitment to build a massive joint plant called the Gigafactory in northern Nevada. Panasonic would build battery cells and Tesla would assemble them into packs for vehicles at this massive facility outside Reno, which was scheduled to grow until it had the largest footprint of any building in the world. The sheer economies of scale provided by this massively centralized supply chain was supposed to deliver the competitive pricing edge that would fuel Tesla's move into more affordable EVs.

Tesla's transformation was complete. In just eighteen months, Musk had brought his car company from the brink of bankruptcy and a seemingly endless cycle of fundraising to the most promising point in its history. Tesla had revived its battery supply business, secured two of the world's leading automakers as customers and investors, revealed its second car, purchased a factory to build it in, and obtained nearly half a billion in low-cost government loans with which to proceed. Most important of all, at least from Musk's perspective, it had done so without taking on private investments that would have diluted his massive stake in the company. Not only was Tesla's future secured as a business, Musk's image as its self-sacrificing and visionary leader had been cemented without the loss of a single share.

Musk would later wax eloquent about the dark days of 2008 and 2009, revealing how close he had come to personal insolvency and even a nervous breakdown. However, the brush with oblivion would not provide the humility and focus that both he and Tesla needed to make the most of their second chance. The story of Tesla's turnaround morphed from a frantic "fake it 'till you make it" grab for government loans and a few lucky breaks into a parable of pluck and grit worthy of Horatio Alger.

Musk would repeatedly blame Eberhard for Tesla's financial and operational shortcomings throughout 2008. Simultaneous problems at SpaceX and the inability to raise more money due to the broader economic collapse added to the narrative of Musk heroically battling forces outside his control. Once Musk had cleaned up the problems that Eberhard had created and which the downturn had amplified, he seemed to believe the government loans and automaker investments that followed were simply Tesla's rightful due.

The actual story, as we've seen, is more interesting than that. Let's recap the measures Musk took to survive the gloomy winter of 2008–2009: Musk prematurely claimed to have secured a $40 million convertible debt round and a DOE loan that Tesla hadn't even successfully applied for yet. He followed that up by raising cash deposits on the strength of a cobbled-together prototype, raising prices, and putting on a misleading show of profitability for a single month to secure the low-cost government loan that he'd already claimed to have secured.

This extraordinary bluffing streak paid off, and Tesla made it out of the Great Recession with a DOE loan larger than all its previous funding rounds combined. Musk seemed to come away from his dark night of the soul more convinced than ever that he could will his vision of Tesla into reality by creating the right perception. The disconnect between hype and reality that would fuel Tesla's most bizarre and controversial moments and lead to persistent debates about its viability was already underway.

Government support proved surprisingly easy to acquire, indicating that political forces would ensure the triumph of the electric car whether the market wanted it or not. Partnerships with two of the most respected automakers in the business showed that the old and lumbering car makers were desperate to emulate Tesla's innovation and startup culture, and would provide parts and even the factory to make the Model S possible. Musk's rising celebrity, now burnished by his heroic passage through the flames of adversity, confirmed that the hundreds of millions of dollars destroyed by Tesla's struggling business had in fact provided massive returns in the form of social capital.

Ever since he fell out with Eberhard over publicity at the Roadster unveiling, Musk had shown that Tesla's social capital dividends were at least as important to him as its financial returns. The image Musk had crafted for himself and for Tesla had been key to the company's rescue, and as soon as they began to emerge from the financial crisis, he began to reinvest his social capital with a vengeance. In June 2009, Musk told a conference in New York City that he was prepared to work his magic on the Detroit automakers who were in the process of being bailed out. "When the mess gets sorted out," he said, "I'd like to have a conversation with whoever's in charge at the time—the car czar or whoever—and say, 'I'd like to run your plants, if you don't mind.'"

At that time Tesla still didn't even have its own factory, it had never fully assembled a complete car, and had not once showed a single dollar of profit. But none of that mattered, and Musk knew it. In the aftermath of capitalism's systemic failure, Musk's brash optimism and willingness to do anything to overcome adversity stood out as a beacon of hope. As long as Musk projected a sense of mission and unfettered optimism, Tesla would continue to inspire faith in the public and overcome any obstacle that stood between it and its destiny.

CHAPTER 7

ZERO TO SIXTY BILLION

I mean, the market is like a manic-depressive.
Elon Musk, December 11, 2013

On June 28, 2010, Tesla Motors went public, raising $220 million in an initial public offering on the technology-focused NASDAQ exchange. When stock commentator and CNBC star Jim Cramer gave the newly listed stock a lukewarm welcome, pointing out that Tesla had lost some $290 million to date, Musk fired back at the entire financial establishment. "Yeah, sure, Jim . . . we're not Bear Stearns," he joked to another CNBC interviewer, invoking the investment bank whose failure had triggered the recent financial crisis. "Jim I think recommended Bear Stearns," he continued, "so frankly he's a contraindicator."

Not many CEOs would consider attacking the wisdom of the markets on the day that their company went public, but Musk had learned the value of doing things unconventionally. The Occupy Wall Street and Tea Party movements had already proven that political fortunes could be built by capitalizing on the loss of faith in public institutions following the financial crisis, and Musk was following the same playbook.

Besides, he argued, Tesla could make money if it wanted. With the Roadster's costs under control and two major manufacturers buying battery packs from it, the foundations of a profitable business were in place. But to take the next step in Musk's master-plan strategy, Tesla had to make major investments in the Model S and its new factories. Profitability would once again have to be delayed for Tesla to grow into its world-changing potential.

This was a familiar pitch to the high-tech investors that Tesla had targeted with its pre-IPO road show. Remember, in the world of software, fixed costs can be extremely high when a startup is first developing its product. But once a piece of software is complete, it costs virtually nothing to produce copies of it, and as soon as the development costs are paid off, each additional sale enjoys an eye-popping profit margin. By presenting Tesla as a "frickin' technology velociraptor" rather than an industrial automaker, Musk convinced investors that the Model S would eventually unleash a similar flood of returns.

In reality, Tesla was still learning just how hard it could be to profitably develop, build, and sell cars. Revenue from the Roadster declined from 2009 to 2010, showing that demand had topped just as Tesla finally brought down costs to the point where they could theoretically be made profitably. Even with $20 million in new revenue from its development contracts with Daimler and Toyota, the rising cost of developing the Model S, purchasing the NUMMI plant, and expanding its sales and service footprint dragged Tesla's net loss from $55 million in 2009 to nearly $155 million in 2010. Tesla's losses would continue to grow in 2011, when it lost more than $250 million, and again in 2012, when it lost nearly $400 million.

Tesla would be able to endure these losses thanks to the $465 million DOE loan it had secured in 2009, investments from Daimler, Toyota, and Panasonic, and the proceeds of its 2010 IPO. But these cash injections, which totaled upward of $800 million, wouldn't be enough to avoid the annual cash-raising rituals: secondary offerings in 2011 and 2012 added $175 million and $225 million to the bonfire respectively.

Though Tesla was able to continue selling new shares to raise cash, its share price grew only modestly during its first two-and-a-half years of public trading.

These steadily growing losses were only one of the factors dampening investor enthusiasm for Tesla's stock. As it turned out, the DOE loan that had rescued Tesla from near-certain death in 2009 was a major factor in the muted response to its IPO. Though the DOE charged Tesla far less interest than any other financier would have at the time, the loan agreement included a number of conditions intended to protect its investment from political pressure, which severely limited Tesla's freedom of action and potential value.

One of these conditions was a warrant allowing the DOE to purchase more than three million shares of Tesla common stock at $7.54 per share; this wouldn't take effect until 2018, but it threatened to dilute existing shareholders, including Musk himself. Other conditions limited the kinds and amounts of new debt Tesla could take on, forcing the company to dilute its shareholders with equity offerings to raise the cash it needed. Along with numerous other financial restrictions and reporting requirements, the DOE also required Musk to retain at least 65 percent of his Tesla ownership stake and prevented the company from being sold.

Given Tesla's struggle to turn a profit on its core business operations, the best opportunity to provide investors with a return on their capital was to sell the company. Either a tech company with automotive ambitions or a major automaker might have been interested in buying Tesla. As long as the DOE remained a partner, however, that was impossible. The DOE's lifeline had become a leash, and as Tesla came ever closer to launching the Model S, its constraints increasingly chafed the company's leadership.

Luckily for Tesla and Musk, the DOE proved to be something of a lax master. In June of 2011, about eighteen months after the loan was finalized, an amendment to the loan agreement was signed. The first amendment was minor and undertaken by both parties, but it would become the first of a series of changes; starting in 2012 the subsequent amendments and waivers became more serious, and all were requested by Tesla. That February, Tesla received its first waiver from required ratios of earnings to debt and interest payments for the last quarter of the year and parts of 2013, suggesting that it saw financial trouble ahead. In exchange for these concessions, Tesla had to agree to pull forward some of its loan payments.

Tesla was still wriggling out of DOE's loosening grip when it officially delivered the first customer Model S at an event held at its new Fremont factory in June 2012. With factory workers, customers, and politicians on hand for the festivities, a string of Tesla executives introduced the vehicle that Musk explained was designed to "break a spell." "The world has been under the illusion that electric cars cannot be as good as gasoline cars," Musk said. "What the Model S is fundamentally about is breaking that illusion."

The Model S would go on to do just that, garnering accolades from car magazines, owners, and fans that would have a profound impact on the way the public and the auto industry related to electric cars. But in the months following the start of deliveries, it became increasingly clear that the Model S was not going to single-handedly transform perceptions about Tesla's business fundamentals. Though Tesla was holding more than $100 million worth of customer deposits when it began delivering the Model S, implying more than twenty thousand reserved vehicles, those reservations were not converting into sales as fast as Tesla needed them to.

With its development contracts for Daimler and Toyota winding down along with Roadster sales, the Model S was not bringing in the cash Tesla needed and expected. Tesla began delivering the Model S at the end of the second quarter of 2012, but by the end of the third quarter, the company's annual automotive sales revenue was more than $20 million lower than it had been in the same period the year before. Production finally ramped up to more than three thousand units in the fourth quarter, but its cost of sales had climbed as well. Tesla's automotive business closed out the year with half as much operating profit as it had the year before. The car that was supposed to transform Tesla's business was falling flat.

Like the Roadster, the Model S was turning out to be considerably more expensive to build than Tesla had assumed. When it first showed off the Model S prototype, Tesla had said the car would be available for about $50,000; in late 2011, it officially set the price of the entry-level Model S 40 at $57,400 (or $49,900 after a $7,500 federal tax credit). Now, in late November of 2012, with production just beginning to ramp up, Tesla hiked the prices by $2,500 for new orders received after the end of the year, arguing that the increase was less than the rate of inflation since the car was announced in 2009. Around the same time, Tesla told reservation holders that the two cheapest trim levels, the (now) $59,900 S40 and $69,900 S60, would not be manufactured until January and March of the next year, respectively.

In quarterly calls with Wall Street analysts, as well as monthly reports to the DOE, Tesla claimed that manufacturing challenges and the desire to ensure that "every customer receives a car of the highest quality" were responsible for its inability to build the five thousand Model S units it had planned for 2012. But despite the slower production ramp, quality problems were evident in the cars that were delivered to customers; threads soon began to appear on Tesla forums complaining of poor body panel fit, creaks and rattles, and missing software features. Musk would later admit to Ashlee Vance that Tesla struggled to convert Model S reservations to sales because "word of mouth was terrible," but at the time Musk said the opposite: "It really is spreading quite wildly by word of mouth," he told analysts on Tesla's Q3 2012 call.

By the end of September 2012, Tesla was running into trouble again. The company had drawn down the last remaining funds from the DOE loan and was left with just $85 million in cash and equivalents, down from more than $210 million at the end of the second quarter. In the last week of the quarter, the DOE granted a waiver from a required ratio of current assets to debt that Tesla would not have been able to comply with. But in return, the DOE demanded a further acceleration of its prepayment schedule.

Earlier in the year, Musk had said that "Tesla does not need to ever raise another funding round." Yet as the company's cash dwindled, it had to sell another $225 million worth of stock in October of 2012. As soon as the latest financial crisis was averted, Musk published a blog post that claimed the company had "raised the funds simply for risk reduction. Barring any disasters internally or with suppliers, Tesla is actually on the verge of becoming cash flow positive and will not have to spend any of the money raised, at least until we embark upon a major new vehicle program." The fact that Tesla had ended the third quarter with less cash than it had burned over the previous three months strongly suggested that the "risk" Musk was trying to "reduce" was more fundamental than the "floods, fires, hurricanes or earthquakes" he invoked in the explanatory blog post.

By the end of December, Tesla was still showing significant operating losses, but it was conserving the cash it had raised, ending the month with positive cash flow and finishing the quarter with over $200 million in the bank. Still, all was not well financially: accounts payable, the amount that Tesla immediately owed its suppliers, grew by $115 million in December alone. It also pulled forward as much demand as it could by contacting reservation holders and asking them to take delivery as soon as possible to receive the $7,500 credit on their 2012 taxes. According to Tesla, the credit would be available even if cars weren't delivered to customers until 2013 despite the fact that the IRS clearly states that tax credits are to be taken in the year the vehicle is "placed in service" by the taxpayer.

The cash pile was cut down to just $84 million by the end of January and dwindled to just $59 million by the end of February. On the Q4 2012 earnings call in January, Musk told analysts, "I do want to emphasize, we are not demand constrained. We are intentionally production constrained." With over fifteen thousand reservations left on the books by the end of the year, that claim seemed to make sense. And yet the company's inventory grew from $160 million at the end of Q3 to just under $300 million at the end of February 2013, even though the factory had been idle for a week in January.

What happened in March 2013 was nothing short of a miracle: With less than $60 million left in the bank at the end of February and yet another solvency crisis looming, Tesla turned everything around. Tesla's automotive revenue, which had grown from just $82 million in January to $150 million in February, suddenly soared to more than $321 million in March. More than half of Tesla's total revenue for the quarter came from that single month of Model S sales, sending its operating profit to $34 million after losing $40 million on an operating basis in the two previous months. With help from $67.9 million in regulatory credit sales and $16 million in windfall gains, Tesla recorded an $11 million profit for the first quarter, its first as a public company.

How Tesla managed such a dramatic reversal in its business over a single month still isn't entirely clear. According to Vance, who has reported the most complete and directly sourced version of events during this period in his book, Tesla's struggle to convert reservations to sales had been "hidden" from Musk until mid-February. When he found out, he fired senior executives, promoted high achievers, and put workers from across the organization to work calling reservation holders and closing deals, telling them, "If we don't deliver these cars, we are fucked." He also issued a resale value guarantee, promising to back the promise with his own personal fortune.

These factors might explain a single-quarter turnaround, which at the time is what Tesla's miracle appeared to be. But an FOIA request of Tesla's monthly reports to the DOE reveals that the entire turnaround had in fact taken place in a single month. Such a dramatic reversal of fortunes is more difficult to explain with some phone calls by Tesla designers and engineers, or a resale value guarantee. There are also some discrepancies between Vance's "official version" of events and other evidence.

For one thing, Tesla sent an email to reservation holders in March outright asking them to pay for their Model S by the end of the quarter, so Tesla could record its first quarterly profit ever. Bizarrely, Musk claimed to not have been aware of this "overzealous" effort despite having supposedly taken charge of the sales conversion effort in mid-February, saying "as soon as I found out, I put an immediate stop to it. That is not how Tesla operates." On the Q1 call, Musk doubled down on the notion that the remarkable sales bump had been organic, saying, "We haven't really tried to push volume super hard yet because I think you need to make sure that the house is in order and the car is being made as efficiently as can be made before you try to push volume."

According to a former factory manager, a lot of Tesla's conversion problems were simply waiting for configurations and options that Tesla hadn't started building yet, and one of the major factors in the 2013 "miracle" was simply making a single color available: red. "[Red paint] wasn't due to launch for like six months," he remembers, "but . . . the VP told me, 'If we don't launch this within the next week we don't have any sales.' So we ran red for like 40 percent for probably three or four months at least. After that he told me 'the red saved the company.'"

Tesla also completely changed its reservation system between the fourth quarter of 2012 and the first quarter of 2013, eliminating the refundable "reservation payment" that simply held a customer's place in line and replacing it with a "customer deposit" prepayment when an order is made. This eliminated the entire problem of reservations that wouldn't convert to orders, and it finally provided Tesla with data about the configurations that customers wanted. That way it wouldn't overproduce configurations that weren't in demand. Tesla conceded that this shift had accelerated cancellations, but contemporary forum posts suggested that at least some of the resulting refunds weren't made until after the March miracle.

Whatever else may have gone into what must be the most miracu-
lous month in auto sales history, the resulting $11 million single-quarter
profit turned out to be the spark that turned Tesla into a stock market
phenomenon. Within days of announcing its Q1 profit, Tesla sold more
than $1 billion worth of stock and convertible bonds and used the pro-
ceeds to pay off the DOE loan completely. Suddenly Tesla's entire image
was transformed from a money-losing ward of the state to a profitable,
independent automaker that Americans could be proud of. After the
painful bailouts of GM and Chrysler and the failure of other DOE loan
recipients like Solyndra, Tesla seemed like a fresh, new beginning for
American automotive ambitions.

With media and political sentiment behind it, Musk told Tesla's PR
staff that he wanted the company to make one announcement per week.
In the following months, Tesla announced an asterisk-laden lease plan
that could make a Model S cost just $500 per month, the goal of mak-
ing its charging stations "zombie apocalypse–proof," a battery-swap
system that would automatically recharge a Model S in less time than
it took to pump a tank of gas, an "Autopilot" system that would be able
to drive itself in 90 percent of road conditions in just three years, and
a claim that the Model S had earned the "best safety rating of any car
ever tested" from the National Highway Traffic Safety Administration
(prompting a statement from the regulator warning it not to overstate
its ratings). Musk also released his plans for a futuristic "Hyperloop"
transportation system, launching what would become a habit of showing off ambitious independent projects. Each of these announcements
struggled to withstand close examination, ranging from mere exaggeration to quasi-delusional fantasy. Still, many outlets reported these developments unquestioningly, and Musk's legend as a twenty-first-century
Renaissance man blossomed.

The flood of hype that followed these announcements cemented
the lesson that Musk had learned during the preceding crises: his
visions for the future were his most marketable product, and they were

Tesla's stock price and trading volume from IPO through 2014

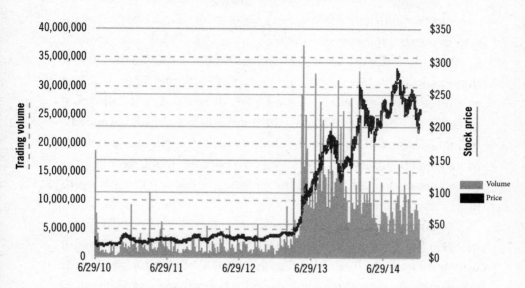

Tesla's transition from a thinly traded and moderately valued company from its IPO until the first quarter of 2013, when it recorded a surprise quarterly profit, freed itself from the constraints of the DOE loan, and became a momentum stock phenomenon. Source: Morningstar

Tesla's operating profit and loss, 2011 through 2014

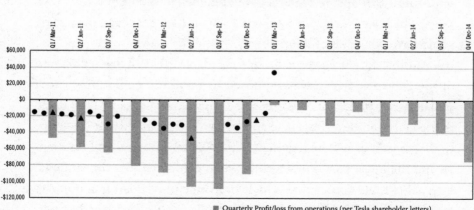

Tesla's Q1 2013 "miracle" turns out to have been a turnaround made in a single month, according to monthly financial data the company reported to the DOE as a condition of its loan. This single anomalous monthly result, in March 2013, launched Tesla into "Ludicrous Mode," making it a momentum stock phenomenon. Sources: company data reported to the DOE and obtained by FOIA request; Tesla Motors, Inc. shareholder letters.

in no way limited by reality. The Elon Musk media circus was just beginning in earnest, and it would forever put Tesla into "Ludicrous Mode."

As Tesla and Musk entered Ludicrous Mode, so too did the price of the electric automaker's stock. At the start of 2013, one Tesla share was worth less than $40, and by the last week of September, it had closed above $190. The value of Musk's share of Tesla had already exceeded a billion dollars in 2012, when the company was struggling to launch the Model S and conserve its dwindling cash pile, and by the end of 2013 (when he was named *Fortune*'s businessman of the year), it was worth more than $5.5 billion.

Tesla's early investors benefited from the explosion of Teslamania in 2013, but both the company itself and the taxpayers who saved it were less fortunate. Tesla ended up losing $74 million during the year it became a stock market phenomenon, a performance it would fail to match every year since. And though taxpayers saw their loan money repaid (with $12 million in interest), the extinguishment of the DOE's warrants on Tesla stock meant that the government missed out on its opportunity for upside. Had the DOE retained its 3,090,111 Tesla warrants, which were priced at between $7.50 and $9 per share, the upside could have exceeded a billion dollars.

Another forgotten casualty: the affordable 40 kWh battery version of the Model S, which was supposed to fulfill the commitment to a $50,000 base price that Musk repeatedly made publicly and Tesla made to the DOE (an early Tesla loan application even claimed that "the price to the consumer will be less than $40,000 after given federal tax credits and the lower cost of ownership when compared to a conventional internal-combustion engine vehicle"). In an end-of-quarter announcement revealing the March miracle, Tesla disclosed that "only four percent of customers chose the 40 kWh battery pack, which is not enough to justify production of that version." But because customers could only order vehicles then in production, at least until Tesla switched its order process at the beginning of 2013, it's not clear that the vast majority of Model S reservation holders had even been able to register their preference. The 40 kWh version was also never capable of using Superchargers, eliminating one of Tesla's most critical advantages.

But nobody was looking backward to count how many amendments DOE had given Tesla, how much upside it had left on the table, or even what it had done to escape the government agency whose loan had saved it. Nobody even seemed to care that Tesla's tiny one-time profit didn't show any real potential for recurring profits, or that its promises for the future couldn't hold up to even the most cursory scrutiny. Just as Tesla had crafted perceptions that in turn shaped its reality, the runaway growth of its stock price created a perception that became stronger than any rational analysis.

After the humiliating bailout of the US automakers and the general gloom of the global financial crisis, Tesla presented a fresh-faced optimism that seemed to reflect the dawning of a new morning in America. While the Detroit automakers went right back to their pre-recession truck and SUV dependence, Tesla was becoming a global leader in electric cars and pointing the way to a high-tech green future. With faith in national institutions irreparably damaged by the mortgage bubble and Too Big to Fail, Tesla gave Americans something to believe in and (just as important) invest in.

CHAPTER 8

THE LOVERS AND
THE HATERS

*Pied Piper's product is its stock. Whatever makes the value of the stock
go up is what we are going to make. Maybe sometime in the future,
we can change the world and perform miracles and all of that stuff.*
"Action" Jack Barker

Once upon a time, when automotive technology was still developing fairly rapidly, the auto industry regularly wowed the public with visions of a future that seemed simultaneously far off and right around the corner. In Detroit's midcentury heyday, automakers nurtured a vibrant sense of modernist expectation. In car shows and world's fair exhibits and on *Popular Science* magazine covers, they showed off flying cars, self-driving cars, and cars powered by jet engines and nuclear reactors. These visions wildly outstripped the R&D developments of the companies. Still, dramatic technological developments in everything from automobiles themselves to aerospace had made science fiction seem plausible, and the public embraced the futuristic potential with which Detroit burnished its brands.

Half a century later, the business had all but completely lost touch with its ability to inspire enthusiasm for the future. The flamboyance and optimism of the post-WWII auto industry had been crushed by brutal competition in things like quality control, manufacturing, and capital efficiency. At the same time, technological developments outside the auto industry—the computer, the internet, the cellular phone, the smartphone, and the app store—were once again transforming everyday life in previously unimaginable ways. There was a new sense of futurist expectation just waiting to be tapped.

If the venture capital fundraising treadmill first triggered Tesla's hype-happy tendencies, this larger public desire cemented them; the public was ready for a car company that could make people feel like a brave new world was right around the corner. Once Tesla became a publicly traded company and Musk launched it into Ludicrous Mode, it became clear that his ambition and optimism filled a very real public need. Musk's splashy announcements generally had nothing to do with the prosaic realities of Tesla's business, which was as profit challenged as ever, but were focused on inspiring speculative optimism about its possible future—the announcements I mentioned in the last chapter, "zombie apocalypse–proof" solar Superchargers, self-driving technology, the Hyperloop, battery swap, even a drive-in restaurant and a music-streaming service. This burnished Tesla's brand, helping it sell more cars, but it also inspired vague but soaring valuations of its speculative future business while distracting from the challenging realities of its present.

By the middle of 2013, the relationship between Musk's real-life sci-fi spectacle and Tesla's soaring stock price was clearly established. This presented a unique opportunity: Musk's visions were a product that anyone could help sell. By making an investment in Tesla stock and then spreading the good news about the bold future Musk was inventing, you could help win over new believers and help fuel the seemingly limitless growth in Tesla's market valuation.

Best of all, selling Musk's vision didn't require industry experience, technological expertise, or the ability to analyze financial disclosures. The novelty of Tesla's approach to the car business meant that belief in Musk was more important than any of the lessons learned in a century of automotive history, which only trapped the established automakers and investors in their uninspiring prison of rationalism. As long as you believed in Musk and his high-tech and environmentally friendly future, you too could join the "winning team" and make money by evangelizing his visions.

The introduction of this financial feedback loop was a game changer. Combined with the power of online forums, social media, and the cheap price of entry into the online media business, Tesla evangelism became an enterprise. As the movement grew, more and more opportunities emerged, from publishing Tesla-specific news to selling Tesla accessories and eventually even selling Teslas themselves, all fueled by a shared belief that for many was becoming a core aspect of their identity.

Prior to Tesla's 2013 miracle, there was a well-established ecosystem of "green car" blogs that covered and promoted the emerging hybrid, plug-in electric, hydrogen fuel-cell, and other low- or zero-emission drivetrain technologies. These sites ran the gamut from outlets that sought to bring balance and credibility to their generally positive coverage of the sector, to less-credible fan blogs and forums dedicated to cheerleading the move toward new technologies. But wherever these sites found a niche on this spectrum, they were first and foremost dedicated to covering and/or promoting the full range of green car options, wherever they came from.

As Tesla rose to prominence, this community started to change. Slowly, almost imperceptibly at first, Tesla's share of green car coverage started to grow. Older generations, whose enthusiasm for electric had been born in the fuel crises and environmental movement, began to give way to younger generations of readers and writers whose belief in Tesla was more rooted in the perception that it made the iPhone of cars. Over time, Tesla outgrew its role as the standard bearer for the broader electric car movement and became a financial and ideological mission unto itself.

This phenomenon first became noticeable at the investor section of Tesla Motors Club, the first independent online Tesla community, which hosted the leading Tesla owner forum since the company's earliest days. The majority of TMC's forums were focused on owner discussions. Though they had an unsurprisingly pro-Tesla culture, they also encouraged owners to share information that other owners would find useful, including reports of poor quality and service experiences. In contrast, the investor section brooked no criticism of Tesla and attacked critical contributions as attempts to spread "FUD" (fear, uncertainty, and doubt). This was also where the practice began of attacking critical coverage as attempts by short investors to drive down Tesla's stock price, eventually becoming a defining feature of Tesla's online discourse.

The difference between the culture at TMC's investor forum and its owner forums was no coincidence: Among the new members who flooded into the investor forum starting in 2013 were a number who had experience creating echo chambers around speculative stocks. One of the investor forum's moderators and some of its most vocal members had come over to TMC from another forum that would become an object lesson in the dangers of such hyperbull online echo chambers.

GT Advanced Technologies, known by its stock symbol GTAT, was a company that grew industrial sapphires for use in special grades of glass. As rumors began to spread that Apple would be using sapphire glass in an upcoming product, GTAT's stock came into focus for speculative investors. At a forum called "The Contrarian Investor," a thread about GTAT quickly developed a consensus that a major order from Apple would boost GTAT stock to many times its price. As more evidence surfaced that seemed to indicate that Apple would indeed use

GTAT's sapphire glass, the culture in the thread became increasingly bullish, with participants putting more and more of their savings into the stock.

Anyone second-guessing the herd mentality was accused of spreading "FUD" and attempting to drive down the share price to make money by "shorting" the stock (betting that its price would decline). Declines in the stock price were blamed on manipulation by "market makers" who, according to the increasingly feverish thread at The Contrarian Investor, were simply trying to buy into the stock at a lower price. Speculation spiraled upward, from rumors that Apple would switch its entire lineup to sapphire glass to other speculative applications for GTAT's technology. When YouTube tech reviewer Marques Brownlee released a video purporting to show a sapphire screen "from Apple's assembly line," GTAT stock looked like a no-brainer.

But in late 2014, Apple finally announced product details for its new iPhone, and it became clear that it had opted for "ion-strengthened glass" rather than GTAT's sapphire glass. It turned out that GTAT had been unable to produce sufficient sapphire on the timeline Apple required, and when the contract was canceled, GTAT's reckless capital structure had brought the company to sudden bankruptcy. Almost overnight, the GTAT thread filled with stories of investors who had overallocated their holdings to GTAT's speculative stock in hopes of a big payday and were suddenly destitute. People lost entire retirement accounts, all their savings, and even their houses.

There had been warning signs: analysis of GTAT accounting would have raised concerns about its capital structure, and a thorough reading of its contract with Apple would have revealed that it was not exclusive. But the echo-chamber culture had shouted down anyone voicing these warnings until it was too late.

Though many GTAT investors "busted out" when the company went bankrupt, others went looking for another hot stock with the potential to make massive gains. Tesla had been mentioned several times as a "momentum stock" in the GTAT thread, and a number of the most active GTAT pumpers shifted focus to the Tesla Motors Club where a similar "hyperbull" culture was forming around Tesla's booming stock.

Like GTAT, Tesla's business was far from a sustainable cash generator, and its stock was rapidly climbing to levels that seemed impossible to sustain with the slim margins of a small-scale car manufacturing business. But what Tesla did have was limitless potential for hype, which increased every time Musk held an event introducing a new feature or capability. Though most Tesla investors were unfamiliar with the brutal realities of the auto manufacturing business, the collective belief that new technology could overturn the established rules of business allowed investors to imagine almost infinite opportunities for growth and profit. And as had been the case with GTAT, even skeptics who brought up very real concerns that Tesla was being overvalued were driven off with the now-familiar accusations of "FUD" and "short manipulation."

As the culture that had fueled the boom and bust in GTAT established itself at the TMC investor forums, it spread across the internet. Along with the aggressive culture of Tesla's own official forums, the Reddit forum known as r/teslamotors became a center for Tesla hyperbull discourse.

A new crop of media outlets emerged that were distinctly different from the green car blogs that had preceded them. Rather than promoting an entire class of technology, these new outlets were increasingly focused on Tesla itself as a "disruptor" that would turn the fundamentals of the car business upside down and in the process establish itself as the major player in the future auto industry. Promoting this vision meant more than just hyping Tesla: it required tearing down every other electric car and the companies that made them.

One of the most prominent of these new outlets, called Electrek, started publishing its distinctive brand of pro-Tesla coverage in the second half of 2013. Founded by Seth Weintraub, the creator of several successful blogs covering Google and Apple and an award-winning former journalist for Computerworld, Electrek ran a mix of content aggregated from social media and online forums and scoops from sources inside the company, as well as news and reviews of non-Tesla electric vehicles. Superficially it resembled many of the established green car blogs, but as its reach exploded, it became increasingly clear that it was a different animal. Like the growing communities at the TMC investor forum and r/teslamotors, Electrek actually criticized most electric cars and the companies that made them, in service of the narrative that Tesla would dominate the electric future of the car business.

Electrek's distinct editorial focus on promoting Tesla and defending it from criticism, even at the expense of other green car companies, was easy to understand in light of its founding staffers' previous experience. Jon Jivan, one of the two original Electrek writers, had promoted Tesla stock via StockTwits, a Twitter-based stock discussion platform, since it started to take off in mid-2013. Fred Lambert, who would go on to become Electrek's editor in chief, had previously written about Tesla's potential as an investment at the stock site Motley Fool and was a moderator at r/teslamotors. Besides promoting Tesla stock and moderating the increasingly hyperbull-dominated r/teslamotors forum, neither had any experience with journalism, the auto industry, or even green technology.

In those early days, neither made any secret of the fact that they owned Tesla stock and that they were bullish on its prospects, nor did Electrek's owner Seth Weintraub. But rather than clearly disclosing a stock position on each story, as Lambert had been required to at Motley Fool and as FTC guidelines require, Electrek's vague disclosure "some writers of Electrek maintain positions in $TSLA and other green energy stocks" was buried in the site's "About" section. Electrek even briefly ran a Tesla stock price ticker on its main page, further reinforcing the perception that its writers and editors—to say nothing of its aggressive base of commenters who followed up every story with fresh layers of hype—were most interested in Tesla as an eminently pumpable stock.

Even after the founding of Electrek, Lambert continued to cross the line between media coverage and stock promotion. In 2015, he was sued by the tuning company Saleen over accusations he allegedly made using a variety of usernames at r/teslamotors, InvestorsHub, his blog *Black Sheep Planet*, and the website for his "research and capital" outfit called Zalkon, after Saleen claimed to be "partnering" with Tesla on a tuned (modified) version of the Model S. (Tuning is alteration of the appearance or performance of a vehicle. Saleen is generally known for making power-increasing modifications, to Mustangs specifically, while the Tesla they modified had only cosmetic changes.) The lawsuit alleged that Lambert had defamed Saleen as a "pump-and-dump" and ponzi scheme, and sought an injunction against further defamation. Lambert eventually settled with Saleen, agreeing to retract his defamatory statements and refrain from making further such statements, but not before soliciting financial support for his legal battle through several crowdfunding sites.

Lambert initially claimed he had researched Saleen in the course of "diligence" for a potential investment, and that his crusade was simply an attempt to warn investors who might be taken in by the "pumpers" trying to boost Saleen's stock price, but his interest in the company was clearly tied to his investment in Tesla. "If they sell some cars and let their customers believe that Tesla will respect the warranty even though they play around with the software and drivetrain, when the car starts having problems, Tesla might experience a backlash," he eventually wrote in a Reddit comment. The incident, which directly preceded his hiring at Electrek, would establish him as one of the most aggressive and prolific pro-Tesla propagandists.

The accusation that Saleen "resembled a ponzi scheme" was particularly interesting given that Tesla had done the exact same thing Lambert accused the tuning company of doing: using customer deposits to fund operations. Several years after the Saleen lawsuit, when the CEO of the car-dealer chain AutoNation suggested that Tesla might be a ponzi scheme, Lambert wrote an Electrek piece defending the company. Lambert's ability to compare Saleen's use of customer deposits to a ponzi scheme while defending Tesla's practices from the same comparison was emblematic of his coverage.

As moderator of r/teslamotors, Lambert was not only well positioned to harvest content posted there for Electrek, but also well connected to others who were eagerly pushing Tesla as an investment. The two sites Lambert was involved with became such a nexus for Tesla investors that the *Wall Street Journal*'s Charley Grant reported that Tesla's Investor Relations team was recommending that investors get their news from r/teslamotors and Electrek. Both sites heavily curated coverage, ignoring or "downvoting" bad news and featuring or "upvoting" good news, with legions of aggressive promoters attacking any sign of criticism in the comments. The most aggressive bulls at r/teslamotors inevitably showed up in Electrek's comment sections, driving up the hype and attacking anyone who dared to question it.

As Electrek's prominence grew, mostly on the strength of its ability to coax scoops out of company sources and be the first to run Tesla's comments refuting critical reporting, other sites like CleanTechnica and Teslarati got in on the act. Eventually the pumping schemes became increasingly blatant: a "rumor" floated by a shadowy investment advisor fund suggesting that Tesla shareholders would get first dibs on an eventual SpaceX IPO was written up as news at Teslarati by one Christian Prenzler, who failed to disclose in the piece that he was in fact a Tesla shareholder. SpaceX quickly denied that it had any such plans, and Prenzler said his investment in Tesla was a "miniscule" twenty shares, but the utterly false story still helped fuel a short-term run-up in Tesla stock.

But stock pumping wasn't the only way to profit from loudly promoting Tesla. A "referral" program quickly became a favorite tool of the new crop of Tesla-touting outlets and content creators that sprouted up after 2013. Using referral codes to order a new Tesla provided benefits like a $1,000 discount or free supercharging to the buyer while also providing a kickback to the link provider. Originally intended as a marketing tool that incentivized Tesla owners to educate potential buyers, referral codes also provided a form of incentive for reporters and "content creators" who effectively became Tesla salespeople (at least according to the California New Car Dealers Association).

Because Electrek presented itself as a media outlet rather than a "fan content" site, its use of referral codes (which eventually earned both Lambert and Weintraub six figures' worth of prizes) came under criticism from other automotive media outlets. But countless other content creators popped up or adapted to take advantage of the program, marrying relentlessly positive reporting and "analysis" with regular calls to use their referral codes to buy new Teslas. From websites that listed Tesla inventory and blogs like Electrek to podcasts and YouTube channels, the internet was flooded with pro-Tesla propaganda as creators competed to generate the most sales.

As the program became more successful, so too did the rewards, which had started with Tesla-branded merchandise and invites to company events but eventually earned the top referrers a free Model X. Weintraub and Lambert each won a $200,000 next-gen Tesla Roadster, among other prizes. As the magnitude of these rewards began to outweigh revenue from ads and other monetization, referral shilling became more ubiquitous and aggressive. Though Tesla did attempt to limit full-time referral shilling by warning that it would shut down "abuse" of the program, the line between acceptable and unacceptable practices was never clearly defined nor did the flood of referral spam noticeably slow as a result.

At a time when making money in the online media business was becoming increasingly difficult, the twin inducements of stock promotion and affiliate marketing had a profound effect on perceptions of Tesla. This approach was especially effective because Tesla and its supporters took pains to highlight the fact that Tesla had only a tiny budget for advertising, marketing, or public relations. The implication was that the legions of passionate fans on social media, forums, and comment sections were part of an organic movement; that they were inspired solely by Tesla's world-changing potential and not by financial interests.

Indeed, one of the key talking points that emerged from this culture was that Tesla's critics must either be shills of the oil and auto companies that the newcomer threatened or "shorts" attempting to manipulate its stock price. Not only did this invalidate even the most on-point and friendly criticisms, it also helped distract from the fact that many of Tesla's most eager promoters had financial interests in either the company's stock or affiliate marketing of its cars. This gambit succeeded, creating the impression that Tesla enjoyed a volunteer "army of Davids" inspired only by its mission of saving the Earth, lined up against the venal self-interest of the powers that be.

Clearly Tesla did have considerable organic support from fans who were largely motivated by their passion for the car's high-tech cool and the company's environmental mission. But just as Tesla itself was sucked into a cycle of overpromising that eventually left it totally dependent on ever-increasing hype, so too did its fan base find itself shifting from purely passionate advocates to investors who could boost a highly lucrative stock and earn rewards while promoting the company they loved and helping it sell cars. Once personal and financial motivations are intermingled, it can become all but impossible to separate them from each other.

For every action there is an equal and opposite reaction, and as Tesla's online empire spread, so too did its detractors. Some of the first were short investors like Mark Spiegel, who started looking at the shaky fundamentals of Tesla's business during the run-up of its stock in 2013, concluding that it would never be able to make enough money to justify its soaring valuation. The more Tesla's legend and stock price grew, the more these hard-nosed money managers came to see it as the leading example of one of the worst sins they could imagine: a misallocation of capital.

Mark Spiegel got his start in commercial real estate before he "talked himself into a job" on Wall Street in 2003 at age forty-two and was successful enough to eventually start his own small fund. A lifelong "car guy," Spiegel first noticed Tesla during its 2013 stock price spike, and upon examining its financials, he concluded that it would struggle to justify its share price, which at the time was in the high nineties. Taking a small short position of about one percent of his fund, Spiegel wrote a series of posts detailing his financial criticism of Tesla at the stock commentary website Seeking Alpha under the username "Logical Thought." His early criticisms were strictly business, casting doubt on Tesla's ability to make a profit on $35,000 Model 3s and arguing that competition would prevent it from achieving the dominant market position fans expected, but as the stock price grew, he became increasingly frustrated.

In 2014, after Musk told the third-quarter analyst call that slower-than-expected growth was due to manufacturing challenges rather than demand challenges, even as evidence of discounting mounted, Spiegel started becoming suspicious of Musk. "It became increasingly clear to me that he's an incredibly deceptive guy, and it became increasingly frustrating to me that the media was letting him get away with it," he remembers. With Tesla's share price now above $200, he made even bigger short bets against the company and became increasingly vocal in his criticisms.

Spiegel's early and outspoken comments about Tesla, and his bets against its inexorably rising stock, made him the bête noire of the Tesla bull community. Unabashed to be taking an unpopular position and utterly convinced that economic fundamentals would win out in the long run, Spiegel embraced the antagonism, sparred with the company's fans on social media and in comment sections, and began acting as a clearinghouse for every piece of news and analysis that was critical of Tesla. The intense passions on both sides fueled each other, creating an increasingly polarized discourse around the company.

Like Spiegel, Jim Chanos also started short selling Tesla stock during the initial 2013 run-up, working from the thesis that its software-style management and culture were a poor fit for the auto manufacturing business. As time went by, his perspective also shifted, from simply being skeptical of Tesla's ability to justify its valuation to actively suspecting serious cultural issues at the company. However for Chanos, a legendary short seller, Tesla's triumph of hype over fundamentals was less of an aberration and more of an extreme symptom of a broader market phenomenon.

"In any environment other than Dotcom 2.0 this company probably would have been dead and buried a couple of years ago," he told me. "The fact that Musk has been able to access billions and billions of dollars to finance his vision is as much the market environment as it is him. If you look at some of the unicorns with business models that I just cannot make work, investors are throwing money at these companies," he said, naming the commercial real estate company WeWork as another example.

Because of this environment, in which it's easy to raise money without a lot of scrutiny of the fundamentals of your business, "there's this general sense that if you believe you're changing the world, you can lie to investors," he argued. "That's a bull market phenomenon . . . A whole generation has forgotten about the late 1990s, and so a lot of people who are buying these stocks or the Bitcoin craziness never saw these things go down 90 or 99 percent like my generation did. We saw a bull market phenomenon in the late 90s, and when the market turned down and the glasses became half empty and not half full, the access to capital dried up overnight. If you have positive cash flow you can survive, but if your burn rate is really high and capital markets shut down for six months, you're dead. That's what investors are underestimating."

Though Chanos would regularly discuss his Tesla short in television appearances and his pseudonymous Twitter account, he tended to be less confrontational than Spiegel. But his far larger fund and long record of picking successful short investments, including the Detroit automakers in the lead-up to 2008 and Enron, made him almost a more terrifying figure in the online bull enclaves. He was regularly imagined to be behind critical coverage of Tesla, paying off journalists as part of a "short and distort" campaign, a theory that even Musk forwarded on Twitter in the summer of 2018, although no evidence ever surfaced to support this.

When asked about this wild-eyed theory, Chanos laughed and said that trying to make facts fit a preexisting short thesis "would not be a very profitable business undertaking . . . Short sellers have been reviled by the market since the 1600s," he said. "There's always been this view that some short sellers are profiting off the misery of others. The fact of the matter is that short sellers are the only market force that have an incentive to ferret out fraud in real time. The regulators and law enforcement are the financial archaeologists, finding out what happened well after the fact and everybody's lost money. It's not a coincidence that [Enron executives] Jeff Skilling and Ken Lay used this defense, that short sellers were in cahoots with financial journalists. It wasn't true then, and it isn't true now in the case of Tesla."

In late 2015, an account known as Montana Skeptic began posting critical analyses of Tesla at Seeking Alpha using an etching of Galileo Galilei as an avatar. Unlike Spiegel and Chanos, Montana wasn't a professional short investor, and he'd been attracted to Tesla because of his fascination with the story rather than through pure financial analysis alone. A former lawyer who now ran a billionaire's family office, Montana never shorted Tesla professionally but after writing about the company for some time, he eventually opened a small "put" position so that he would have some "skin in the game."

In many of his more than one hundred posts on the subject, he actually warned readers against shorting Tesla for the very reason he was so interested in the company: the almost religious faith of Tesla's fans and investors made it virtually impossible to say when confidence in the company might be lost. An erudite, self-described classical liberal, Montana said he had been looking for a writing project when he found Tesla, and it provided a rich vein of material to mine. From debunking Musk's claims to dissecting Tesla's financials, the subject lent itself

perfectly to the research and analytical skills he'd once briefly practiced
as a reporter and later developed as a lawyer.

As Montana emerged as one of the most persistent and cutting critics of Tesla, both at Seeking Alpha and later on Twitter, he also became
something of a community organizer for like-minded thinkers. Comments under his posts turned to email correspondence, and soon he
was the hub of a small network of investors and researchers whose spe-
cialized work he would feature or expand on in his posts. As word of his
writing spread, journalists and analysts at big banks began to regularly
read his posts, and the attention motivated him to dig ever deeper.

Montana's prolific writing set him apart from Spiegel and Chanos,
who preferred Twitter and television as mediums for their Tesla criticism, as did his pseudonymous identity. As interactions between Tesla
bears and bulls on Seeking Alpha and Twitter inevitably grew more
heated, Montana's secret identity became an opportunity to hit back.
Working from the assumption that he wouldn't use a pseudonym unless
he had something to hide, several regular posters at the TMC investor
forum began to research his true identity in the summer of 2018.

Before long they deduced his real name, as well as the name of the
billionaire whose wealth he managed, and they found out that he'd
made investments in oil and natural gas. These investments were part of
a diversified and conservative investment strategy that he'd pursued on
behalf of his employer, but to Tesla investors in the midst of an online
war for the company's image, they were evidence of a dastardly hidden
agenda. Tesla threatened these investments, their logic went, which is
why Montana had started writing about Tesla and allegedly made up
unspecified falsehoods about the company.

Then, one day, shortly after his true identity began circulating on
pro-Tesla forums, his office received an unexpected call from Elon
Musk himself. According to Montana, Musk complained to his colleague about his critical writing and said that if he didn't stop, he would
retain counsel and sue. Though Musk never specified the grounds on
which he threatened to sue, and though Montana was eager to defend

himself against any claim Musk might make, he ultimately agreed to stop publishing on Seeking Alpha and delete his Twitter account to avoid entangling his publicity-shy employer in a public relations and legal battle. Even after he had done so, Tesla PR representatives continued to circulate his identity and his office's phone number to reporters, and Musk taunted him by posting an image of Miley Cyrus twerking on Twitter (a reference to Cyrus's Hannah Montana character).

When I spoke with him just days later, Montana admitted that the intensity of the debate around Tesla had surprised him, and he said he was at least partly relieved to have been forced out of it. "It's a little unnerving to have these people who are so passionate and crazy out there knowing who I am, and you know I worry for my family a little bit," he said. He has asked me not to identify him here. "Let them vent their hate somewhere else for a while . . . it will only become more intense if the share price continues to erode."

The crowdsourced doxxing of Montana Skeptic and Musk's call to his employer may have ended his career as an online Tesla critic, but it hardly put an end to the criticism itself. As the news of Montana's forced retirement spread, so too did his Galileo avatar, which multiplied across Twitter in a show of solidarity that revealed how big and passionate the community of Tesla shorts had become. This act of defiance catalyzed this loose association of individuals, some of whom were pure financial speculators like Chanos and Spiegel and others who were primarily motivated by factors other than money.

In the weeks and months that followed, the sense of identity among Tesla critics and short investors on Twitter flourished, increasingly becoming a kind of open-source research and analysis operation. Several new accounts rose to prominence in the community, which increasingly referred to itself as $TSLAQ, since companies in bankruptcy proceedings must add a "Q" to the end of their stock ticker. Eventually a "Shorty Air Force" (complete with a mock unit patch) flew air reconnaissance over parking lots to count stored vehicles, and a "Shorty Ground Force" tracked vehicles being shipped from the factory and delivered by Tesla stores. News stories, research, rumors, and jokes were traded around the globe twenty-four hours a day.

If Montana Skeptic had been the head of this community, by cutting him off, Musk inspired many more to get off the sidelines and take his place, which deepened its conviction that Tesla had something to hide. Ironically, Tesla and its fans were so eager to fight the shadowy conspiracy they believed to be working against their noble mission that they actually turned a disparate group into the very conspiracy they feared, only it was working out in the open on Twitter.

The company's issues with transparency weren't just limited to financials, of course. From 2013 onward, Tesla's effort to be at the forefront of automotive technologies—solar power, battery swaps, and Autopilot—would bring the contrast between its public image and its actual practices into stark relief.

CHAPTER 9

SOLAR, SUPERCHARGERS, AND SWAP

If you travel less than 350 miles per week, you will therefore be "energy positive" with respect to your personal transportation. This is a step beyond conserving or even nullifying your use of energy for transport—you will actually be putting more energy back into the system than you consume in transportation!
Elon Musk, in the 2006 Top Secret Master Plan

"You'll be able to travel for free, forever on pure sunlight," Musk said, as the crowd assembled at Tesla's Hawthorne facility broke into cheers. "So I think it's pretty hard to beat that, y'know?" He smirked. "Free long distance? You're not going to get that with gasoline."

"Or AT&T," quipped someone in the crowd.

"Yeah, exactly, or AT&T," said Musk, pausing to chuckle. "So . . . I think this day will actually go down as being quite historic. I think at least on par with SpaceX docking with the space station earlier this year." His expression had suddenly become deeply earnest. "I mean, I really think this is important. And really, I want you to go out there and spread the word."

It was June of 2013, and Musk was sharing the stage with a giant obelisk that looked like a modernist sculpture of a rocket ship. This striking object was a Supercharger, Musk had explained, and it was Tesla's answer to the biggest challenges facing electric cars. Common arguments against EVs are that they tie drivers to a much shorter range than conventional vehicles, and that driving one doesn't actually cut down your carbon footprint—because an electric car has a figurative "long tailpipe" that shifts the source of emissions from the vehicle itself to the power plant. Not only would Superchargers eliminate "range anxiety" by providing a network of convenient fast refueling stations, it would also eliminate the criticism that coal-fired power means electric cars simply have that "long tailpipe," providing 100 percent solar power thanks to panels from Musk's firm SolarCity. Best of all, it would provide clean, convenient recharging power at no cost to Model S owners who had bought the bigger 85 kWh battery or added Supercharging as a $2,000 option on the 60 kWh version.

No automaker had ever built its own branded charging stations before, and Tesla promised that by the end of 2013, its network would allow its cars to drive from Los Angeles to New York. In a company press release, Musk called the Supercharger network "a game changer for electric vehicles," that would "[provide] long-distance travel that has a level of convenience equivalent to gasoline cars for all practical purposes." The release also fleshed out Musk's most audacious claim to date: that every Supercharger would provide more clean solar energy than Tesla drivers would use.

The electricity used by the Supercharger comes from a solar carport system provided by SolarCity, which results in almost zero marginal energy cost after installation . . .

Each solar power system is designed to generate more energy from the sun over the course of a year than is consumed by Tesla vehicles using the Supercharger. This results in a slight net positive transfer of sunlight generated power back to the electricity grid. In addition to lowering the cost of electricity, this addresses a commonly held misunderstanding that charging an electric car simply pushes carbon emissions to the power plant. The Supercharger system will always generate more power from sunlight than Model S customers use for driving.

This promise was the first step Tesla had taken toward the zero-emission energy bullet point in Musk's Top Secret Master Plan, while addressing the other major electric car challenges Musk had laid out six years before. As chairman and chief funder of SolarCity, Musk also had access to all the panels and installation capabilities Tesla might need to realize this vision of a "green transportation ecosystem." With the hype around Model S just starting to take off, the prospect of free, fast zero-emission charging seemed like proof positive of the electric car's inherent superiority.

A significant portion of the public clearly wanted to believe that Superchargers would be as "game changing" as Musk promised, and media coverage was almost universally glowing. Even though shareholders had seen their shares diluted by a $220 million secondary offering on the day of the announcement, enthusiasm for Superchargers helped boost the share price. The fact that Superchargers represented a new (and potentially massive) capital expenditure that showed little promise of returning revenue couldn't hold back enthusiasm for Musk's next big thing.

Even then, there were signs that Superchargers weren't everything Tesla had promised. The striking, if somewhat phallic, obelisk that towered over Musk on the stage in Hawthorne was nowhere to be found in videos showing Teslas charging at the first six Supercharger sites. Sure enough, the sculpture was never seen again after the event, although the Hawthorne Supercharger did eventually get a more understated columnar monument.

More seriously, Musk's most important promise of the night—that every Supercharger would not only be solar powered but in fact generate more solar power than Tesla drivers would use—never came close to materializing. Though Tesla rapidly expanded its Supercharger network, first across the US and then in Europe, not a single station had solar panels until 2015, when one was opened in Rocklin, California.

This hadn't stopped Musk from grabbing headlines in 2013 by making that extraordinary claim about the ostensibly grid-independent Supercharger network. "So, I was joking with someone that even if there's the zombie apocalypse, which is a popular theme these days, even if there's a zombie apocalypse, you'll still be able to travel throughout the country using the Tesla supercharging system," Musk had said to wild applause. His confidence on this point certainly convinced elements of the media: by the time the first solar-powered Supercharger opened, media reports could still be found claiming that every Supercharger was in fact solar-powered.

At the 2015 Tesla shareholder meeting, Musk confirmed that the goal of solar-powered Superchargers was still well off. "Most of the Superchargers do not yet have solar and a battery backup," he said. "So over time we're going to put solar on every Supercharger where that's possible. Or, if that's not possible, make sure we're purchasing power that is generated in a renewable manner so that the entire Supercharger network is powered by sunlight." When asked in mid-2015 how many Superchargers were in fact solar powered, a Tesla spokesman declined to provide a number but said the company's European Superchargers were powered by renewables.

Questions about the environmental impact of coal- and other nonrenewable-powered Superchargers that Musk had been addressing since the 2006 master plan have continued to pop up. Only "a half-dozen or so" of the firm's eight hundred charging stations would sport solar panels of any kind by June 2017, and none of them claimed to have the grid-independent capabilities Musk bragged about four years earlier. When he was told on Twitter that a coal plant powering a North Carolina Supercharger could be seen from the site of the charger, Musk replied, "All Superchargers are being converted to solar/battery power. Over time, almost all will disconnect from the electricity grid."

How exactly Musk envisions generating enough solar power to deliver on this oft-repeated promise has never been explained, and the whole idea falls apart under even the most cursory and conservative analysis. A Supercharger station with ten stalls, each providing an average of ten 50 kWh charges per day, would require solar arrays capable of generating 5 mWh per day. Even in the most consistently sunny parts of the world, where solar panels can generate about 1 kWh per square meter, more than an acre of panels would be required to even come close to this level of output. Beyond the obvious space constraints, the high cost of so many solar panels as well as the massive array of storage batteries required to handle higher peak loads make the economics of such a plan a nonstarter.

Tesla's inability to even come close to delivering on Musk's promise of "zombie apocalypse–proof" 100 percent solar Superchargers is a classic example of Musk's hubris. Most studies conclude that electric cars powered by even relatively dirty mixes of coal and natural gas pollute less than gasoline cars, so any Tesla should be an improvement on the status quo. Indeed, this was the core insight that led Eberhard and Tarpenning to create Tesla in the first place. But Musk's hubris drove him to overlook these meaningful improvements and promise the impossible, hurting both his credibility and that of Tesla as a company.

Even Musk's more prosaic promises about the Supercharger network turned out to be a stretch. Though Superchargers can charge Tesla's cars faster than most other electric car charging networks, no battery electric vehicle can genuinely provide the "long-distance travel that has a level of convenience equivalent to gasoline cars for all practical purposes" that Musk promised in 2012. When operating at full potential, a Supercharger still takes half an hour to provide an 80 percent charge, with a full charge taking more than an hour. Practically speaking, this translates to between two and three hours of driving for every hour spent charging.

Tesla fans and owners downplay the impact of charging time, arguing that a break for food or restrooms every few hours makes for a more enjoyable road trip experience. Though this may be the case for well-off vacationers traveling at a leisurely pace, it simply can't be compared to the five minutes it takes to refuel a car with gasoline. Once again, it wasn't enough for Tesla to simply tout the fact that Supercharging is more practical than other electric cars, Musk had to claim that Supercharging would be as convenient for road-tripping as a gasoline car, which it simply isn't.

Tesla seemed to acknowledge this reality a year after the Supercharger premiere, when it held yet another event in Hawthorne to unveil a battery-swapping system. "When you come to a Tesla station," Musk said from the event stage, "you have the choice of the Supercharger, which is and always will be free. Or, you have the choice of a battery swap, which is faster than you can fill a gas tank. So the only decision you need to make when you come to one of our Tesla stations is: do you prefer faster, or free."

With the drop of a techno beat, a Model S drove onstage and stopped directly above a rectangular opening. Simultaneously, a video feed showed an Audi pulling up to a gas station where it began to fill up. After a minute and a half of unseen activity under the stage, the Model S drove away with its instrument panel showing a fully charged battery, raising a hearty cheer from the audience. "Looks like we've got some extra time," said Musk. "Let's do another one." A second Model S drove up and completed a second swap before the Audi had finished filling up, as the crowd roared its approval.

"Voilà," said Musk when the demonstration was over. "So our goal here was really to eliminate the objections that people have," he explained. "What we really wanted to show here is that you can actually be more convenient than a gasoline car. We just did two Model S in the time it took to fill up, and we honestly try to make the gas station stop go as fast as it could. It only took just about four minutes at the gas station, but it only took about ninety seconds for a pack swap. So hopefully this is what convinces people finally that electric cars are the future."

At first it looked like Musk had succeeded. Like the Supercharger event, Tesla's battery swap generated reams of glowing headlines heralding the bold new future that had been displayed on the stage in Hawthorne. Very few words were wasted wondering why the swap mechanism was concealed throughout the demonstration, or speculating about what precisely lay behind the metaphorical curtain. If Musk said that a fully automated swap system would soon be an option at Tesla Supercharger stations, surely that would be the case.

The transformational promise of battery swap was largely forgotten until December 2014, when a company blog post announced that the first Tesla swap station was beginning pilot operations at Harris Ranch, California. Almost halfway between Los Angeles and San Francisco, in California's Central Valley, Harris Ranch seemed like the perfect place to test the system. An 85 kWh Model S could make it to Harris Ranch on a single charge, quickly swap batteries, and then continue on to its destination. With this capability, travel between two of Tesla's biggest markets could be done as quickly and conveniently as with a gasoline car.

But in the months that followed the announcement, the Tesla forums that religiously followed and documented the company's latest features were conspicuously devoid of battery-swapping reports. By Memorial Day weekend, there was only one report of a customer swapping batteries to be found online and only a few reports of Tesla inviting customers to try the system. Having been fascinated by battery swap since covering the abortive swap company Project Better Place, I decided to spend the long holiday weekend at Harris Ranch to see if I could witness a battery swap in person. AAA had projected that those four days would have some of the highest traffic in recent years, making it a likely opportunity to see the station in action.

Over the course of that long weekend, I witnessed lines for the on-site Superchargers that were three vehicles deep at times. Because each vehicle in line required as much as an hour of charge time, people were stuck at Harris Ranch for hours waiting to recharge their Teslas. Families with children faced lengthy waits before resuming what was already a long road trip; many told me they would love to have the option of quickly swapping out their spent battery for a full one, and they would be willing to pay a good deal of money for such a service. But despite the obvious need for a faster solution during peak hours, Tesla had not made the battery-swap "pilot program" available to any-one I spoke to making the drive that weekend.

Instead, it took a different approach. On Friday, the first day of obser-vation, a Tesla employee showed up at the swap station, where he began hooking up two pairs of extra Superchargers to diesel generators. Over the rest of the weekend, Tesla and Harris Ranch employees directed owners waiting for the permanent Superchargers to the diesel-powered backups—while it's possible that there were some, owing to my bath-room breaks, I did not witness a single battery swap.

When reached for comment, a Tesla spokesman confirmed that the swap station was open for pilot operations and that customers who regularly charged at the Harris Ranch Superchargers had been invited to try it. However, not a single driver I spoke with over four days of observation had received an invitation, although many of them regu-larly used Harris Ranch Superchargers. Then, days after I wrote a series of blog posts describing the situation, suddenly forum reports flooded in of Tesla owners receiving invitations to use the swap station.

Just two weeks later, the battery-swap story was over. At the 2015 Tesla shareholder meeting in mid-June, Elon Musk was asked how own-ers could participate in the swap program, to which he replied, "We have the LA to San Francisco pack-swap capability in place, and I believe all Model S owners in the sort of California area have been invited at this point to try it out. And what we're seeing is just a very low take rate for the pack-swap stations. So we did an initial round of invitations where we did basically like two hundred invitations, and I think there were a total of four or five people that wanted to do that and they all did it just once. So, like OK, clearly not very popular."

Musk continued to say that he believed that sample group was indicative of Tesla customers as a whole—he thought people "don't care" about pack swap, and that the free Superchargers were preferred. Further, he claimed, "We built the pack swap into the car because we weren't sure if people would want to choose the pack swap or not. We thought people would prefer supercharging but we weren't sure so that's why we built the pack-swap capability. And based on what we're seeing here it's unlikely to be something that's worth expanding in the future, unless something changes."

If Musk had always been skeptical of consumer desire for fast battery swaps, he'd done an amazingly good job of hiding it at the premiere event where he'd said he thought it would convince skeptics that electric cars were the future. And if every owner in California had been invited to try the swap station only to universally reject the service, why had tens of drivers told me that they'd have been happy to pay for swap but hadn't received an invite just a few weeks earlier? Like his decision to cancel the entry-level 40 kWh Model S, thus eliminating the lower price point that was at one point the raison d'être for the "first affordable Tesla," Musk's claim that he was simply responding to weak demand for battery swap didn't add up.

There was, however, an explanation that did make sense. In 2013, California revised its Zero Emissions Vehicle credit system so that long-range ZEVs that were able to charge 80 percent of their range in under fifteen minutes earned almost twice as many credits as those that didn't. Overnight, Tesla's 85 kWh Model S went from earning four credits per vehicle to seven. Moreover, to earn this dramatic increase in credits, Tesla needed only to prove to CARB that such rapid refueling events were *possible*. By demonstrating battery swap on just one vehicle, Tesla nearly doubled the ZEV credits earned by its entire fleet even if none of them actually used the swap capability. Recall that, under the

ZEV mandate, at least one percent of every automaker's California sales must be vehicles with no tailpipe emissions; ZEV sales earn their makers credits while non-ZEV sales earn debits, and at the end of the year the ZEV sale credits must offset the non-ZEV debits. If an automaker fails to sell enough ZEVs in a given year to earn a positive credit balance, it must purchase credits from an automaker with excess credits or face a fine. Since the fine for each credit shortfall was $5,000, Tesla could sell these three additional credits to other automakers for as much as $15,000 in marginal profit on each car it made.

As it turned out, the California Air Resources Board staff had become concerned about the potential for Tesla's battery-swap program to "game" this provision by the end of 2013. For the 2015 to 2017 model years, CARB created a new rule requiring Tesla to actually document a certain number of battery swaps to prove that the capability was actually being used. This development just so happened to coincide with Tesla's half-hearted "pilot program" and its subsequent decision that its customers had no interest in fast, convenient battery swaps.

Though Musk repeatedly downplayed the importance of these credits to Tesla's finances, the company earned some $217 million from ZEV credits in 2014, when it turned an overall loss of $294 million on $3.2 billion in revenue. Tesla's pivotal Q1 2013 (non-GAAP, or Generally Approved Accounting Practices) profit of $11 million, which allowed the firm to borrow the cash to pay off its DOE loan and sent its stock price soaring, would have been a loss without the $68 million in ZEV credit revenue it earned that quarter. Tesla's only other quarterly profit, which brought in $22 million during the third quarter of 2016, was similarly made possible by $139 million in ZEV credit revenue.

It's safe to say that none of Tesla's recorded profits would have been possible without the ZEV program. By exploiting CARB's fast-refueling rules, Tesla appears to have earned as much as $100 million in additional revenue by demonstrating and hyping a system it seems to never have intended to commercially deploy. The episode demonstrates the challenge of creating incentives that encourage the deployment of electric vehicles and not cynical exploitation of the credit system. It also shows how Tesla's ability to game CARB's rules underpinned its only two profitable quarters, both of which were instrumental in boosting its stock price.

Tesla's cynical use of battery swap echoed its claims to be taking huge amounts of carbon off the road while failing to deliver on its solar power promises and even using diesel generators at Harris Ranch. Tesla regularly releases updates on the amount of carbon its vehicles have saved, which it calculates based on the assumption that the electricity used to power its cars is carbon free, but when pressed for details, Tesla admits that it is not. This pattern of repeatedly promising environmental benefits and then not fully delivering on them but claiming the benefits for publicity purposes suggests that Tesla's use of environmentalism is less purely principled than Musk claims.

Now, of course, none of this changes the fact that electric cars are almost always better for the environment than gas cars. But rather than sticking with more modest but defensible and deliverable commitments and claims, Tesla continually overstates its environmental and technological benefits to prop up the mythology that Musk has built around it and the hype that has made him billions on the company stock. Absent any public fact-checking of these claims, or accountability for these promises, both continue to grow apace.

Five years after promising Tesla owners they could drive anywhere using only the power of the sun, Tesla still had yet to provide proof that even a single Supercharger was actually fully solar-powered . . . and yet new promises of off-grid Superchargers were still coming. Whether these promises are noble aspirations or cynical lies almost doesn't matter at this point. The promises themselves, rather than their realistic fulfillment, seems to be what Tesla owners and investors want from Tesla. And Elon Musk is only too happy to deliver.

CHAPTER 10

THE AUTOPILOT PIVOT

If one set a standard that you couldn't have loss of life, then there would be no transport. You wouldn't even be allowed to walk.
Elon Musk, September 29, 2011

n retrospect, Tesla's soaring stock price made its 2013 leap from DOE loan dependence to stock market sweetheart look all but inevitable, but it was another high-stakes gamble that could easily have ended in disaster. In fact, the gambit was so risky that Musk had developed a backup plan in case public markets weren't taken in by a single profitable quarter. This backup plan might have been a trivial footnote in the history of Tesla, had it not given birth to Tesla's most important and controversial "pivot": the Autopilot program.

Turning from the government to friends in Silicon Valley, Musk had approached Google founders Sergey Brin and Larry Page in early March of 2013 with an offer to sell the company. As Ashlee Vance tells it:

He proposed that Google buy Tesla outright—with a healthy premium, the company would have cost about $6 billion at the

*time—and pony up another $5 billion in capital for factory
expansions. He also wanted guarantees that Google wouldn't break
up or shut down his company before it produced a third-generation
electric car aimed at the mainstream auto market. He insisted that
Page let him run a Google-owned Tesla for eight years, or until it
began pumping out such a car. Page accepted the overall proposal
and shook on the deal.*

By the end of March, it was clear that Musk had pulled off Plan A;
Tesla was out of the DOE loan, it showed it was capable of recording a
quarterly profit, and its stock price was lifting off like a SpaceX rocket.
With no further need for a billion-dollar safety net, Musk called off
the deal while lawyers for both sides were still negotiating the details.
Within five months, Tesla's market cap would be more than double the
$11 billion Google had agreed to pay for it.

At the time, nobody knew how close Musk had come to selling
Tesla (and Musk himself disputes that there was a formal offer). The
deal wouldn't become public knowledge until years later when Vance's
book came out, by which time it was an interesting but seemingly
inconsequential footnote in Tesla's history. Though it does illustrate
how close Tesla came to busting out in 2013, as well as Musk's ability to
manage the perceptions that fed Tesla's stock market tear, it also marked
the beginning of a fundamental pivot in the company's strategy.

There was more than friendship behind Google's interest in Tesla.
Since 2009, Google had been developing a technological play that held
even more transformative potential for the auto industry than Tesla's
batteries and electric motors: self-driving car technology. Headed up by
Sebastian Thrun, the German innovator and computer scientist who had
led a Stanford University team to victory in the 2005 Defense Advanced
Research Projects Agency Grand Challenge, Google's self-driving car
program (which would be spun off into a company called Waymo in
December 2016) was the undisputed leader in a technology that threatened to make EVs look like old news.

Autonomous-drive technology is actually a collection of technologies, each serving different aspects of the driving task. Sensors like radar, lidar, and cameras perceive the road and its occupants, machine-learning algorithms classify each potential obstacle and predict their movements, pathfinding algorithms plot a course through the predicted flow of traffic, and mechatronics translate the actions to the vehicle controls. Some of the core challenges of autonomous drive are related to the work Google had done for its map products, which involved multisensor scanning to create realistic models of roadways and machine learning to derive turn-by-turn directions from them. But the near-infinite complexity of traffic made it an order of magnitude more challenging, and until 2013, Google's self-driving car program was widely seen as a speculative moon shot funded by its massive ad revenues.

The first public clue that Google's self-driving cars were moving beyond mere experimentation came in early May 2013, when Musk revealed that Tesla was discussing possible collaboration on autonomous-drive technology with the search giant. But, in typical Musk fashion, collaboration with Google was only one option, and Tesla would go its own way if necessary. Whereas Google was under no financial pressure to turn its nascent autonomous-drive technology into a viable consumer product, Tesla needed something to bolster demand for cars it was already selling.

"I think Tesla will most likely develop its own autopilot system for the car, as I think it should be camera-based, not Lidar-based," Musk told Bloomberg News, referring to the pricy laser scanner sensor that crowned Google's autonomous test vehicles. "However, it is also possible that we do something jointly with Google. The problem with Google's current approach is that the sensor system is too expensive. It's better to have an optical system, basically cameras with software that is able to figure out what's going on just by looking at things."

At the time, Musk said, "We're not focused on autopilot right now . . . Autopilot is not as important as accelerating the transition to electric cars, or to sustainable transport." But by the end of the summer it was clear that his ambitions were expanding as rapidly as Tesla's market cap. On September 18, 2013, Musk tweeted, "Intense effort underway at Tesla to develop a practical autopilot system for Model S," and a Tesla ad surfaced soliciting an engineer to oversee "vehicle-level decision-making and lateral and longitudinal control strategies for Tesla's effort to pioneer fully automated driving." "We should be able to do 90 percent of miles driven within three years," Musk told the *Financial Times* in an article headlined "Tesla moves ahead of Google in race to build self-driving cars." That timeline positioned Tesla to become the first automaker to sell an autonomous vehicle, ahead of Nissan who earlier in the summer had committed to deploying an autonomous vehicle by 2020.

This was a stunning pivot for Tesla, which had never mentioned autonomous-drive technology in Musk's Top Secret Master Plan or anywhere else. (Marc Tarpenning would later say the technology "was not really on our radar screen at all.") Inside Google, sources close to the company's founders say Musk's decision to start competing with his erstwhile friends—especially after they agreed to a generous acquisition deal—soured the relationship. In their view, Musk saw Google's progress on autonomous-drive technology as a threat to Tesla's status as the preeminent Silicon Valley mobility technology company. Having generated enormous hype for Tesla's electric vehicles, Musk wasn't going to let autonomous vehicles upstage them as the hot new Silicon Valley trend.

But stealing a march on Google wouldn't be easy for Tesla. Google had a four-year head start on the technology and a team stacked with the top names in the field. After years of development, Google was still years away from reaching its goal of developing a car capable of driving itself with zero human input even using the latest and most expensive sensors. This forced Tesla to move in a different direction. Instead of trying to beat Google to full autonomy, Tesla had to develop a product that would create the impression of a self-driving car as quickly as possible without tackling the toughest safety challenges that still held back fully autonomous cars. To pull this off, Tesla would have to create a far cheaper and less capable system than Google's, and Musk would have to redefine public perceptions of autonomous-drive technology around the new system.

Musk began reframing autonomous-drive technology by arguing that Google's full self-driving strategy was unnecessary, telling Bloomberg News, "I like the word autopilot more than I like the word self-driving. Self-driving sounds like it's going to do something you don't want it to do. Autopilot is a good thing to have in planes, and we should have it in cars." In "Autopilot," Musk found his opportunity to create a new brand that could capture the excitement just beginning to build around self-driving car technology without having to follow Google down a seemingly endless rabbit hole of obscure problems and expensive sensors. It was a term that was familiar to the public, but it was also undefined outside of aviation, allowing Musk to create a unique definition to match the capabilities of a new Tesla system that was close to, but not quite, autonomy.

This familiar but ambiguous branding would become Autopilot's greatest strength, allowing Musk to create the impression that it was the first autonomous-drive system available for sale to the general public while avoiding the toughest technological challenges and massive legal liability risks associated with true autonomy. But at the same time, the vague nature of the Autopilot brand and Musk's inconsistent statements about its constantly shifting capabilities introduced massive safety risks that would plague the system's rollout. Like Kleenex, Autopilot was a brand that became synonymous with a unique product category . . . but unlike with tissues, the definition of Autopilot could be changed to serve Tesla's interests.

The public's confusion about Autopilot was rooted in the term itself. Rather than being the single integrated system that the brand implied, Autopilot is a collection of Advanced Driver Assistance Systems (ADAS), each of which performs a different task. For example,

Forward Collision Warning (FCW) warns the driver when an obstacle appears ahead, and Automatic Emergency Braking (AEB) applies brakes to mitigate an imminent crash. These systems are available on automobiles from a number of brands and only manifest themselves during a collision or a near miss. Another subsystem of Autopilot, Traffic Aware Cruise Control (TACC), is an advanced cruise control system that uses radar to prevent forward collisions and match vehicle speed with surrounding traffic. TACC was deployed by a number of carmakers starting in the late 1990s, and it's increasingly available in more affordable nonluxury-brand cars.

The most unique feature of Autopilot is the one that dominates perceptions of it: Autosteer. An advanced lane-keep assist system, Autosteer keeps the vehicle within lane markings without driver input, theoretically allowing the driver to remove his or her hands from the steering wheel. Though other automakers offer versions of lane-keep assist, they either don't allow or heavily limit hands-free operation due to safety concerns. Though testing has shown that Autosteer performs better than competitive lane-keep assist systems, the key to Autopilot's success was not an overwhelming technological advantage but Tesla's risk tolerance. In addition to allowing longer periods of hands-free driving than other automakers, Tesla permitted owners to use the system on any road even while warning that the system was only safe on divided highways with no cross traffic.

While Tesla's official representatives consistently emphasized the fact that Autopilot was not autonomous and required constant driver engagement, Musk had always danced around the contradiction at the heart of the Autopilot gambit. In 2014, well before Autopilot functionality was released to the public, Musk told Tesla shareholders, "In one year we will have a car that drives on Autopilot from freeway on-ramp to freeway off-ramp." Noting that Autopilot was tested on highways between San Francisco and Seattle, he said before release that the system was "almost able to go [between the two cities] without touching the controls at all." He even slipped up in the Autopilot release press conference, saying, "It's $2,500 to activate the autonomous features forever," after repeatedly insisting Autopilot was not autonomous.

In the Tesla blog post announcing the release of Autopilot capabilities, the company stated, "While truly driverless cars are still a few years away, Tesla Autopilot functions like the systems that airplane pilots use when conditions are clear. The driver is still responsible for, and ultimately in control of, the car." Musk echoed the warning at a press event announcing the new feature, while introducing the first hints of ambiguity that would prove so problematic. "We tell drivers to keep their hands on the wheel just in case, to exercise caution in the beginning," he said. "It works almost to the point where you can take your hands off . . . but we won't say that. Almost."

Tesla started building every car with Autopilot hardware shortly before it first announced the system in October 2014, but full functionality didn't arrive until an over-the-air software update a year later. After a year of steadily building hype, TACC and Autosteer were pushed to every car that had been ordered with a "technology package" that unlocked these "Autopilot convenience features." This unprecedented delivery method only heightened the sense of exuberant futurism that had surrounded Autopilot since its announcement, and Musk's promise of continuing updates suggested that even if Autopilot wasn't yet truly autonomous, future updates could make it so. "Over time, long term, you won't have to keep your hands on the wheel," he said.

The ambiguity between Musk's hype and Tesla's warnings burst out into the open in the first wave of media coverage that accompanied the public release of Autopilot. "I went hands-free in Tesla's Model S on Autopilot, even though I wasn't supposed to," confessed a Mashable headline that captured the uncertainty that Tesla had created. "Tesla's Cars Now Drive Themselves, Kinda" added *Wired*. From Slate to *Car and Driver*, it seemed that every blogger and journalist who got time with Autopilot during the launch campaign was told not to remove his or her hands from the wheel but did it anyway. Videos and gifs of reporters waving their hands above the steering wheel of an Autopilot-equipped Model S flooded the internet, accompanied by earnest paeans to a *Jetsons* future that seemed to have already arrived.

For more than six months, concerns about the risks presented by hands-free use of Autosteer were buried under an avalanche of gee-whiz optimism fueled by a series of quotes and tweets from Musk hyping Tesla's nonautonomous autonomous-drive system. Then, suddenly, the concerns resurfaced with a vengeance when Tesla published a blog post on June 30, 2016, revealing that the National Highway Traffic Safety Administration (NHTSA), which regulates auto safety in the United States, was investigating a fatal crash involving Autopilot. In an instant, any ambiguity about the proper use of Autopilot was a distant memory.

On May 7, 2016, Joshua Brown's beloved black Model S collided with a semitruck that was turning across a Florida highway. The car was in Autopilot mode and traveling at a high rate of speed at the time of the collision, and Brown had taken no action to correct the car's lethal course even though he'd had plenty of time to see the truck blocking the road. Tesla's blog post hinted at the likely problem: with only a camera and radar system, the Autopilot sensor suite could not distinguish "the large, white side of the tractor trailer against a brightly lit sky." The fact that one of Google's lidar sensors, which Musk had been disparaging since 2013, would not have been fooled by this kind of scenario was a huge hit to Tesla's burgeoning image as a leader in autonomous-drive technology.

But ultimately the Brown crash was not so much about a technical failure on the part of Autopilot, but the deadly risk Tesla was running by marketing an ADAS system as a nearly autonomous car. Had Brown followed Tesla's legal disclaimers and official warnings and remained as engaged and alert as any other driver, he would have seen the truck turning and taken a course of action that was safer than the high-speed collision that mangled his Model S. Instead, Brown was following in the path that the media launch for Autopilot had set: breaking Tesla's rules to find out just how autonomous and futuristic the experience could be. And he'd been egged on by Elon Musk himself, who just months earlier had tweeted a video that Brown had posted to YouTube, showing Autopilot "saving" his Model S from a crash without his intervention. Musk's caption credits Tesla's "Autopilot steering to avoid collision with a truck," potentially reinforcing Brown's tragically mistaken belief that the system could keep him safe.

In that blog post about Brown's death, Tesla doubled down on Autopilot's supposed safety benefits. "This is the first known fatality in just over 130 million miles where Autopilot was activated," the post claimed. "Among all vehicles in the US, there is a fatality every 94 million miles. Worldwide, there is a fatality approximately every 60 million miles." Two and a half months later, it was revealed that a twenty-three-year-old Tesla owner named Gao Yaning had died months before the Brown crash, when his Model S slammed into a slow-moving street sweeper on a highway. Though Tesla insisted that the crash had damaged the communication devices that transmit telemetry data to their servers, and thus argued that it had no way of knowing whether Autopilot was engaged, the crash reflected Autopilot's inability to track slow-moving or stationary objects as well as its tendency to make drivers less alert and engaged.

By the time Gao's family filed suit against Tesla, alleging that Autopilot had encouraged irresponsible driving and contributed to his death, Tesla's credibility on Autopilot was melting down. When *Fortune* magazine questioned why Tesla had not disclosed the Brown crash when it sold more than $2 billion in stock earlier that year, Musk lashed out in response to *Fortune*'s request for comment, writing, "[I]f anyone bothered to do the math (obviously, you did not) they would realize that of the over 1M auto deaths per year worldwide, approximately half a million people would have been saved if the Tesla autopilot was universally available. Please, take 5 mins and do the bloody math before you write an article that misleads the public."

But there was far more to Musk's statistical defense of Autopilot's safety than just "doing the bloody math." Musk was comparing a tiny number of Teslas, none of which was more than four years old or cheaper than about $70,000, to a much larger US car fleet with an average age of eleven years and an average price of $35,000. Moreover, Autopilot was supposed to be used only on divided highways, whereas the average car operates in far more complex environments, making crashes more likely. Autonomous car experts derided Musk's safety statistic comparisons as "ludicrous on their face" and "[having] no meaning," severely damaging Musk's credibility as a man of science and advocate of the safety benefits of autonomous cars.

As Musk's meaningless and misleading statistics further eroded his credibility on Autopilot, it became increasingly clear how much the public depended on Tesla's word about what exactly happened in crashes where drivers said Autopilot was involved. Because Tesla's data-recording capabilities did not fit the precise definition of an event data recorder (like the black box on an airplane), the company did not have to comply with legislation that gave ownership of the data to the vehicle's owner and required that they make a third-party data reading tool available. In numerous cases, Tesla used that data to publicly refute customer accusations of Autopilot involvement in a crash without ever offering access to the data itself. If Musk could tout misleading statistics about Autopilot's safety, could the public trust Tesla's unverifiable statements about what vehicle data said? Until the company finally released a data-reading tool in 2018, in the wake of a lawsuit in which the owner was able to maintain custody of onboard vehicle data and demand a third-party reading, they had no choice but to trust the company.

After all, numerous Tesla owners had blamed Autopilot for a crash only to be told by Tesla that the drivers had been at fault. One such owner, profiled in the *Wall Street Journal*, had crashed into a car parked on a highway while Autopilot was activated. Her experience exemplifies the double bind that Autopilot users faced. Tesla said vehicle data showed that she had hit the brakes before the collision, disengaging Autopilot before the crash took place. "So if you don't brake, it's your fault because you weren't paying attention," she explained. "And if you do brake, it's your fault because you were driving." With Musk peddling questionable safety statistics and Tesla denying any owner or third-party review of vehicle data, this "damned if you do, damned if you don't" approach made it all but impossible to trust Tesla's statements about crashes involving Autopilot.

After a summer of almost uniformly negative media coverage of Autopilot, Musk's frustration boiled over in an October conference call. He had been asked whether Tesla would be liable for crashes involving its autonomous cars, and after giving his usual answer (not unless the crash was tied to a specific design defect), he let his anger flow. "One of the things I should mention that frankly has been quite disturbing to me is the degree of media coverage of Autopilot crashes, which are basically almost none relative to the paucity of media coverage of the 1.2 million people that die every year in manual crashes," he said. "[It is] something that I think does not reflect well upon the media. It really doesn't. Because, and really you need to think carefully about this, because if, in writing some article that's negative, you effectively dissuade people from using an autonomous vehicle, you're killing people."

Musk was correct in the sense that the media's Autopilot coverage had contributed to a death. By encouraging the hands-free use of Autopilot and heralding it as the first (sort of) autonomous car when it launched, the media had helped create the overconfidence in Autopilot's abilities that ultimately killed Joshua Brown. If anything, the wave of negative coverage that followed Brown's death was a long-overdue examination of the risks inherent to Tesla's Autopilot strategy, which should have been given a more thorough airing at launch. As Tesla's own supplier of Autopilot-enabling hardware and others pointed out, Tesla's decision to rush Autopilot to market, push the technology to the limit, and overhype its capabilities was what put lives—and the future of autonomous-drive technology itself—at risk. By conflating criticisms of Autopilot with criticisms of autonomous vehicles, Musk's rant proved that he still didn't get it.

In the end, Musk's bluster and bad statistics won the day. On January 19, 2017, the last day of the Obama Administration, the day before Donald Trump was sworn in as president, NHTSA closed its investigation of the Joshua Brown crash with the conclusion that Autopilot should not be recalled. Not only did NHTSA's final report exonerate Autopilot, both in the Brown case and more generally, it included a breathtaking endorsement of the most controversial part of the system: "The data show that the Tesla vehicles crash rate dropped by almost 40 percent after Autosteer installation." This astounding revelation effectively put an end to the controversy around Autopilot, giving Tesla a powerful cudgel against its critics.

But like Musk's statistics about Autopilot safety, NHTSA's claim does not hold up well to close scrutiny. Shortly after the report came out, a company called Quality Control Systems (QCS) filed a Freedom of Information Act lawsuit for the data the agency had used to make its determination. In May 2018, NHTSA finally admitted that its crash rate comparison was "cursory" and did not "evaluate whether Autosteer was engaged" or "assess the effectiveness of this technology." In February 2019, after two years of Tesla and NHTSA fighting QCS's calls for transparency about the 40 percent claim, the data and analysis NHTSA had used was made public in a report that revealed the finding to be based on incomplete data and inept statistical analysis. Using the relatively small amount of complete data that Tesla had provided to NHTSA, the far more rigorous analysis that QCS ran concluded that "Autosteer is actually associated with an increase in the odds ratio of airbag deployment by more than a factor of 2.4."

For two years, Tesla defended the system with the argument "Autopilot was found by the U.S. government to reduce crash rates by as much as 40 percent," even after yet another Tesla crashed while on Autopilot, killing its driver. That this explicit government endorsement was based on yet more demonstrably inaccurate data and statistical analysis is bad enough, but the fact that Tesla and NHTSA had argued that both the data and the analysis should be exempted from the Freedom of Information Act out of fear of "competitive harm" is more shocking still.

Worst of all, the National Transportation Safety Board had conducted a thorough investigation of the Josh Brown crash, and its report blew apart Musk's entire approach of comparing human and Autopilot safety. According to the NTSB report, the cause of the first fatal Autopilot crash was neither the human nor the Autopilot system, but a dangerous mix of the two. Autopilot's design "allowed prolonged disengagement from the driving task" due to the lack of a driver monitoring system that would turn off assistance if it noted driver distraction, the report said, and allowed the system to be used on roads where it wasn't safe, due to a lack of hard operational design domain limits. Autopilot had worked perfectly when it slammed into a truck at seventy miles per hour, but Brown had been lulled into a fatal overreliance on Autopilot while using it in a situation it hadn't been designed for.

Autopilot engineers would tell the *Wall Street Journal* that they had pushed for better driver monitoring during the development of Autopilot, suggesting both gaze-tracking cameras and more sophisticated sensors to ensure the driver's hands remained on the wheel. According to these engineers, Musk personally rejected their suggestions due to cost, a claim Musk called "false" in a tweet claiming eye tracking had been "rejected for being ineffective." Musk's ultimate defense was that Autopilot is simply safer than human drivers, but Tesla's record compares poorly to that of the Cadillac Super Cruise system, which does exactly what NTSB called for: limits use to mapped freeways and tracks the driver's gaze to prevent distraction. Not a single crash has been reported in a vehicle with Super Cruise activated.

Had Tesla designed Autopilot to ensure that the system was being used safely, by limiting its use to divided highways and more accurately monitoring driver attention, Josh Brown might still be alive. But the very lack of these features, which allowed Autopilot to "drive" through any kind of road or traffic condition without driver input, is precisely what made the system seem more advanced and autonomous than any-thing else on the market. If Tesla were to completely eliminate the risks that killed Josh Brown, Autopilot would be almost impossible to dis-tinguish from any other ADAS system, and Tesla's supposed advantage in autonomous-drive technology (and the billions in market valuation that it brings) would disappear.

Ultimately, Autopilot points to a dangerous contradiction at the heart of all automated driving technology. Though ADAS and autonomous-drive technologies are almost always presented as safety-enhancing features, what people actually want out of them are both the ability to pay less attention when behind the wheel and the high-tech cool factor of a car appearing to drive itself. Though Tesla was the first and most prominent company to understand and exploit this reality, the lack of regulatory action even after the NTSB diagnosed Autopilot's glaring safety issues leaves the door open for others to follow.

CHAPTER 11

X MARKS THE SPOT

[The Model X] program has been challenging. I particularly
need to fault myself for a fair bit of hubris for putting
too much technology all at once into a product.
Elon Musk, May 31, 2016

"When we designed the Model S, we created a platform," said Musk from the familiar stage in Hawthorne. The screen behind him showed Tesla's flat battery "skateboard" chassis. "So it's not just a single car. We created something on which we could build many cars. And we're able to leverage that and really bring a car to market fast . . . and that's what the Model X is all about." It was February 2012, four years before the Brown crash, and Tesla was still months away from delivering the first Model S. But Musk was already back in Hawthorne unveiling Tesla's next big thing. Sales of SUVs had been booming as the economy recovered from the global financial crisis, and Tesla was scrambling to tap into the growing segment. After all, not only were SUVs in high demand with customers, but they also delivered a disproportionate percentage of automaker profits.

Musk's pitch to prospective buyers was that Tesla's Model X SUV would combine the utility of a minivan, the capability of an SUV, and the performance of a sports car, all wrapped in the slick styling and high-tech details that had become Tesla's calling card. But by referencing the Model X's use of the Model S platform, Musk was also sending an unspoken message to Tesla's investors: the Model X could become Tesla's first real cash cow.

From its earliest days, the auto industry had been dogged by a persistent challenge: smaller, cheaper cars are no less expensive to develop—and nearly as expensive to build—as large, expensive cars. In particular, the upfront investment to create a body/frame, suspension, engine, and transmission, as well as tooling needed to build the vehicle, is staggeringly high whether it's for an affordable car with slim profit margins or a luxury car with relatively strong profit potential.

The industry's solution to this challenge is called "platform strategy." Each major investment in a "platform," which encompasses the chassis dimensions, drivetrain, and manufacturing system, should yield an entire line of vehicles, each of which shares as many underlying components as possible. Thus, a single massive investment in (for example) a compact platform would allow an automaker to develop compact sedan, hatchback, station wagon, minivan/MPV, and SUV variants at relatively low incremental cost. Because the huge initial "platform" investment is spread across a range of models, an automaker can develop "loss-leader" affordable versions whose losses are offset by more profitable SUV or MPV variants.

The key to this platform strategy is to differentiate each model from its platform mates as much as possible while sharing as many parts as possible. It's a tricky balance: differentiate too much and you lose meaningful efficiencies of scale, but differentiate too little and you end up with "brand engineering," in which identical cars are differentiated only by badges, grilles, and other details. Finding this balance is like blackjack: the more shared parts the better, right up to the point where the illusion of differentiation is shattered and premium models and brands lose their appeal.

Thus far, Tesla had only built two cars—the Roadster and Model S—each of which used its own platform. With the Model X, Tesla was taking its first step into the core challenge of the modern auto industry, and its ability to differentiate the X from the S while improving profit margins through platform and parts sharing was a major test. A properly executed Model X had the potential to generate more demand and higher profit margins than the Model S, all while improving margins on its sedan cousin. A Model X with too many or too few parts in common with the S would be a massive missed opportunity and a sign that Tesla would struggle to turn around its hefty losses as it grew into a full-line automaker.

As soon as the prototype Model X rolled out from behind the curtain and onto the stage to a thumping techno beat and cheers from Musk's chorus of the faithful, there were signs that Tesla's SUV would fail to strike the all-important balance between commonality and differentiation. On the one hand, it looked a lot like a Model S with a higher roofline and the awkward proportions of a people mover, suggesting that it might struggle to stand out on a lot filled with Tesla's sedan. On the other hand, its key differentiating feature was a unique double-hinged, roof-mounted "falcon wing" rear door system that looked extremely complex and expensive to make.

Roof-mounted, swing-up doors, known in the industry as "gull-wing doors," had been around since the 1952 Mercedes 300SL race car. Though eye-catching, the subsequent half-century proved that this design had serious shortcomings: they made roofs harder to seal against the elements, they required extra reinforcement for side-impact protection, they prevented egress in rollovers, and they tended to be much less reliable than standard door configurations. Because of these challenges, roof-mounted doors have remained a rare feature, typically appearing on low-volume sports cars like the Delorean DMC-12, the Bricklin SV-1, and most recently the Mercedes SLS.

Tesla's version of the gull-wing layered extra complexity on top of these issues by making the doors double hinged and packing them with sensors and actuators. This complexity actually made Tesla's "falcon-wing" doors far more useful than a typical gull wing; they could sense obstacles and fold up in ways that created giant door openings even in tight parking spaces and small garages. It also transformed the X from an awkwardly proportioned, almost pregnant-looking Model S to a high-tech transformer, a party trick that cemented Tesla's status as the coolest automaker in the world.

The doors were a product of Musk's direct involvement in the Model X's development, and they represented an attempt to marry stunning design with the solution to a very real problem. According to Ashlee Vance, Musk and Tesla's design boss, Franz von Holzhausen, discussed the challenge of accessing the rear seats of SUVs and minivans while walking the floor of an auto show and agreed to pursue an innovative solution to this problem for Model X. After reviewing "forty or fifty" door concepts, they settled on what von Holzhausen termed "one of the most radical ones."

As Vance puts it,

Like Steve Jobs before him, Musk is able to think up things that consumers did not even know they wanted . . . As he sees it, all of the design and technology choices should be directed toward the goal of making a car as perfect as possible. To the extent that rival automakers haven't, that's what Musk is judging. It's almost a binary experience for him. Either you're trying to make something spectacular with compromises or you're not. And if you're not, Musk considers you a failure.

This perspective goes a long way toward explaining the intense passion that consumers feel for Tesla, and it reinforces the perception that "legacy" automakers simply lack the innovative creativity of a high-tech, California-based startup. But the reason established automakers don't offer flashy features like falcon-wing doors is not a lack of design talent or creativity, as evidenced by decades of concept cars featuring outrageous designs that rival anything Tesla has produced. Rather, the reason production cars never look as flashy as the design concepts you see at car shows is that automakers have all learned the lesson that Tesla was about to learn with the Model X.

From the very beginning, Tesla's engineers had trepidations about transforming Musk's falcon-wing vision into reality. "Everyone tried to come up with an excuse as to why we couldn't do it," one engineer told Vance. But the debate between Musk and his engineers centered on the falcon-wing system's utility to consumers, and Musk demonstrated that the concept not only looked distinctive but genuinely improved access to back seats. It was only after the design engineers had been convinced and the development work began that it started to become clear that the core challenge lay in actually manufacturing the falcon wings.

Tesla began taking reservations for Model X on the day Musk unveiled the prototype, and at the time Musk said the first deliveries would begin "toward the end of next year," with volume production ramping up in 2014. A year later, Tesla's annual report for 2012 revealed that Model X production had been pushed back to late 2014. By the end of 2013 it was delayed again, this time until the second quarter of 2015. But even that timeline would prove unrealistic, and the first "Founder Series" deliveries to early reservers and Tesla investors didn't start until the final quarter of 2015.

In January 2016, with Model Xs still only trickling out of Tesla's Fremont factory in tiny volumes, Tesla filed a lawsuit against the US division of a Swiss automotive supplier called Hoerbiger that would drag the falcon-wing door's troubled gestation into the public eye. According to Tesla's complaint, the two firms had reached an agreement to develop a hydraulically actuated falcon-wing door system in 2014, but that

> *The parties never entered the production phase because, although HOERBIGER had represented it could produce a production-ready hydraulic actuation system, HOERBIGER failed to deliver a product that met TESLA's specifications or that fulfilled HOERBIGER's promises. On numerous occasions, TESLA notified HOERBIGER of the multitude of defects with its product. While HOERBIGER insisted it could fix the problems, HOERBIGER failed to do so.*

The suit alleged the doors had been riddled with deficiencies: they were prone to overheating and would shut down, they didn't open fast or symmetrically enough, they sagged, they continually leaked oil.

It's rare for disagreements between automakers and their suppliers to spill out into the open, but by this time the Model X delays had become a nagging PR issue for Tesla, and the lawsuit helped explain why development had dragged on for so long. The lawsuit generated numerous media reports on the day it was filed, suggesting that (as a source with knowledge of the situation later confirmed) Tesla had leaked the suit to reporters. Hoerbiger was blindsided. Tesla's version of events had been widely reported by the time the supplier issued its own statement several days later, saying that it had been fully prepared to start production and had never been in breach of its contract with Tesla—that Tesla owed Hoerbiger money after backing out of their agreement. And further,

> *Media reports implying HOERBIGER was responsible for the design of the Tesla Model X doors are misleading. From the beginning, HOERBIGER was only tasked with the development and production of the hydraulic door actuation system. HOERBIGER was never responsible for the electronic controls associated with symmetry and overheating problems cited in the complaint.*

Tesla's lawsuit, which sought a judicial declaration that it had not violated its contract with Hoerbiger as well as claims against the supplier for negligence and misrepresentation, was eventually settled in mediation for undisclosed terms after Tesla dropped eight of its ten claims. None of those claims alleged breach of contract, however, suggesting that Hoerbiger had indeed requested compensation it was contractually owed when Tesla backed out of their contract. Such an arrangement is customary in auto industry supplier relations, where a supplier must invest in tooling, labor, and materials needed to deliver on its obligations. In any case, Tesla's lawsuit had its intended effect by making Hoerbiger out to be the scapegoat for Model X delays.

After all, when Tesla dropped Hoerbiger in 2015, it didn't simply choose a new supplier. After spending five months selecting Hoerbiger and another fifteen months iterating hydraulic falcon-wing doors with the supplier, Tesla decided to build the falcon-wing doors itself using electromechanical rather than hydraulic actuation. Despite incurring millions in additional development and tooling costs, a Tesla team, headed by former MIT researcher (and later head of Tesla's Autopilot program) Sterling Anderson, was able to wrangle a design that Tesla could put into production in less than a year. If the Hoerbiger debacle had highlighted the unforeseen challenges of developing the falcon-wing doors, Anderson's team proved that Tesla's prowess at hacking together creative solutions on short notice was still one of its greatest strengths.

Model X production volume remained below three hundred units per month in January and February 2016, and the delays were beginning to take their toll on Tesla's stock price. By the end of March, production had finally ramped up, and the nearly two thousand deliveries recorded in the month suggested that the worst of the Model X's manufacturing challenges had been overcome. But as customers began to receive their long-awaited SUVs, their forum posts soon made it clear that Model X was not out of the woods yet.

Many of the early posts described problems similar to the ones that plagued the Model S, including poor paint quality, door and window seal problems, interior squeaks and rattles, misaligned body panels and trim, and generally poor fit and finish. But the early Model Xs also had a host of unique problems, including faulty air-conditioning compressors and weird double- and triple-vision illusions from the windshield in low light conditions. And just as the Model S's pop-out door handles had been a major source of early quality problems, the X's signature combination of self-presenting front doors and falcon-wing rear doors proved deeply problematic.

The front doors had done away with the Model S's pop-out door handles, opening themselves when the owner either pressed the handle or simply walked up to the car with the "self presenting" option turned on. Like the falcon-wing doors, they were both practical and appealing in concept . . . and a nightmare in practice. The complexity of the Model X's front and rear falcon wing caused countless problems: doors didn't align properly with the frame, refused to open, shut, or lock, stopped self-presenting, and even opened themselves randomly. A few even broke themselves by opening into obstacles that they were supposed to have sensed and avoided.

A number of early owners reported multiple trips to service centers, and in some cases even sold their cars back to Tesla under state lemon laws. As Tesla struggled to get a handle on the multifarious problems with the Model X's recalcitrant doors, owners would share the latest suggestions from their local service centers with varying degrees of success. Eventually Tesla issued a firmware update that disabled "pinch sensors" that it said were responsible for much of the falcon-wing door malfunctions, which seemed to improve their performance but created new safety concerns—as popularly illustrated with YouTube videos showing the doors chopping vegetables.

Even when Tesla fixed all the major problems that prevented normal function, the Model X's overly ambitious design inspired almost as much embarrassment as it did awe. Because the front and rear door handles were designed to meet up, even relatively minor misalignments were instantly identifiable since the handles didn't quite mirror each other. Even in cases where Tesla assured owners that they had realigned falcon-wing doors and panels to be within specification, a mismatch was easy to see. There was simply no getting around the fact that Musk's design ambitions had radically exceeded Tesla's manufacturing capabilities.

Musk paid a heavy price for his hubris, telling investors on the first quarterly earnings call of 2016 that he'd been personally overseeing the troubled Model X production line. "My desk is at the end of the production line," he revealed. "I have a sleeping bag in a conference room next to the manufacturing production line that I use quite frequently." It was the kind of heroics that his fans loved, playing directly into their image of Musk as a deeply involved genius who spent his days personally guiding everything aspect of the company.

In the offices of the major automakers, however, Musk's revelation inspired little more than an eye roll. Seasoned auto executives had predicted that Tesla would struggle with the Model X's doors from the moment they saw the first prototype, and Musk's almost penitential tour of duty in quality control came across as theater rather than a serious attempt to fix the situation. Musk's antics might repair the damage that the Model X debacle had done to his reputation, but any improvement they might have had on Tesla's manufacturing quality only proved how troubled the company really was.

Car companies are massive organizations, and as such they must operate in a systematic manner. Quality in particular must be baked into every step of the design, development, and production of a new car, and a commitment to quality must come from every level of the organization—think back to what I told you in chapter 5 about the Toyota Production System and values. Any car company that must rely on the physical presence of its CEO to manufacture vehicles to an acceptable quality standard is essentially admitting that its culture isn't committed to quality.

This systematic approach to quality and efficiency is precisely why no automaker would have attempted to make the Model X.

Manufacturing engineers would have been involved early in the design process to assess the manufacturability of the design and would have anticipated many of its problems. A cost accountant would also have forced the design's "champion" to weigh the additional cost of the falcon-wing doors against the potential increase in demand or profit margin that they hoped to bring in. Finally, if the four-year process of development, testing, and preproduction had identified persistent quality or profitability issues, the design would have been canceled or sent back to the drawing board.

These layers of hard-nosed analysis and validation represent the "compromise" that Musk appears to so disdain, slowing the product cycle and replacing unique artistic visions with the "dumbed down" and "generic" vehicles that he and his followers decry. And as the Model X proved so dramatically, they exist for good reason: The most brilliant design in the world is worth very little if it can't be made efficiently, profitably, and at competitive quality. These "compromises" aren't the products of generic corporate mediocrity, but of survival of the fittest—the car companies that didn't embrace them have all gone out of business.

Musk would later admit that the entire first half of 2016 had been a "production hell" that had cost him "a whole lot of mental scar tissue," but the Model X–related pain didn't end there. After Model X "production hell" ended, the ill-fated SUV remained stuck near the bottom of most reliability surveys, dragging down the brand's mediocre-at-best reliability ratings. When the X was rated "much worse than average" in the 2018 *Consumer Reports* survey, combining with the merely "average" Model 3 and the "below average" Model S to secure the third-worst brand rating, Tesla protested that "while the earliest production Model S cars encountered quality inconsistencies, this is simply not a concern for Model X cars being built today."

Over time Tesla did beat some of the most egregious quality problems out of the X through its iterative engineering changes, but Tesla's contention that "quality inconsistencies" were only found in early builds flies in the face of countless owner accounts. Even after years on the market, reports of problems with both the self-presenting and falcon-wing doors, seals, windows, panel fit, half-shaft consumption, squeaks, whistles, and various other issues kept the Model X sections of Tesla forums stubbornly well-stocked with complaints.

Even more important, the Model X had failed at the most fundamental task of an SUV: It hadn't printed the profits Tesla so desperately needed. "In order to make the X great, we had to go to the point where maybe 30 percent of the parts are in common between the S and the X," Musk admitted. Such low percentage of parts commonality meant that Tesla had ended up spending huge amounts on parts that might have been carried over from the S had the X design been more restrained. The entire logic of making a sedan-based SUV, namely the ability to earn more margin with a fraction of the investment, had been lost to Musk's grand ambitions.

Nor had the "greatness" of Musk's uncompromised vision made the Model X—one of the highest-priced entries in the luxury midsize SUV class upon its release—a sales success. At a time when SUVs were solidly outselling sedans in the US, where Tesla makes the majority of its sales, the Model X never once outsold its sedan sibling. Tesla's SUV may have brought in a few buyers who weren't already sold on the Model S, but in general the Model X served only to deepen Tesla's fan base at a time when it desperately needed to broaden it.

As early as 2016, Musk admitted that the Model X's failures were the result of his own "hubris," a self-criticism he would repeat in the following years. "A big mistake we made with the X, which is primarily my responsibility, there was way too much complexity right at the beginning," he said in 2017. "That was very foolish."

The Model X may have taught Musk hard lessons about modern vehicle design, engineering, and economics, but even at his most reflective and self-critical, he seemed to miss the larger issue. The core problem wasn't that Musk let his ideas run away with him; it was that Tesla's internal culture couldn't empower its cost accountants, manufacturing engineers, and suppliers to stand up to their CEO, chief product architect, largest shareholder, spokesman, and mascot. The scale and complexity of modern automobiles has made the car business the ultimate team sport, relegating all-powerful automotive auteurs to either tiny luxury-brand workshops or the history books.

Tesla has a clear leader and it has a clear mission, but what it doesn't have is what allows the best automakers to manage massive scale and complexity: clear cultural principles and practices. Tesla's stated mission is profoundly motivating for many of its employees, and its work culture is correspondingly intense, but "accelerating the transition to sustainable transport" only explains the company's ends, not its means—the why but not the how. As a result of this cultural vacuum, almost every decision that management makes at Tesla ends up coming down to a single consideration: Will Elon approve?

In the absence of constraints, ambition must always find its limits, and in the Model X Musk found his. But despite his repeated self-criticisms over the debacle, Musk showed no signs of stepping back or tempering his impulses with tested auto industry expertise. There was even a note of insouciant pride in some of his public penances about the Model X, as if Tesla's biggest product flop had almost been worth the countless millions in easy profits that were left on the table, or the quality problems that marred countless customer experiences.

The Model X "is like a Fabergé egg of cars," he said at the 2017 shareholders' meeting. "It's really an amazing product, but it has way too many cool things in it that should have really been rolled in with version two, version three. We got overconfident and created something great that probably will never be made again. And perhaps should not be."

CHAPTER 12

DEFECTS, DISCLOSURE, AND DRAMA

The word "recall" needs to be recalled.
Elon Musk, in a since-deleted tweet from January 2014

ometime in early 2014, Keith Leech was looking through pictures of wrecked Tesla Model S vehicles at an auction house website when he started noticing a pattern: in almost every photo, the car's wheels had sheared off from the suspension. Once he noticed it, he started to see it in nearly every picture of a wrecked Tesla he could find. Eventually he started an album on the photo-sharing site Flickr, dubbing the collection "whompy wheels." Thus a one-man crusade was born.

Leech says he hadn't set out to look for safety problems with Teslas. Several years earlier, when he'd been building a solar panel system for his off-the-grid home in the Australian bush, he discovered something called the "SunCube" on the internet. The SunCube's creator promised it would revolutionize solar energy generation, and at first Leech was taken in, but as time went on, it became clear that there was no actual product. In the online confrontations that followed, the SunCube's inventor called Leech a fraud and a criminal; Leech sued him for defamation and won. The SunCube, which had secured an AUD$450,000 contract with the South Australian government, collapsed into bankruptcy and infamy. For his part, Leech had found a new hobby: uncovering green scams.

As one of the most high-profile green companies at the time, Tesla quickly hit Leech's radar screen, but his initial investigation was simply looking at the company's environmental claims. When he noticed the broken wheels and suspensions, however, he was sure he'd found his next SunCube. Though he didn't have an engineering degree, he had done a mechanical and electrical engineering apprenticeship through the UK Ministry of Aviation and considered himself an "eyeball engineer." Given the weight of the Model S and its use of cast aluminum suspension components, which he knew was unusual due to its brittleness and tendency to casting defects, he smelled a problem.

Convinced that the Model S was underengineered and poorly manufactured, Leech launched a one-man online campaign to document what he saw as evidence of a dangerous problem. As his Flickr folder of images of Model S vehicles with broken suspensions and "whompy wheels" grew, and he became more certain he had uncovered a public danger, he began to post warnings on various Tesla forums, even reporting potential failures to the National Highway Traffic Safety Administration's complaint database.

Though Leech only comes across as somewhat eccentric on the telephone, his quirky usernames, trollish turns of phrase, and combative persistence can make him come across as downright crazy on the internet. When his crusade collided with the paranoid, defensive culture of Tesla forums, the combination was explosive. Leech played right into the stereotype of an anti-green provocateur spreading anti-electric car "FUD" on behalf of shadowy forces. The immediate hostility of the forums in turn triggered Leech's inner bulldog, and each time he was banned, he'd just register a new username and go right back to it.

By early 2016, Leech had become the boogeyman of the Tesla forums, reviled and feared to the point where anyone obliquely referencing a suspension problem was immediately accused of being one of his accounts. The entire subject of suspensions had already become radioactive when a Tesla owner named Peter Cordaro posted a thread at the Tesla Motors Club forum that read (excerpted exactly as posted):

> I have owned my Model S since May of 2013 and truly love the car. With that said, I must tell everyone about a recent problem I experienced this past Sunday while driving on a back road at a very low rate of speed, about 5 MPH. The road was rough so my airride was at it max lift. As I was proceeding down a steep hill I heard a snap and felt my steering wheel pull to the left. I stopped the car for further inspection only to discover that my left front hub assembly separated from the upper control arm. Needless to say the car was inoperable due to a loss of steering. Thank goodness I was not traveling at a high rate of speed. This could of been a tragic accident causing injury or even death.
>
> I contacted Tesla and they towed the car to a service center. They just informed that this is not covered under warranty, stating that the cause was due to normal wear and tear. I have owned many cars in my life and have never experienced such a failure. My car has been driven 73000 miles.

Forum members immediately began questioning whether or not his complaint was real and suggesting that he had abused his vehicle, causing the suspension to break. When he supplied images and claimed he had not done anything more than drive the car at low speeds on a rough road, other owners began to add accounts of suspension breakage to the thread. Even after the accounts began to pile up from around the world, many of the forum members seemed more interested in uncovering the motives of a trollish poster going by the handle Wivaneef, who had showed up in the thread to share his findings (it would turn out to be Leech).

I had been following the thread as part of my daily Tesla forum reading, but I hadn't considered it worthy of reporting. That is, until one day when Mr. Cordaro posted something that instantly caught my attention. Cordaro had previously reported that Tesla was refusing to repair the damage under warranty; now, suddenly, he revealed that the company had agreed to perform the repair for 50 percent off. But in exchange for this beneficence, Tesla had required him to sign a "Goodwill Agreement," which he subsequently posted.

The agreement stated that in exchange for goodwill repairs, the customer releases Tesla from any claims or damages, promises not to sue Tesla for anything related to the problem being fixed under goodwill, and agrees to keep the entire incident confidential. The sweeping confidentiality clause covered everything about the incident: the problem being fixed, the events that led up to the problem, the fact that Tesla was providing goodwill repairs for the problem, and even the Goodwill Agreement itself.

The agreement's language immediately struck me as being deeply problematic from an auto safety regulation perspective. NHTSA has two main sources of information about potential defects in new cars. First, automakers can self-report defects and initiate a Technical Safety Bulletin for non-safety-critical defects or perform a recall in the case of safety-critical defects. Second, vehicle owners can report defects directly to NHTSA's defect database, which the agency uses to determine whether or not to investigate a potential defect. If Tesla was making owners with potential safety-critical defects sign Goodwill Agreements that amounted to nondisclosure agreements (NDAs), that practice effectively cut NHTSA off from its sole source of independent defect reporting and made it reliant on manufacturer self-reporting.

Having covered several auto safety scandals, most recently the trumped-up Toyota "sudden unintended acceleration" scare and the decade-old unrecalled GM ignition switch problem, I knew that proving whether or not a defect exists was all but impossible without large amounts of data or a forensic engineering lab. A manufacturer policy like the nondisclosure clauses in Tesla's Goodwill Agreement, on the other hand, would be a clear and provable sign of a cover-up. Even if no underlying defect were ever provable, the mere existence of an NDA that could prevent an owner from reporting a defect to NHTSA was a serious safety concern.

I began looking around the internet for other reports of Tesla requiring nondisclosure agreements for customers with potential defect complaints, and it didn't take long to find two more. One also came from a TMC thread, where an owner complained of a number of issues with his Tesla including "the loss of control and abs, steering, traction etc." After directly contacting Tesla's then VP of worldwide service and deliveries, the owner reported that Tesla had agreed to repair his vehicle in exchange for an NDA. A third report was found at the Better Business Bureau, which claimed that Tesla had required an NDA before repossessing a defective Model X:

Tesla refuses to make me whole on its repossession of the defective vehicle sold me unless I sign a hush up agreement with $150,000 penalty violation.

Tesla sold me a defective Model X. Tesla then took back possession of the vehicle and cancelled its registration without my knowledge. Tesla is now refusing to make me whole on the monies I am out unless I sign an agreement where I can not report the defects to agencies or others or the repurchase terms. If I violate Tesla says I am liable for $150,000. Tesla now has possession of the Model X and I am not being made whole for what I am out. Vehicle was riddled with defects.

Having found three separate examples of Tesla requiring owners of potentially defective vehicles to sign NDAs in exchange for "goodwill repairs" or repossession of the vehicles, I wrote a story on my blog titled "Tesla Suspension Breakage: It's Not the Crime, It's the Coverup." Though not all the examples I found had involved suspension breakage, Mr. Cordaro's report had been the most complete and had included a word-for-word copy of the agreement. I also made it clear in the text of the story that only experienced investigators could perform the forensic analysis needed to conclusively identify a defect, and even then only NHTSA could conclusively determine whether or not a safety defect exists in a car.

When I was finally able to reach a NHTSA spokesperson for comment on the story, he laughed and told me that several of the most experienced auto reporters were trying to catch up with my reporting. Then he gave me the following official agency statement, which I subsequently added to the story:

> NHTSA is examining the potential suspension issue on the Tesla Model S, and is seeking additional information from vehicle owners and the company.
>
> NHTSA learned of Tesla's troublesome nondisclosure agreement last month. The agency immediately informed Tesla that any language implying that consumers should not contact the agency regarding safety concerns is unacceptable, and NHTSA expects Tesla to eliminate any such language. Tesla representatives told NHTSA that it was not their intention to dissuade consumers from contacting the agency. NHTSA always encourages vehicle owners concerned about potential safety defects to contact the agency by filing a vehicle safety complaint at SaferCar.gov.

The next evening, I was relaxing in bed when my phone began spasming. I had scheduled one of the first interviews for this book early the next morning, but as soon as I checked my Twitter notifications I realized that I wouldn't be getting to sleep as early as I had planned. Tesla had just written an official response to my story on its company blog, and my mentions were filling up with a combination of recrimination and support. I had just become part of the story.

Given NHTSA's unequivocal statement about Tesla's use of NDAs, I had assumed the company would keep a low profile. There was really nothing it could say about the problem that I had clearly identified as being the issue: not the "crime" of broken suspensions, but the "cover-up" that had impacted owner defect reporting. Instead, the company blog post twisted my story to make it seem like I had been trying to prove that a dangerous and unrecalled suspension defect existed in its cars.

Titled "A Grain of Salt," the blog post began by stating, "a few things need to be cleared up about the supposed safety of Model S suspensions."

"First," it read, "there is no safety defect with the suspensions in either the Model S or Model X." This was unambiguous language that any other automaker likely would have avoided given NHTSA's statement that it was "examining the potential suspension issue." But the important part of this statement was not whether it was true or false, but its ability to change the subject. Because there was no way to defend its NDA policy after NHTSA declared it "troublesome" and "unacceptable," Tesla's only play was to focus on the question of suspension breakage.

"Second," the post went on, "NHTSA has not opened any investigation nor has it even started a 'preliminary evaluation,' which is the lowest form of formal investigatory work that it does." At best this was a semantic quibble: Not only had NHTSA told me it was "examining the potential suspension issue," but reports from outlets like the *New York Times* and Reuters confirmed that NHTSA's "review" and "data collection" were ongoing. That meant that until the safety regulator concluded that no further review was necessary, the matter remained unsettled. Musk also subsequently tweeted that NHTSA had "found no safety concern with the Model S suspension and have no further need for data from us," which was widely taken to confirm that no investigation was necessary, when in fact NHTSA confirmed to other sources that it was still collecting data as part of its "screening" procedure.

"Third," the blog post continued, "Tesla has never and would never ask a customer to sign a document to prevent them from talking to NHTSA or any other government agency. That is preposterous." This was self-evidently false, as proven by the text of the Goodwill Agreement and NHTSA's statement about it. Tesla went on to claim that the facts actually proved how proactive Tesla is when it comes to safety, listing the voluntary recalls it had performed in the past. "There is no car company in the world that cares more about safety than Tesla," the post argued, as if examples of its compliance with defect-reporting laws were somehow extraordinary and not the minimum legal behavior for a company selling new cars.

But Tesla was saving its best material for last, calling me out by name as "the blogger who fabricated this issue" and casting doubt on my impartial stance by mentioning the "Tesla Death Watch" series I'd been assigned to write at *The Truth About Cars* eight years prior. "We don't know if Mr. Niedermeyer's motivation is simply to set a world record for axe-grinding or whether he or his associates have something financial to gain by negatively affecting Tesla's stock price," the post read, "but it is important to highlight that there are several billion dollars in short sale bets against Tesla. This means that there is a strong financial incentive to greatly amplify minor issues and to create false issues from whole cloth."

This was not the first time that Tesla had attempted to discredit a critical reporter or commentator, and it certainly hasn't been its last blatantly defamatory smear of a journalist. The claim that I had "fabricated" the story was obviously contradicted by NHTSA's statement and Tesla's subsequent decision to comply with the regulator's demand that it modify its Goodwill Agreements. Nor did Tesla provide any evidence of any kind to back its claim that I had "fabricated" any part of the story, beyond its similarly fact-free speculation about my motives.

The suggestion that I had reported on (or "fabricated") this issue to financially benefit from "short selling" Tesla's stock was also presented without evidence. This was an accusation that Tesla's supporters had leveled at me and others in the past. I had denied that I was shorting the stock before, but in hopes of making it abundantly clear that Tesla's accusation was false, I took the unusual step of writing a blog post attesting "under penalty of perjury" that I had no financial interest whatsoever in the success or failure of Tesla.

It didn't make much of a difference. Tesla's smear was repeated as fact in forums and comment sections across the internet, where I was excoriated as a fabricator in the employ of either Tesla "shorts" or the oil and auto companies that Tesla was supposedly on the verge of "disrupting." Though a number of journalists and commentators defended my reporting and blasted Tesla's unfounded personal attack against me, their measured analyses could not budge the majority of fans who took Tesla's assertions at face value.

I wasn't alone in facing attacks over the story. Tesla's post also sought to blame Peter Cordaro for the damage that led to his TMC blog post, noting that Cordaro's car had "very abnormal" rust that they had never seen on another vehicle. Cordaro, they claimed, lived down a long dirt road, and that those conditions led to the problem.

Cordaro debunked this claim in his TMC thread, writing (excerpted as posted):

> They have my address and should of googled earth my address before making such an outrageous statement. [...] The above statement is an out and out lie. I live on a paved road in the city of Connellsville pa. The car was towed from a dirt road as I stated earlier because I was out morel mushroom hunting that day with my wife. We were traveling about 2 miles an hour on a bumpy back road. Most of my 70k miles are on the highway. Telsa shame on you.

Like me, Cordaro was viciously attacked by TMC members. Several members who were most active on the site's investor thread led the charge, casting doubt on the credibility and motivations of anyone who had helped bring potential safety and disclosure issues to light. Some TMC members fought back, arguing that their interests as owners were in seeing a thorough and independent investigation, and that the potential public safety concern outweighed the investors' interest in silencing even legitimate criticism of the company they had invested in.

This split between the interests of owners in open information sharing and the investor interest in silencing or discrediting any negative information about Tesla's quality or business practices had been opening for some time. A separate TMC thread, which had been started in 2013, highlighted the extent to which Tesla investors and hard-core fans themselves pressured owners not to report defects to NHTSA. A parade of commenters scorned concerned owners for even considering "tattling to Mother," arguing that Tesla would proactively fix any defects without the need for complaints that might impact the company's image.

In fact this "code of silence" only raised fresh questions about Tesla's safety culture. Because Tesla's NDAs prevented both reporting of defects and reporting of the very existence of the company's Goodwill Agreements, it was all but impossible to get a solid read on how many defects Tesla owners may have endured even before factoring in the self-imposed and self-enforced culture of nondisclosure. The fact that Tesla forums had as many reports of problems as they did, especially in light of how few Teslas were on the road compared to mainstream vehicles, was something of a miracle given these factors.

NHTSA's investigation into Tesla's suspension problems never got past the "screening" step, and the issue faded away as Autopilot safety grabbed the media and NHTSA's attention. Reports of suspension failures continued to trickle in, and Leech carried on his online campaign, but without enough money to fund real forensic engineering work, his investigation was doomed. Having been banned from every Tesla forum, multiple times in some cases, he continued to submit NHTSA complaints and troll Elon Musk from a series of oddly named Twitter accounts. Without an NHTSA investigation to show for his efforts, his bizarre online presence gave off an increasingly kooky vibe.

In the face of the NDA drama, I had almost forgotten about the underlying suspension issue, when I found myself at lunch several months later with a former automotive engineer. Almost as soon as Tesla came up, he asked me what I thought about the possibility of a suspension defect in its cars. I told him that I had my suspicions, but that proving it would be all but impossible so I had dropped the subject entirely.

He smiled and explained that he had worked on the redesign of a large, heavy vehicle that had replaced steel control arms with cast aluminum for weight savings. The switch had delivered the desired results, but ensuring quality for these safety-critical parts was a major challenge. Aluminum castings are highly prone to porosity, caused by air trapped in the liquid metal while it is being cast or gas bubbles in the metal forming as it cools. These tiny pores can weaken castings, and the intense, repetitive fatiguing pressures in a heavy vehicle's suspension can cause them to break.

"Do you know what we had to do?" the engineer asked. "We had to x-ray every single control arm the supplier made, just to be sure they met our specifications . . . and even then, we ended up replacing way too many of them under warranty." He laughed. "We ended up going back to steel for the next redesign. The cost and quality problems just weren't worth the weight savings."

"So," I asked, "do you think this Keith guy is onto something?" He didn't even have to stop to think. "Between the weight of the vehicle, the use of cast aluminum, and Tesla's lack of experience with manufacturing . . . yeah, I do," he replied. I was stunned. I had not expected an experienced automotive engineer who had been through the wringer with cast aluminum suspension components to validate the hunch of a guy who was widely considered to be an internet crazy.

NHTSA ultimately never determined that there was a specific defect in Tesla's suspensions, but then, it would have been all but impossible to do so. Musk regularly bragged about the hundreds or even thousands of engineering changes that Tesla made to its cars on a weekly basis, suggesting that Tesla could be more agile than a traditional automaker, which would typically wait until a model-year change to make a significant engineering modification in the car. Musk liked to cast this "iterative engineering" approach as a software-derived innovation that made better cars, but these constant changes also had a little-understood and less-positive impact on auto safety regulation.

In addition to the complaint data they receive from owners, NHTSA needs to know the "population" of vehicles that use the problematic part or system. Only by comparing reported failures with the potentially affected population can NHTSA independently determine whether or not the complaints are statistically significant. But thanks to Tesla's iterative engineering, which continuously changes the parts in cars without consistently reporting them, regulators never know for sure how many vehicles have a specific version of a given part.

NHTSA has struggled to effectively regulate safety, even among the established automakers who generally make engineering revisions every two years at the most. Incidents like the GM ignition-switch scandal, which killed 124 people over ten years before the safety regulator uncovered it, show the extent of the safety regulator's struggles in a much slower-moving context. It also showed that it was all but impossible to catch parts changes that weren't denoted by a parts number change. How the same regulator could possibly keep up with Tesla's constant engineering changes, even without owner nondisclosure agreements and a fan culture that tries to prevent open discussion of problems online, is hard to imagine.

Tesla's ability to effectively flout auto safety regulations is vividly illustrated by its handling of an earlier problem that caused its vehicles to suddenly lose power and throw error codes. The problem, which was reported by the website Edmunds.com as well as numerous owners around the world, had a similar effect as the defective GM ignition switch: suddenly turning the car's power off. But in spite of the clear safety implications of this failure mode, which in many cases were reported on freeways at relatively high speeds, Tesla didn't recall any cars for the problem.

I was alerted to the situation when a French taxi driver who had bought a Model S, thinking it would be good for business, contacted me with a bizarre story. After he'd experienced a sudden terrifying power loss, Tesla had replaced the car's high-voltage contactors, but instead of describing the problem he had reported, the service invoice simply noted: "As part of providing peace of mind and a great ownership experience, Tesla vehicles are equipped with telematics systems to provide remote diagnostics support. We have been notified this vehicle has been remotely diagnosed that the Power Switch and Power Supply would benefit from the latest generation components."

I began researching reports of similar problems in the online forums, and a pattern quickly emerged: Not only had a number of owners experienced a similar sudden power loss, there were also over a dozen related reports from around the world of the mysterious boilerplate language about proactive repairs in service of "a great ownership experience." Tesla had told one owner that his sudden power loss had been caused by a firmware issue, but the company sent him an email several months later with the exact same message that the French taxi driver had noticed on his invoice. Another owner reported an email saying, "Engineering has identified your car as potentially benefiting from a switch and power supply update," while others reported similar requests under the guise of "ensuring your vehicle is consistently being improved with the most updated parts available."

In its only communication to regulators about the problem or the worldwide campaign to repair it, Tesla filed two versions of a Technical Service Bulletin for a high-voltage contactor "upgrade" intended to correct an issue that could prevent a car from starting. By calling the repair an upgrade and suggesting that the worst-case scenario was a failure to start a car, Tesla eliminated any reference to a safety issue that might have required a recall. According to a later report by the Department of Transportation's inspector general, GM had prevented NHTSA from discovering its lethal defect by using a similar trick.

By reaching out to owners, Tesla was effectively performing a "stealth recall" of a part it knew could cause vehicles to stall dangerously. By telling them it was proactively improving their cars and refusing to document their complaints about stalling, it was hiding a paper trail that might allow NHTSA to uncover the truth. And because it was still requiring that owners sign NDAs that said they couldn't talk to anyone about problems repaired under "goodwill," NHTSA was effectively cut off from any data that might have alerted them to the issue.

Though I wasn't able to tie any injuries or deaths to this problem, there was no doubt in my mind that Tesla should have recalled cars to fix it. NHTSA has considered such a fundamental loss of performance to have intrinsic safety implications since the 1970s, and between 2004 and 2013, some ninety-one recalls were carried out to address defects that caused stalling. One of these, the 2013 recall of the Ford Focus Electric, fixed a problem with almost identical symptoms to the Tesla contactor problem and was undertaken after NHTSA opened a formal investigation.

In 2015, Toyota and Daimler separately recalled the RAV4 EV and Mercedes B-Class E-Cell, whose powertrains were developed and built by Tesla during their partnerships, for problems causing sudden loss of drive power. Both problems involved incorrect signals in the Tesla-made drivetrain regarding the status of the high-voltage contactor (in the case of the Mercedes) and the speed of the motor (in the case of the Toyota), and both companies worked with Tesla to identify the problem. Only Tesla could fully understand what, if anything, might have contributed to these problems, and its actions to conceal the truth hardly inspire confidence.

Tesla's motivation for concealing real or potential defects or safety problems can be found in the "risk factors" section of its annual report to the SEC, under the heading "we may be compelled to undertake product recalls or take other actions, which could adversely affect our brand image and financial performance." Recalls, Tesla notes, could "involve significant expense and diversion of management attention and other resources, and could adversely affect our brand image in our target markets, as well as our business, prospects, financial condition and results of operations."

Given the speculatively high valuation that Tesla was able to inspire, and the resulting volatility in its stock price, it's safe to assume that Tesla could be hit especially hard by a recall. Anything that was critical to the safe performance of its self-developed drivetrain had to be even more closely protected, lest its unique selling point be called into question. Even after the events surrounding its high-voltage contactors, and the recalls of its drivetrains in Toyota and Daimler products, Tesla proudly noted that "none of our past recalls or corrective measures have been related to our electric powertrain."

Tesla also had the opportunity to hide problems with its cars because of its unique in-house sales and service operation. Since franchised dealers represent every other automaker in the US to their customers, warranty repairs and service complaints are all documented and billed by a third party. Because Tesla owned its own stores and service centers, it had a unique ability to order "stealth recalls" and keep actual customer complaints off of service invoices to evade legal reporting requirements. By recording repairs as "goodwill," it could also avoid having to raise the amount of money it set aside for warranty reserves.

Tesla is outspoken about the safety of its cars, taking immense pride in their high crash-test scores and personal reports from owners who credit their Tesla's engineering with protecting them in wrecks. (As I've mentioned, it has even drawn NHTSA's ire by suggesting that its cars have scored higher than the five-star top score in crash testing, inspiring repeated rebukes from the regulator.) With the exception of Autopilot engineers, some of whom felt that Tesla didn't do enough to ensure the safety of its driver-assistance system, every Tesla engineer I have spoken to was proud of the lengths that Tesla goes to design cars that are as safe as possible.

Tesla's problems on safety come down to some of the unique attributes that it brings from the software world into the highly regulated, life-and-death world of automobiles. One could speculate that its high-flying stock price gives it extra incentives to conceal any problem that might lead to a recall, even though recalls are the responsible (and legally necessary) response to any safety-related issue. What's more, its approach of launching with a "minimum viable product," and then iterating the vehicle's engineering over time not only makes it more likely to bring an undertested and potentially problematic vehicle or component to market, it also means regulators can't properly track vehicle populations to oversee safety. Tesla's seemingly systematic evasion of NHTSA's independent investigatory capabilities also brings to mind Silicon Valley's cultural disregard for fussy regulations and slow-moving bureaucrats.

Though automakers regularly produce defects, and the industry endures a full-blown safety scandal at least once a decade or so, there's also a real understanding in the industry that regulation is a fact of life. Automotive engineers and executives generally recognize that the products they produce are intrinsically dangerous, and that a strong record of compliance with safety regulations can help prevent and mitigate potentially devastating civil liability lawsuits. Almost every single automaker has a shameful moment in its history that left an indelible mark on its collective memory of what happens when safety problems are ignored or concealed. As a result, most of the defects that do cause tragic injuries or deaths are byproducts of the massive scale and complexity of these companies, their products, and their supply chains rather than conscious skulduggery.

For all its futuristic vision, Tesla's position is too precarious for it to have the same approach. Having built up so much hype and anticipation around itself, the brand damage caused by a single recall could lead to a loss in confidence in its prospects. Without a solid business to support its heady valuation, a loss of confidence could have catastrophic, cascading consequences that could affect its ability to hire talent, raise fresh capital, and ultimately survive.

This precariousness, along with Tesla's world-saving mission, is part of what feeds an "ends-justify-the-means" culture inside the company. The powerful twin motivations of survival and salvation make it easy to wave off issues like regulatory compliance and cover up defects with nondisclosure agreements. They also make convenient cudgels with which to attack critics, shifting the focus away from the company's questionable actions to speculation about the critic's motivations for wanting to destroy a company that is only trying to save the planet.

The problem, of course, is that this cultural feedback loop would eventually devolve into outright hostility toward huge swaths of the media. I saw my own experience play out again and again, as reporters realized Tesla had stories worth digging for, Tesla and its fans responded to their investigations with attacks, and the cycle of mutual antagonism repeated itself.

CHAPTER 13

THE REMASTERED PLAN

In ~2 years, summon should work anywhere connected by land &
not blocked by borders, e.g., you're in LA and the car is in NY.
Elon Musk, January 10, 2016

You can summon your Tesla from your phone. Only short distances
today, but in a few years summon will work from across the continent.
Elon Musk, November 28, 2018

The storm clouds swept up by the nondisclosure-agreement scandal and the Josh Brown crash were still swirling around Tesla when an Elon Musk tweet suddenly blew them away one Sunday morning in the summer of 2016. "Working on Top Secret Tesla Masterplan, Part 2. Hoping to publish later this week."

The message was retweeted nearly four thousand times. After months on the defensive over various scandals and investigations, a new master plan promised a return to the Tesla fan base's bread and butter: getting excited about the transformative power of Musk's latest bold vision of the future. The company's stock jumped 4 percent in anticipation.

But as was the case with so many of his promises, Musk's second master plan took longer than expected to arrive. Six days later, Musk tweeted, "Sunday is the end of the week :)"—revealing that he was sleeping less than six hours a night and joking that he was staying focused with the help of "large amounts of crack." The next day he delayed again, tweeting "Have to focus on tonight's @SpaceX launch. Will post Tesla (master) product plan afterwards."

Several days and anticipation-building tweets later, Musk finally delivered. Titled "Master Plan, Part Deux," the post opened with a recap of the substance and rationale of the 2006 master plan, which noted that it had failed to prevent attacks on Tesla's strategy but still provided a context for decisions that might otherwise have seemed "random." That context, noted Musk, "was, and remains accelerating the advent of sustainable energy so that we can imagine far into the future and life is still good."

To continue making progress toward this far-off yet unassailable goal, Musk could no longer be held back by the promises he'd made a decade before. After all, the "affordable" Model S that was supposed to start at half the price of the Roadster enjoyed a comparable six-figure average transaction price; Model X cost even more than the S. Yet in spite of these persistently high prices, none of Tesla's cars ever actually generated enough cash flow to fund development of the subsequent model as envisioned in the original plan.

Still, Tesla had introduced the long-promised "more affordable" Model 3 in prototype form several months earlier, and Musk was ready to make new promises. First, Tesla and SolarCity would have to merge to create an integrated solar roof and battery product that would "empower the individual as their own utility." This new solar roof could not be produced if Tesla and SolarCity remained separate companies, explained Musk. The 100 percent solar-powered Superchargers Musk had repeatedly promised since 2012 apparently did not play a meaningful role in this proposed merger, as Musk failed to reference them even once.

With clean energy solved, Musk turned to vehicles. Acknowledging that Models S and X only "addresses two relatively small segments," Musk promised that the upcoming Model 3, Model Y crossover variant, and an electric pickup truck would "address most of the consumer market." Then Tesla would turn to the commercial vehicle segments, which it would address with an electric semitruck and a "high passenger density urban transport." With these seven vehicles—large car/large SUV, small car/small SUV, pickup truck, semi, and minibus—Tesla would cover every mobility need that Musk could imagine in the future.

The key to success with these vehicles would lie with the "machine that builds the machine," which Musk said Tesla's engineers were "heavily" focused on. By starting with a "physics first principles analysis of automotive production," Musk predicted Tesla would be able to iterate its production system every two years and improve it "5 to 10 fold" by approximately 2022. "What really matters to accelerate a sustainable future is being able to scale up production volume as quickly as possible," argued Musk, ignoring the quality and capital efficiency problems that had plagued Tesla's manufacturing thus far.

The biggest divergence from the original master plan was that Musk was no longer calling for Tesla to continue making electric cars cheaper and cheaper. Indeed, Musk specifically stated that a vehicle cheaper than the $35,000 Model 3 "is unlikely to be necessary" due to the autonomous-drive technology that Tesla was increasingly orienting its business around. Musk promised that every Tesla would be built with the hardware for full self-driving, but warned that regulatory approval for autonomous-drive software would be likely to take another five and a half years.

Once that approval was given, however, Musk foresaw a world where anyone could afford a sensor-packed Tesla costing more than the US new car average-transaction price. Freed from the need to oversee a system like Autopilot, Musk argued, Tesla owners would be able to make their cars work for them:

> *You will also be able to add your car to the Tesla shared fleet just by tapping a button on the Tesla phone app and have it generate income for you while you're at work or on vacation, significantly offsetting and at times potentially exceeding the monthly loan or lease cost. This dramatically lowers the true cost of ownership to the point where almost anyone could own a Tesla. Since most cars are only in use by their owner for 5% to 10% of the day, the fundamental economic utility of a true self-driving car is likely to be several times that of a car which is not.*

In effect, Musk was arguing that Teslas were about half a decade away from becoming economic perpetual-motion machines. As long as you could qualify for a loan of $35,000 or more, you could own an asset that could not only pay for itself, but possibly even earn its owner a net profit. Though Tesla owners would be forbidden from renting out their autonomous vehicles using Uber and Lyft, a "Tesla Network" would facilitate these private robotaxis, and Tesla would even provide its own fleet in localities where demand exceeded supply.

Having pivoted from electric drive to autonomy, Musk was now following his Silicon Valley peers into the promised land of shared autonomy. But because Tesla was a traditional car company built on private ownership, it couldn't simply shift overnight from sleek, expensive, powerful status-endowing cars to the anonymous shared mobility pods that Google and others in the space envisioned. Instead it promised that private ownership of Teslas would be subsidized by revenue from shared mobility, which your car would earn while you worked or slept.

But Musk was trying to fit a square peg into a round hole: a car designed for private ownership would never be optimal for taxi duty, particularly not the fast but fragile premium cars Tesla built. A purpose-built robotaxi from one of Tesla's mobility service competitors would be designed to optimize efficiency, durability, and interior space, making it able to operate at the lowest possible cost per mile. Unable to compete on price or amenities, a privately owned Tesla would be unlikely to earn enough through robotaxi duty to pay off its owner's loan or lease.

The only way Tesla's scheme could work as promised is if it had a monopoly on autonomous mobility that was competitive with the ubiquitous human-driven mobility services. Even in such an unlikely scenario, Tesla owners could hardly be assured of earning enough from their vehicles' robotaxi services to cover the vehicle loan and reduced resale value resulting from the extra miles, let alone the relatively high cost of maintaining, repairing, and insuring a Tesla. And if there was indeed a reasonable chance of making money by operating a Tesla as a robotaxi, the company would likely do so itself; there would be no economic incentive for Tesla to sell the cars to private owners.

This unlikely vision was especially audacious in light of Tesla's ongoing and well-publicized struggles with autonomous-drive technology. Tesla had the dubious distinction of being the first maker of automated driving technology to have one of its owners die in a crash while the system was activated, and the NTSB's investigation clearly identified design decisions that had contributed to Josh Brown's death. The perception that Tesla was a leader in autonomous-drive technology, which had boomed following the public release of Autosteer, was now being called into question.

But behind the scenes, Tesla's autonomous ambitions faced an even greater challenge. Though Tesla's aggressive PR offensive managed to contain much of the damage in the eyes of the public, the fallout ended Tesla's partnership with its key Autopilot supplier Mobileye, which provided the EyeQ3 image-analysis chip that was the heart of the Autopilot system.

During a quarterly earnings call in July of 2016, Mobileye CEO Amnon Shashua explained that the relationship ended because "I think in a partnership, we need to be there on all aspects of how the technology is being used, and not simply providing technology and not being in control of how it is being used."

Musk fired back, telling the *Wall Street Journal* that Tesla's work on a more advanced version of Autopilot had threatened its supplier, which was more comfortable with the auto industry's slower pace of innovation. According to Musk, "Mobileye's ability to evolve its technology is unfortunately negatively affected by having to support hundreds of models from legacy auto companies, resulting in a very high engineering drag coefficient."

The war of words continued into September, with Shashua arguing that Mobileye's chip wasn't designed to handle the kind of cross traffic that had caused the Brown crash and Musk contending that Mobileye was threatened by Tesla's research into computer vision. The conflict came to a head when Musk claimed that Mobileye had "attempted to force Tesla to discontinue this development, pay them more and use their products in future hardware . . . When Tesla refused to cancel its own vision development activities and plans for deployment, Mobileye discontinued hardware support for future platforms and released public statements implying that this discontinuance was motivated by safety concerns."

Mobileye responded with a press release accusing Tesla of ignoring its safety warnings and pushing its technology beyond its safety limits.

In its communications dating back to May of 2015, between the Mobileye Chairman and Tesla's CEO, Mobileye expressed safety concerns regarding the use of Autopilot hands-free. After a subsequent face to face meeting, Tesla's CEO confirmed that activation of Autopilot would be 'hands on.' Despite this confirmation, Autopilot was rolled out in late 2015 with a hands-free activation mode . . .

Mobileye's deeply held view is that the long-term potential for vehicle automation to reduce traffic injuries and fatalities significantly is too important to risk consumer and regulatory confusion or to create an environment of mistrust that puts in jeopardy technological advances that can save lives.

Indeed, Mobileye had been working on computer vision for autonomous vehicles for more than a decade, and it supplied the same EyeQ3 chip to so many automakers that its contract with Tesla made up only 1 percent of its revenue. Though Tesla's Autopilot initially showed how capable Mobileye's technology could be when pushed to its limits, the Brown crash suggested that Tesla was willing to sacrifice safety for the perception of a lead in the "race to autonomy." With its head start on computer vision and supply contracts with half the industry, Mobileye had no need for the kind of risks Tesla was taking.

A month after the last verbal salvo from Mobileye, Tesla announced that its new post-Mobileye Autopilot hardware was complete. The sheer speed with which the new hardware suite was made ready seemed to validate Tesla's side of the story: clearly they had started working on the system before the Mobileye breakup, and it was already prepared to replace Mobileye's deep experience within a fraction of a typical auto-industry product cycle. More important, Tesla was claiming that its new Autopilot hardware made it a leader in the "race to autonomy."

"All Tesla Cars Being Produced Now Have Full Self-Driving Hardware" screamed the headline of Tesla's blog post announcing the updated system. Not only could the so-called "Hardware 2" provide what Musk called "Enhanced Autopilot" capabilities, which would finally deliver on his promise of a system that could handle freeway travel "from onramp to offramp" for $5,000, but for an additional $3,000, customers could also unlock a "full self driving" capability. Tesla had officially become the first company to sell a car that claimed to be capable of full autonomy.

There was just one catch—though customers could pay for "full self driving," it wasn't actually available yet. In a conference call with reporters, Musk explained the situation: Every Tesla vehicle leaving the factory had the hardware necessary for full self-driving autonomy. It would take time to get the necessary regulatory approval for those features, but, Musk claimed, "The important thing is that the foundation is laid for the cars to be fully autonomous at a safety level we believe to be at least twice that of a person, maybe better."

Once again the announcement and the video dominated headlines, wiping away the nearly six months of ambiguity and doubt that had swirled around Autopilot since the Brown crash. In its place was the unambiguous promise of full "Level 5" autonomy—meaning the car can drive itself anywhere on Earth with zero human input—which could be purchased immediately and would be delivered on a stunningly short timeline. The only downside was that the system was lacking core Autopilot features at launch, but there too Musk promised a rapid rollout of capabilities, telling reporters they expected their Enhanced Autopilot to reach feature parity with the original Mobileye-based Autopilot in two to three months—and that there would be continuous improvement thereafter. Musk concluded with the grandiose claim that by the end of 2017, Tesla could demonstrate a car driving all the way from Los Angeles to New York City "without the need for a single touch, including the charger."

To prove that this extraordinary claim could be believed, Tesla released a video depicting a Model S driving itself from a residential home to the company's headquarters near Stanford University as the Rolling Stones' "Paint It Black" played. "The person in the driver's seat is only there for legal reasons," the opening frames of the video proclaimed. "He is not doing anything. The car is driving itself."

According to eyewitnesses, Tesla filmed the car driving the route multiple times over several days and even stopped filming during rush hour. By repeatedly driving the same route and avoiding traffic peaks, Tesla had made its demonstration video look far better at negotiating what it called "urban traffic" than it really was.

Several months later, when the state of California released the "disengagement reports" required for fully autonomous vehicles testing on public roads, the video began to look even less convincing. Tesla had only tested its "fully autonomous" system on public roads for a grand total of 550 miles during 2016, almost all of which coincided with the filming of the demonstration video between October 14 and 17. And despite its claims that the driver in the video was "only there for legal reasons," Tesla recorded 182 system disengagements—incidents where the human driver was forced to take over control—over those four days.

Though this revelation didn't definitively prove that Tesla's test car had failed to drive the depicted route without intervention, it did prove that on average the system could drive only about three and a half miles before a human had to take over control. These numbers suggested that Tesla's system performed far less effectively compared to Waymo's average of more than 5,000 miles between disengagements and BMW's single disengagement in 638 miles of testing. It also proved that Tesla was testing its "self-driving" system far less than its competitors: just 550 miles, compared to Google's 635,868 miles, the automotive supplier Delphi's 16,662 miles, and VW's 14,945 miles in the same year. The fact that the vast majority of Tesla's "test" miles came while it was filming its demonstration video only added to the impression that Tesla was spending more time hyping its newest unfulfilled promise than it was working toward delivering on it.

By the time these facts came to light, Tesla was already behind on its promised timeline. As 2016 came to a close, it was clear that Enhanced Autopilot had not achieved feature parity with the original Autopilot, and the Tesla forums were full of reports detailing the system's weak performance. In January, Musk was asked when "Full Self Driving" features would noticeably depart from "Enhanced Autopilot" features, to which he replied, "3 months maybe, 6 months definitely." By this time, Tesla's head of Autopilot, Sterling Anderson, had left the company, at least in part due to the belief that the new Autopilot hardware was not designed to achieve the "Full Self Driving" capabilities Musk had promised, and he was followed by a wave of departures of like-minded engineers.

By May, Tesla owners were still complaining that "Enhanced Autopilot" wasn't even as good as the original system, so Musk promised that the next update would make the system feel "smooth as silk." That update didn't satisfy owners either, and Musk stopped making promises about the development of Autopilot software. By August, Tesla fan site Electrek was reporting that Tesla had already replaced its "Hardware 2.0" suite with a new sensor suite. Though Electrek called the new system "Hardware 2.5," a Tesla spokesperson argued, "The internal name HW 2.5 is an overstatement, and instead it should be called something more like HW 2.1. This hardware set has some added computing and wiring redundancy, which very slightly improves reliability, but it does not have an additional Pascal GPU."

Though the update was framed as yet another example of Tesla's relentless iteration, it also seemed to confirm Anderson's belief that the Hardware 2.0 cars Tesla had been selling for nearly a year may not have been truly able to deliver on the promise of full self-driving capabilities. That was certainly the picture that was forming on Tesla forums, where frustration festered over the weak performance of the new Enhanced Autopilot and the slow rate of improvement, along with a growing distrust of Musk's promises. By the summer of 2018, Tesla was hyping a third iteration of Autopilot hardware, this time featuring a new processor that it was developing in-house. These repeated revisions to hardware that Musk had said was capable of Level 5 autonomy, as well as his tweets predicting the rollout of "full self driving" capabilities, cross-country "summon" capabilities, and a cross-country autonomous demonstration drive, were becoming monuments to his exaggeration and inability to deliver.

In the meantime, the perception that Tesla had a meaningful advantage in autonomous-drive technology remained an important talking point for analysts and investors seeking to justify Tesla's sky-high valuation. Even before Musk's Master Plan Part Deux, Morgan Stanley analyst Adam Jonas predicted that the firm would announce an on-demand autonomous mobility service and valued that service alone at $124 a share, making the entirely hypothetical division worth around $20 billion. Pointing out that the on-demand mobility market could be worth

$2 trillion, ARK Invest's Catherine Wood argued repeatedly that Tesla should be worth "many multiples" of its $50 billion valuation.

The key differentiator underlying these massive valuations was that every vehicle Tesla sold had a sensor suite and compute system the company said were capable of "full self-driving": a front-facing radar, three front-facing cameras, four side-facing cameras, a rear-facing camera, and 360-degree ultrasonic sensors. This sensor suite was incredibly cheap compared to those used by Waymo and other autonomous-drive programs, having been initially designed and specced for Autopilot's driver-assistance features. It also allowed Tesla to collect data from every car in its fleet. Tesla claimed that it could run its self-driving software in "shadow mode" on these cars, recording when and how the system would have acted, theoretically giving it millions of miles of real-world data with which to train and validate the algorithms used to perceive road conditions and plan its path through them.

Though fans and bullish Wall Street analysts latched on to the notion that Tesla's "shadow mode" fleet miles made it a leader in autonomous-drive technology, autonomous-drive technology experts were almost unanimously skeptical of Tesla's ability to deliver on Musk's promises, let alone challenge Waymo for leadership in the space. Nobody quite understood how much data Tesla was really pulling from its fleet of cars, whether that data could really show what was safe and what wasn't, or how "shadow mode" really drove improvements in the self-driving software. Rather than demonstrating and demystifying these capabilities to the media, as nearly every other autonomous vehicle developer did to some extent, Tesla preferred to let its fans and investors project their optimism onto these open questions.

But the core of Tesla's strategy, the relatively low-cost suite of sensors, was also its Achilles' heel. Where Tesla had only one forward-facing radar, Waymo used four radars located around the vehicle as well as a whole suite of the lidar sensors that Musk had long claimed were too expensive and unnecessary for autonomous drive. Tesla's sensor suite only had redundant and diverse sensors in the front of the car where its radar and cameras overlapped, whereas Waymo and others had 360 degrees of redundant sensor coverage from cameras, radar, and lidar.

Each sensor type has advantages in different tasks. For example, radar and lidar excel at determining an object's range, while cameras are generally superior at recognizing and classifying objects. Multiple overlapping sensors give an autonomous vehicle a larger and more detailed view of the world around it. They also give it a much higher level of certainty about what it's perceiving, making it less likely to miss or misclassify an object or situation it needs to avoid. Multiple sensors also allow the system to perceive objects that might be invisible to just one sensor type due to physical occlusion—say, from weather like rain, snow, or fog, or even the failure of one sensor.

The importance of diverse and redundant sensors, as well as the computing power needed to process the huge amounts of data they generate, only increased as autonomous vehicles took to public roads and moved closer to reality. The initial wave of public demonstrations showed how far the technology had come, inspiring a surge of optimism about the imminent arrival of the next great technology revolution. But as time went on, it became increasingly clear that the hardest part was still to come. The fundamental problem turned out not to be driving itself, but maintaining a high level of safety in the unpredictable mess that is human-driven traffic in the real world.

If you think about it, most of the time you spend behind the wheel doesn't require the utmost of your physical capabilities or driving skills. The fundamental challenge of driving is that most of it is boring and predictable routine, punctuated by the sudden appearance of unexpected situations—an animal crossing the road, a bale of hay falling out of the truck in front of you, a distracted driver plowing through a red light—that require skill, experience, and presence of mind to safely navigate.

These situations, called "edge cases," can arise from a single actor or a complex interaction of actors and circumstances, and their sheer randomness makes them an extremely difficult challenge for autonomous car development. Not only are they randomly distributed, meaning you can drive for thousands of miles without ever seeing one, but they are also intrinsically random events, meaning it's incredibly difficult to design an artificial intelligence system to handle them. This "long-tail risk" means that the closer an autonomous-drive system gets to being "perfect," the harder it becomes to anticipate and address the remaining edge cases.

In 2016, when Tesla first started selling a Full Self Driving option, autonomous-drive technology was at the peak of its hype. After the Josh Brown incident and the fatal crash of an Uber autonomous test vehicle into a pedestrian in March of 2018, popular perceptions of autonomous cars turned negative and developers began to take the edge case problem a lot more seriously. Silicon Valley's "move fast and break stuff" ethos, which fostered innovation in non-safety-critical software, was beginning to look like a poor approach to developing self-driving car systems, which hold the power of life and death.

Using a sensor suite designed for a driver-assist system came across as the ultimate example of Silicon Valley's "minimum viable product" paradigm, applied not to a smartphone app but to an activity that is a leading cause of death. Any plan to simply update software whenever an underbaked autonomous-drive system runs into a situation it can't handle has to assume that a number of those situations will involve a customer dying. The challenge of self-driving car development was not simply convincing the public that a car could "drive itself," which could theoretically be achieved with as little hardware as a brick placed on the accelerator, but by making a car drive itself *safely*.

As this reality sank in, the rest of the autonomous-drive space dialed back expectations. In the summer of 2018, the research and advisory company Gartner released its latest "hype cycle" analysis, which showed that autonomous-drive technology had passed peak hype and was entering the "trough of disillusionment." Increasingly, the entire goal of a Level 5 vehicle, capable of full autonomy anywhere, was being

dismissed in favor of Level 4 vehicles, which operate fully autono-
mously but only in a limited "geofenced" area. By restricting the operational design domain of an autonomous car to a specific thoroughly
mapped area and optimizing the system for the conditions found there,
you could reduce the possible scope of edge cases to a manageable level.

This retreat from the hype of 2016 isolated Tesla in an awkward contrast. Companies developing autonomous vehicles that had vastly more
sophisticated sensor and compute systems than Tesla's were saying that
Level 5 was a fantasy . . . while Tesla continued to collect payments for
a Level 5 system. Even as Waymo approached the late 2018 launch of
the first-ever autonomous ride-hailing service in a suburb of Phoenix,
Arizona, CEO John Krafcik publicly admitted that autonomous vehicles might *never* work in all locations and weather conditions, and that it
would "take longer than you think" for autonomous vehicles to become
ubiquitous. Most top autonomous-drive developers had been saying
the same thing in private for months or even years, and only Tesla continued on as if nothing had changed until October 2018 when it made
Full Self Driving an "off menu option," without any further explanation.

But then, as one former Autopilot engineer put it to me, what could
Tesla do? If it admitted that Autopilot was unsafe or that Full Self Driving would never happen, it would open itself to untold legal liability and
a massive decline in its stock valuation. In the case of Full Self Driving,
consumers knew from the beginning that there was no delivery date for
the option they had paid for and that it might never arrive if regulators
didn't approve it. For many owners, it was simply an expression of faith
in Tesla's technological prowess, as well as a way to help pad the company's profits.

In many ways, Tesla's entire experience with autonomous-drive
technology showed how its hype- and perception-driven strategy was
beginning to fall apart. Having developed Autopilot to create a stop-
gap impression of autonomous-drive technology, the lethal consequences had blown up its relationship with Mobileye. Since it couldn't
simply replicate the Autopilot capabilities that Mobileye had enabled,

Tesla had to promise that its replacement hardware would make it a leader in autonomous drive. Then, having already taken money for this wildly optimistic promise, it had to stick to its guns even as every other autonomous-drive technology company admitted that self-driving car hype had been overblown.

Worst of all, there were signs that Full Self Driving was having a corrosive effect on one of Tesla's core assets: the faith fans invested in Elon Musk. Almost every other criticism of Tesla could be offset by some unique advantage the company offered: Its cars may have been unreliable and poorly made, but they looked cool and drove well; the battery swap and solar Supercharger promises might be unfulfilled, but Tesla still had the best charging EV infrastructure; the company might not have been profitable, but revenue was exploding and it was investing in growth. With Full Self Driving, all Tesla fans could do was hope that their faith in Musk would be rewarded even as evidence piled up suggesting that it wouldn't.

Meanwhile Tesla's struggles with the traditional auto industry competencies of manufacturing and service, as well as the low market valuation of every other automaker, meant Tesla's all-important valuation was more dependent on autonomous-drive technology than ever. If you believed Tesla's promise, it was not only the sole automaker offering the hottest option on a new car, but it was also a potential disruptor of the hottest companies in the mobility technology space: Uber and Lyft. If you didn't, the brazenness of Tesla's ploy to collect money for a feature it couldn't possibly deliver on raised huge questions about what else the company was bluffing about and what it was really worth . . . and once you started down that line of questioning, there seemed to be no end to it.

Tesla's entire automated driving strategy also showed that there was a serious cost to being on the leading edge of mobility technology. When Tesla started, the big idea was simply to switch from gas to electric drivetrains. Yet within a decade of its founding, the rise of smartphone-based ride-hailing and autonomous-drive technology were opening up entirely new and more fundamentally disruptive possibilities. Tesla tried to co-opt these ideas to maintain the impression that it was a leader of this broader movement, but because it was already stuck in the traditional automaker business, its applications were little more than tacked-on compromises. Unlike a sustaining innovation like electric drive, companies based on technologies with truly disruptive potential must be built from a clean sheet of paper.

Nothing illustrates this trap quite like the timing of Tesla's 2016 full self-driving announcement. Not only was Tesla bouncing back from its blown-up relationship with Mobileye, it was also struggling to control the discounting it needed to keep sales of Model S and X growing. After reports of heavy discounts during the third quarter of 2016 led to record sales and a profit that Musk said would serve as a "pie in the face" to Wall Street doubters, Tesla had to reset market expectations. By announcing that the new Autopilot hardware would be capable of "full self driving," Tesla could end discounts without hurting demand by creating repeat business from its wealthiest customers.

Using the promise of Level 5 autonomous driving to sell new luxury cars is a classic paradox of technological transition, right up there with Uriah Smith's 1899 patent of a car with a horse's head. Even if Tesla does somehow deliver on Musk's promise to make every one of its cars truly self-driving, they will always be high-end cars designed to appeal to private ownership values with features like blistering acceleration, sexy design, and a status-conferring badge. Robotaxis, on the other hand, will be designed for constant utilization, high wear, easy cleaning, efficient operation, and low costs.

Part of the appeal of Tesla's brand is that it is both a familiar concept, a sexy boutique automaker, and a pioneer of an exciting new movement, the high-tech assault on mobility. Though we are conditioned to think that "first movers" have a fundamental advantage in a new technological space, Tesla showed that the blessing and curse of being so far ahead of its time was that it would fit new technologies into an existing mental model. But as time revealed the true possibilities of these new technologies, Tesla looked more and more like it was caught in limbo between the traditional auto industry and a new generation of companies that had been built from the ground up to exploit the possibilities of autonomous drive and on-demand mobility technology.

CHAPTER 14

THE MACHINE THAT BUILDS THE MACHINE

You can create a demo version of a product ... with a small team in maybe three to six months. But to build the machine that builds the machine takes at least a hundred to a thousand times more resources and difficulty ... I would say I only fully came to that realization maybe even just two or three months ago.
Elon Musk, May 31, 2016

"The Model S and X I think are generally regarded by critical judges as technologically the most advanced cars in the world and so we've done well in that respect," Musk told analysts and reporters as he introduced Tesla's earnings call for the first quarter of 2016. Hot off the reveal of the Model 3, and with hundreds of thousands of preorders for the company's most important vehicle ever, Tesla was riding high.

On the strength of the unprecedented volume of preorders brought in by the Model 3, Musk wanted to keep his foot on the accelerator.

As Musk said, Tesla's existing cars were warmly received as triumphs of design, performance, and technology, but the company's image had been marred by the Model X's lengthy delays and quality problems. To shore up Tesla's weak manufacturing image, Musk was about to make what he called the firm's "biggest change strategically."

"The key thing we need to achieve in the future," he continued, "is to also be the leader in manufacturing. We take manufacturing very seriously at Tesla." Following the emerging pattern in Musk's leadership style, his plan to achieve this goal was rooted in a breathtakingly ambitious challenge to his team. The Model 3, which at that point still only existed in prototype form, would reach half a million units of production by 2018, two years sooner than originally planned. Not since Ford's Model T had an automaker ramped production of a car so far so fast.

To achieve this historic feat, Tesla was breaking from its practice with Model S and X: Model 3 would be "designed for production," said Musk. "With Model 3 we are being incredibly rigorous about ensuring that we don't have anything that isn't really necessary to make a very compelling version one of the car," he explained. "We also have a much tighter feedback loop between design engineering, manufacturing engineering, and production, and so no elements of Model 3 can be approved unless manufacturing has that this is easily manufactured, and the risk associated with manufacturing it is low."

For a moment, it seemed like Musk was starting to "get it." Tesla's brilliance at designing and engineering cars was undeniable, but it was also constantly undercut by the company's lack of focus on manufacturing. The higher volumes and lower profits that Model 3 would bring threatened to eliminate Tesla's margin for error unless it got a handle on quality. Musk may have been shooting for the stars by declaring his desire to make Tesla a "leader" in manufacturing, but as usual fans hoped he would at least land Tesla on the moon . . . or at a minimum, improve on the Model X's performance.

As the scope of Musk's ambitions for Model 3 came into focus, it became clear that Tesla still had a hubris problem. Within three months of the earnings call, Musk wanted Tesla's designers to have the production version finalized, with production starting just twelve months later. According to the plan, Model 3 would then take no more than eighteen months to reach a 500,000-unit-per-year rate of production and earn the company 25 percent gross margins. By 2020, Musk hoped to produce between 800,000 and a million Model 3s every year.

Musk hadn't even discussed these new plans with key manufacturing executives before announcing them to the world in the quarterly call. The plan that had been in place up to that point had been fairly typical for Tesla: extremely ambitious, but theoretically possible if the team pushed itself to the breaking point. Tesla's manufacturing team had been preparing for that challenge, so when Musk publicly committed them to a far more ambitious plan, it hit morale hard. "Impossible is one thing," one former Tesla manufacturing executive told me, echoing what others had said. "We were used to impossible. This was something else completely."

Musk's runaway ambition, technophilia, and "physics first principles analysis" had led him to pursue goals that puzzled manufacturing experts both inside Tesla and out. In repeated public comments, Musk cited line speed and volumetric density as the major areas for improvement in manufacturing, and by solving these, he imagined a factory populated completely by densely packed robots moving so fast that no human could keep up with them—the "machine that builds the machine" he would reference in the Top Secret Master Plan Part 2. On call after call with analysts, he mocked the slow speed of the industry's assembly lines, saying "grandma with a walker can exceed the speed of the fastest production line."

To achieve this goal, Musk called for the Model 3's production system to constantly iterate over the course of production. When the Model 3 production began in 2017, "Version 0" of the assembly line would be roughly comparable to the industry standard. A year later, "Version 1.0" would debut with more automation and higher speeds, and by the time "Version 3.0" came out, Musk envisioned a factory unlike anything seen before. By the time the final version debuted, Musk predicted, Tesla's production robots would be moving so fast that they would be impossible to see without the help of a strobe light, and limited only by air friction. Humans would be relegated to maintaining the robots in these fully automated factories of the future.

Musk's growing obsession with manufacturing speed and density had led to an entire series of meetings about his advanced automation goals, termed "UAD" for "unstoppable alien dreadnought." But managers who had cheerfully battled through a million manufacturing challenges for Tesla were starting to become increasingly disillusioned with Musk's inexplicable manufacturing fixations. Musk seemed to be looking for some kind of quantum leap that would boost Tesla's manufacturing prowess the way its car designs boost its engineering prowess, rather than inculcating TPS's boring continuous-improvement philosophy into Tesla's day-to-day culture. The problem was that there was no way to tell Musk no, regardless of whether his latest demands made any kind of sense or not.

Nobody could figure out why Musk cared so much about speed and density. The Toyota Production System that the entire auto industry follows (as do most other forms of manufacturing) emphasizes the reduction of all forms of waste as a core guiding value. As a result, car factories move at a deliberate speed that standardizes work processes, allows workers to spot defects, and gives suppliers time to coordinate just-in-time parts delivery, reducing wasteful scrap and parts inventories. Neither time nor factory floor space limits profit margins to a meaningful extent in any modern factory, making them baffling values to optimize for. Moreover, industrial tooling is incredibly expensive, meaning any plan to replace a mass-market car's entire production system every year or two was a recipe for profound capital inefficiency.

Meanwhile, the "Gigafactory" that Tesla was building outside Reno, Nevada, to house battery-pack production, as well as cell manufacturing by its supplier Panasonic, was showing the dangers of Musk's theatricality. The factory's entire purpose seemed to be to impress the observer with the sheer scale of Musk's ambitions, but even at a fraction of its planned size, it was straining the local road infrastructure and labor and housing markets. Shortages of skilled workers, culture clashes between Tesla and Panasonic, power outages, and poor quality control were already pointing the way to the trouble ahead, even before its own overautomation problems took hold.

From the outside, too, the Model 3 manufacturing strategy looked like a recipe for disaster. With only twelve months between the design freeze and the start of production, and just three months of validation followed by an aggressive ramp, the possibility of Tesla improving on its quality performance did not look good. With the faster production rates Musk was calling for came not only a greater risk of defects, but also the risk that huge numbers of parts or cars might be made before inexperienced workers caught the defects. And if just one supplier (or one of Tesla's insourced lines) couldn't keep up with the Model 3's blistering speed, Tesla could burn eye-watering amounts of cash while it rushed to get production back online.

Meeting the demands of these goals would require more than simply hiring "the best minds" that Musk invited to join the Model 3 program; it would require a manufacturing culture that could coordinate the efforts of thousands of people and hold the line on quality in the face of Musk's intense pressure to meet unheard of timelines. Given that Tesla forums continued to feature a steady stream of reports of quality problems, including some like Model S door handles and seals that had haunted the company for years, it was clear that this culture still wasn't able to stop the company from delivering subpar quality. Shifting from a "garage hacker" startup mentality toward the kind of culture Tesla would need to execute Musk's Model 3 plan could take years—indeed, it had taken the Detroit automakers nearly half a century to reach the point where their quality could compete with Toyota's.

It turned out that questions about Tesla's manufacturing fitness were well-founded.

"Tesla was in disarray when it came to knowing what they wanted," explained a source—let's call him Tom—at one of the industrial tooling suppliers that Tesla hired for part of the Model 3's body line.

Tom worked on the finance side of the supplier, keeping both engineers and clients on budget. The company was working with several major established automakers, involved with some of their highest priority projects: designing, building, testing, and installing body shops and other sections of their assembly lines. Because he handled the project budgets, Tom was exposed to many different aspects of the Tesla project, and he says the contrast between Tesla and the established automakers was stark.

Speaking on condition of anonymity for fear of retribution, Tom remarked that the chaos of the Model 3 project was reflected in the sheer number of changes it underwent. Tesla revised the project's purchase order five times before the order was even signed, he said, and then revised it four more times for good measure. And though the supplier was able to keep to Tesla's timeline, Tom couldn't figure out how Tesla was going to be able to keep its promises. Tom had just worked on a Detroit automaker's truck project, which had been built, tested, and shipped before the Model 3 line was done, and that was for a project that wouldn't start regular production until 2019 . . . by which time, Tesla hoped to be making more than half a million Model 3s per year.

Musk's manic deadlines meant that "manufacturing engineers were pressuring us to work on a design that was not yet approved," according to Tom. This lack of coordination between design and manufacturing was becoming clear even as Musk promised investors that the Model 3 would be "designed for production" and that there was "a much tighter feedback loop between design engineering, manufacturing engineering, and production." Tesla's engineers and their supplier counterparts did their best to follow Musk's stricture, but there simply wasn't enough time to work through all the issues.

This chaotic situation was exacerbated by turnover within the ranks of Tesla's manufacturing staff. The supplier that Tom worked for had helped Tesla develop its second production line, which integrated S and X production, and despite problems with the X, he said there was real improvement in the working relationship over time. But by the time Tesla started working on Musk's accelerated Model 3 plan, much of the manufacturing talent working on Tesla's side of the relationship had left in frustration, taking years of institutional knowledge with them. "We started again at square one," Tom remembers.

Tesla announced the start of Model 3 production at one of its trademark extravaganza events at the Fremont factory, featuring employees and executives extolling the company's accomplishments in front of rows of cars lined up for delivery. In typical fashion, the denouement featured Musk driving a Model 3 onto the stage where he received his usual rockstar welcome. Musk appeared unusually downbeat (he had recently broken up with the actress Amber Heard and told *Rolling Stone* that he was "in severe emotional pain" at the time). Still, he introduced the car, explaining its features and capabilities, before giving an unexpected warning.

"The thing that is going to be the major challenge for us over the next six to nine months is how do we build a huge number of cars," Musk revealed. He paused and then made several attempts to continue speaking, before chuckling and blurting out, "Frankly, we are going to be in production hell." Still the only person laughing, Musk made an exaggerated gesture to signal that he was joking. "Welcome," he said as the audience began to laugh with him, "welcome to production hell."

At the beginning of 2017, Musk told investors that Tesla would be ordering parts for one thousand cars per week following the July start of production, ramp up to two thousand cars per week in August, and achieve four thousand per week by September. Shortly after the delivery event, with production already nominally underway, Tesla dialed those targets back in its Q2 investor letter. "Based on our preparedness at this time, we are confident we can produce just over fifteen hundred vehicles in Q3, and achieve a run rate of five thousand vehicles per week by the end of 2017," the revised guidance read. "We also continue to plan on increasing Model 3 production to ten thousand vehicles per week at some point in 2018."

By the end of September, even those dramatically reduced goals were in tatters as Tesla revealed that it had built a total of just 260 Model 3s in the quarter, just over one-sixth of the goal it had set just months before. "It is important to emphasize that there are no fundamental issues with the Model 3 production or supply chain," the company said in a statement. "We understand what needs to be fixed and we are confident of addressing the manufacturing bottleneck issues in the near-term."

Even as Tesla claimed the situation was under control, reporting was starting to trickle out that suggested the situation was worse than anyone had imagined. The *Wall Street Journal* reported that "as recently as early September major portions of the Model 3 were still being banged out by hand," with workers welding bodies together in the Fremont plant's pilot area, called "Area 51," while automated tooling was still being installed. Tesla responded with a blistering statement accusing the *Journal* of "relentlessly [attacking] Tesla with misleading articles that, with few exceptions, push or exceed the boundaries of journalistic integrity" but didn't specifically deny the story's stunning claims.

As it turned out, Tesla had announced the start of production of its first mass-market car well before Fremont was ready to build them in any kind of volume and had simply put on a show for the public. "That black Model 3, that first production one—that Elon *said* was the first production one? That was a crock of shit," one former employee told me. "I walked that thing through the shop, I watched the dudes build it in the back area, the little cave area [Area 51], and he drove it off."

Another employee confirmed that the cars lined up in front of the stage at the event were "sitting there as props" to create the impression of volume production. "If you were able to test those cars . . . realistically, only a percentage of those cars actually ran," he explained. This was because "the first batch of cars were the trial run for literally all the parts. They were all concepts and trial runs, and once they made it and everything communicated and was functioning, they would order one-hundred-thousand-piece batches on everything."

This is similar to what the auto industry calls "preproduction," in which a company manufactures a limited number of "production intent" vehicles to test the production equipment, parts, and the vehicles themselves. Actual production doesn't begin until the tooling and processes have been fully validated, ensuring that production ramps up quickly and with minimal drama once the company announces a car's availability. Announcing the start of production before a design is finalized would be unthinkable in the auto industry, but thanks to Tesla's forgiving customers and constant iteration it seems to have done just that.

Musk told analysts that the initial production run units were "not engineering validation units. They're fully certified, fully DOT approved, EPA approved production cars. These are not prototypes in any way," but subsequent evidence suggested that the design wasn't fully baked at the start of production. The following January, Tesla released a technical service bulletin stating that all Model 3 drive units should be replaced because an improved version had been developed "that meets Tesla's high standards for performance and durability." Tesla had apparently launched production with a drive unit that hadn't met its standards, a decision that may not have been uncommon in light of multiple reports saying that a stunningly high percentage of its cars needed to be reworked after rolling off the assembly line.

Unsurprisingly, employee sources say early Model 3 production was "nothing but nightmares." Problems ranged from faulty parts to poor integration, with symptoms including faulty charge ports, dome lights delivered with the wrong connection port, misaligned "frunk" (front trunk) trays, and wiring harnesses that had to be recut to fit into cars. But perhaps most troubling were the problems with the one thing Tesla was supposed to be better at than anyone: the battery packs.

"Production hell" had hit the Gigafactory, where Panasonic made battery cells and Tesla assembled them into packs for cars. Ambitious automated battery-pack production lines weren't working, forcing Tesla to press Panasonic employees into service to help build them by hand. Shipments of the packs to Fremont slowed to a trickle. A former employee recalls that "a freightliner truck that was supposed [to] hold five pallets at ten batteries a pallet would come in with only two pallets, and not all of those batteries were good. What the fuck are we supposed to do? That's the how it was for months." These quality issues with the Gigafactory's battery production were corroborated by reports published at BusinessInsider, CNBC, and Bloomberg, alleging chaos, waste, dependence on manual assembly, high scrap rates, and a host of other problems at the sprawling Nevada plant.

Once Tesla began missing production deadlines, the scramble to get back on schedule only created more problems. Good manufacturing workers had been in short supply at the Fremont plant for years, and as the pressures of "production hell" mounted, former employees say corners were cut on training and maintenance. This in turn made the factory less safe and more wasteful, and it led to problems that were all but unheard of at the established automakers.

Cuts in maintenance hit the paint shop especially hard. Insufficient cleaning of a skid that carried car bodies through the paint process led to a Model S body falling into a dip tank, forcing employees to completely drain the eighty-thousand-gallon tank and causing a shutdown that lasted eight hours. An overhead conveyor dating to the NUMMI days failed suddenly after a maintenance worker warned his boss about it, dropping a 1,500-pound battery tray.

There were a series of least four fires in the plant's paint shop during 2017 and the first half of 2018. When a robot changed paint color, the system would spray excess pigment into a hopper. Paint built up in this hopper, causing paint to back up and leak onto the spray arm. At the same time, overspray caked on the straps that grounded cars during the electrostatic spray sequence, causing sparks to jump off the car and start fires on the paint that had backed onto the spray arm. Fire would then travel up the arm until it hit the mist of paint, turning the sprayer into a flamethrower. "Literally it's a torch fucking flying around, the paint spraying, the paint's on fire, scorching the car," one former paint shop employee remembers.

Just as he had during the troubled Model X production ramp, when Model 3 "production hell" hit, Musk took to spending days on the Fremont plant's assembly, and sleeping on a couch or air mattress in a nearby conference room. Though his dedication was popular with fans who imagined him personally solving the company's problems, employees are nearly unanimous that his presence added more stress than it relieved.

"He says it himself—he's not a manufacturing guy. He's an engineer, he's an innovator," explains one former manager. "The problem with him and the plant is he's only really putting the pressure on the management team. He doesn't really understand where the true bottlenecks are because most of [the managers] who have a true bottleneck are not going to tell him. Therefore, when he's there it just causes animosity between the rest of the management team, and he's not benefiting himself or the company or the stockholders by being there." Even Musk himself seemed not to enjoy the experience, telling a manager during the troubled Model X launch, "I could be in Bora Bora right now fucking an actress, and instead I'm here babysitting you guys on the line."

Tesla eventually hit its goal of producing five thousand Model 3s per week in the summer of 2018, after nearly a year of "production hell" and a handful of blown deadlines. Musk's plan had called for the first production system automation upgrade at that point, but instead of making progress toward "alien dreadnought" status, Tesla actually had to reduce the level of automation to achieve its long-overdue goal. Tesla built two entirely new Model 3 general assembly (GA) lines: with the original GA line paralyzed by more automation than the company could make work, a second, less-automated line was built inside Fremont, followed by a third built in a giant tentlike structure just outside the plant using scrap from its other lines.

Battered by reports of worker injuries, targeted by union organizers, and roiled by executive turnover, the wave of momentum that Tesla enjoyed after the Model 3's "iPhone moment" all but dissipated over the course of the first year of production. Quality problems showed up from the very beginning, with owners of early cars reporting service bulletins for problems with cracking suspension ball joints, a "battery breather," front window regulators, touchscreen replacement, and the high voltage controller. Other quality issues that had plagued Tesla's previous cars showed up as well, including poor panel alignment, inconsistent and poorly placed seals, mismatched and blemished paint, spontaneously cracking glass, and drive unit failures.

By the time the company hit the five-thousand-per-week production goal, its service centers were overwhelmed. Repair delays, parts shortages, and long lines for service were reported in high-density markets like California and Norway. Tesla took steps to address the crisis, opening a new parts distribution center and call center, piloting a network of body repair shops, and expanding its mobile repair service, but word of the chaos inside the company was spreading.

In the summer of 2018, Tesla faced a set of circumstances not unlike those it had faced leading up to its pivotal 2013 "miracle." Though the Model 3 was earning rave reviews from road testers who praised its design and engineering, Tesla's slow production ramp and its shortcomings in manufacturing quality and service were scaring customers off with just under 20 percent of reservations canceled by the end of the third quarter. Just as important, the critical $35,000 "standard range" version of the Model 3 wouldn't be delivered before 2019, by which time the $7,500 federal tax credit would be sundowning, and meanwhile the cheapest Model 3 cost $49,000. The dream of a genuinely "affordable" Tesla, which had made the Model 3 seem like the culmination of Musk's master plan and fueled its massive order book, now seemed to be slipping out of reach.

The fundamental tragedy of Tesla's situation a year after it started Model 3 production was how familiar it was. The company had been here before with every car it had ever made: enjoying all the theoretical demand in the world, but being unable to deliver cars on time, at high quality, and at the promised entry price. Meanwhile, the cash burn from its duplicative tooling investments and labor-intensive manufacturing were threatening its consistently vulnerable financial situation.

This set of circumstances nearly killed the company several times during the launch of the Model S, and yet it couldn't prevent itself from falling into the same trap. The main difference was that Musk's hubristic timeline and out-of-touch manufacturing vision had led to this crisis, whereas with the Model S, Tesla was more legitimately struggling with its first real production challenge. Not only was Tesla not learning from its past, it was finding new ways to bury its profound promise under an avalanche of self-inflicted wounds.

CHAPTER 15

THE EMPIRE STRIKES BACK

I do think it's worth thinking about whether what you're doing is going to result in disruptive change or not. If it's just incremental, it's unlikely to be something major. It's got to be something that's substantially better than what's gone on before.
Elon Musk, March 9, 2013

Different is everything.
André Citroën

In 1933, the French automaker Citroën revealed one of the most revolutionary cars ever made. Called the Traction Avant, this extraordinary machine pioneered three features that would define the vast majority of modern cars for the next century: unibody design, front-wheel drive, and fully independent suspension. Lighter, lower-sprung, and more efficient than any other car on the road, the Traction Avant sold three-quarters of a million units and for a time made the Citroën brand nearly as synonymous with automobiles as Kleenex is with facial tissue.

The father of the Traction Avant, André Citroën, would have found himself at home in the Silicon Valley of the twenty-first century. He had an eye for innovation, quickly identifying novel engineering solutions like the herringbone gears whose shape gave birth to Citroën's double chevron logo. But he also possessed a genius for marketing, turning the Eiffel Tower into the world's largest advertising billboard and creating toy versions of his cars so that "the first words that a baby should learn to pronounce are Mummy, Daddy and Citroën."

But in spite of the Traction Avant's world-changing innovations and an audacious marketing campaign led by André Citroën himself, the Traction Avant ultimately showed that innovation and hype were a dangerous combination absent the ability to execute them. The high cost of the car's development and the construction of its massive new factory consumed Citroën's available cash, and in the rush to produce the cars fast enough to bring revenues back into the company, problems arose with the car's brakes and transmission. These issues would ultimately be resolved, and the Traction Avant would go on to sell extremely well, but not before bankrupting the Citroën company and leaving its founder penniless.

Citroën would come back from bankruptcy reorganization under the ownership of its largest creditor, Michelin, and would remain a leader in unibody, front-drive vehicles for several decades. But as the market grew more competitive and other firms increasingly adopted Citroën's key innovations, the firm's "first mover advantage" fell apart. Today, Citroën is just one of many purveyors of front-drive unibody cars, slowly losing ground to competitors whose much later mastery of its inventions have not prevented them from eclipsing the pioneering firm.

Throughout the history of the auto industry, this pattern has repeated itself again and again. Before Citroën, Henry Ford's moving assembly line earned the Ford Motor Company a few decades of utter dominance before the entire industry adopted it, removing it as a competitive factor. More recently, GM's innovation of connected vehicle telematics (OnStar) and Ford's early voice-control infotainment (SYNC) lead have failed to translate into durable competitive advantages. Again and again, automotive innovations quickly shift from competitive advantage to industry-standard equipment.

This pattern repeats itself so regularly because almost every innovation in the automotive space is what is known as a "sustaining innovation" rather than a "disruptive innovation." Clayton Christensen, the Harvard Business School professor who coined these terms, defines sustaining innovations as "innovations that make a product or service perform better in ways that customers in the mainstream market already value," which indeed describes the evolution of the auto industry. "Disruptive innovations," on the other hand, "create an entirely new market through the introduction of a new kind of product or service," which are out of step with the values of both established consumer markets and industry leaders.

Though Tesla is widely portrayed as a "disruptive innovator," its major innovations are in fact of the sustaining variety. Electric drive can improve an ownership experience by eliminating emissions, reducing fuel costs, and improving acceleration, but it doesn't fundamentally alter any of these consumer values, which have been present since the dawn of the industry. This makes electric drive no more "disruptive" than any of the technologies that have steadily improved the efficiency and emissions of internal combustion vehicles over the last century, most of which have been widely diffused across the industry without leaving a single automaker with a sustainable technological advantage.

One of the great ironies of Tesla is that it is so widely seen as being a disruptive innovator when in fact it just barely missed the opportunity to fully capitalize on what is likely to be the first truly disruptive innovation to hit the auto industry in a century: shared autonomous vehicles. By enabling an access model instead of an ownership model, in which privately owned cars are replaced by on-demand access to fleets of self-driving mobility pods, autonomous drive has the clear potential to disrupt both consumption patterns and the fundamentals of the business.

Musk's awkward attempt to bend Tesla's private ownership model to fit the new autonomous-drive–enabled paradigm in the Master Plan Part Deux illustrates how closely Tesla missed this historic opportunity to disrupt the auto industry. To truly lead this disruption, Tesla would have to walk away from core brand values—performance, styling, prestige—and reinvent the company around low-cost, highly reliable, shareable pods with an emphasis on its weakest points: interior comfort and durability. The one area where Tesla has had undeniable success, namely creating electric cars with performance and styling that appeals to existing customers, proves that its innovations are sustaining rather than disruptive.

One of the fundamental cornerstones of the Tesla mythology is the belief that established automakers either can't or won't build electric cars in meaningful volumes. This theory relies heavily on crude interpretations of what Clayton Christensen called "The Innovator's Dilemma," which suggests that investments in existing technologies and business models make "incumbent" companies less able to establish new businesses in response to innovations.

Christensen and his coauthors explain this dilemma in an article called "Innovation Killers: How Financial Tools Destroy Your Capacity to Do New Things":

> *Executives in established companies bemoan how expensive it is to build new brands and develop new sales and distribution channels—so they seek instead to leverage their existing brands and structures. Entrants, in contrast, simply create new ones. The problem for the incumbent isn't that the challenger can outspend it; it's that the challenger is spared the dilemma of having to choose between full-cost and marginal-cost options. We have repeatedly observed leading, established companies misapply fixed- and sunk-cost doctrine and rely on assets and capabilities that were forged in the past to succeed in the future. In doing so, they fail to*

make the same investments that entrants and attackers find to be profitable.

This logic is popularly applied to the incumbent automakers, which are presented as having to adapt new technologies to their existing structures and capabilities, whereas Tesla is able to make itself in the image of new technologies and new possibilities. Put simply, this view holds that Tesla need not compromise or destroy an established business based on internal combustion technology to create a new business based on batteries and electric cars. As Tesla's market cap climbed to match or exceed that of "incumbent" automakers whose production volume and profits eclipsed the upstart, this logic was increasingly trotted out as justification for its frothy valuation.

But the perception that automakers wouldn't invest as aggressively in electric vehicles as an unencumbered startup like Tesla was just that: a perception. This belief may have matched the popular understanding of The Innovator's Dilemma, but it simply didn't match the facts on the ground.

———————

Apparently nobody ever told Nissan that its core internal combustion–powered car business should prevent it from developing and deploying new technologies and products. The Japanese automaker built its first electric car, the Tama, in 1947 as a response to postwar oil shortages, and it never stopped developing the technology. Though initially limited by stagnant lead-acid battery technology, Nissan was one of the first automakers to embrace new chemistries like nickel-cadmium, which it demonstrated in a concept car in 1991, and eventually lithium-ion, which it put on the road in small numbers a decade before Tesla delivered its first Roadster.

By 2011, when Tesla was still tooling up to produce Model S at a rate of 20,000 units per year, Nissan was leveraging its deep experience with electric cars into a far more ambitious program. Carlos Ghosn, then CEO of both Nissan and its Alliance partner Renault, had ordered the two automakers to jointly invest over $5.5 billion in a global manufacturing footprint capable of producing half a million electric cars—as well as the batteries needed to power them—every year starting in 2013. With the first generation of these electric cars—the Nissan Leaf and the Renault Zoe—starting at less than $30,000, Ghosn was skipping ahead to the affordable endgame of Musk's master plan years before Tesla even began work on the Model 3.

In the years before the Model S made Tesla a household name, this level of investment in any electric vehicle was a massive gamble. It was especially unexpected from a CEO who was better known for his hard-nosed turnarounds of struggling automakers (which had earned him the nickname of "Le Cost Cutter" at Renault) than big bets on future technologies. But in the wake of gas price spikes in 2008, Ghosn believed that 10 percent of the new car market would be pure electric cars by 2020, and he wanted his Alliance to be ready for the shift.

Rather than following Tesla's strategy of starting at the high end of the market where large initial costs would be amortized by wealthy buyers, Ghosn wanted to dive right into high-volume mass-market sales. This aggressive strategy, as Ghosn explained it to *Wired* magazine, showed that the "innovator's dilemma" was hardly a factor: "Everyone understands in our industry that if you can't get to scale in terms of production, it's difficult to compete." Ghosn continued, "We want to get to 500,000 cars as soon as possible so it cuts the costs of the battery and we begin to compete with our own combustion engines. If we don't get to scale, that's very difficult."

By targeting production volumes that would make electric cars cost competitive with its internal combustion offerings, Ghosn was threatening to gut his core business to capture a leading position in what he expected to be a high-growth electric car business. And once the investment in such high-volume production capacities was made, Ghosn's companies were fully committed: publicly traded companies don't invest billions of dollars into new products only to consciously sabotage them to protect their older products. In one fell swoop, Ghosn proved that automakers didn't have to be intrinsically risk averse let alone constrained by their existing internal combustion businesses.

Contemporary coverage shows that Ghosn could easily have assumed the position as EV evangelist-in-chief that Musk would eventually occupy; *Wired* said he was "either a brilliant visionary or crazy as a loon" and "possessed of an enthusiasm bordering on fanaticism." Certainly his bet on electric cars was bigger than anything Musk had attempted up to that point, and it made affordable electric vehicles more widely available than Tesla ever has. Yet over the next five years, public perceptions of Tesla and Musk as the champion of electric mobility eclipsed Ghosn and the Nissan-Renault Alliance, even as the Alliance delivered more electric vehicles at much more attainable prices.

There is a wealth of potential explanations for this development. Musk and Tesla certainly benefited from their association with Silicon Valley's high-tech disruption, positioning themselves as another Silicon startup that was poised to do to the established automakers what Apple had done to BlackBerry and Nokia. Musk also had a better handle on the levers of cultural power, cultivating a celebrity clientele that endowed Tesla's vehicles with prestige that appealed more deeply than environmentalism alone. Musk's huge ambitions fit perfectly with the perception that cars were stagnating technologically, and his ever-escalating promises tapped into the belief that the Model S was just the beginning of a revolution.

Tying all of this together was the fact that Tesla's cars were expensive, appealingly styled luxury vehicles that could drive hundreds of miles and drag race any car on the planet. By contrast, Nissan's Leaf was a modest hatchback with unexciting acceleration, a limited range, and styling that was simultaneously quirky and bland. Ghosn had taken the public at its word when they said they wanted to drive a car with zero emissions and delivered a competent and affordable but ultimately boring appliance.

As it turned out, mass-market demand for an affordable electric car was far lower than Ghosn had imagined. Instead of selling 500,000 plug-in vehicles per year as envisioned by Ghosn, the Nissan-Renault Alliance sold only about that many plug-ins *cumulatively* between 2011 and 2017. Though this was about twice what Tesla sold in the same period, it was still a dramatic underutilization of the production footprint the Alliance had invested in. The biggest gamble on electric cars of the twenty-first century was also one of its biggest automotive flops.

The contrast between Nissan-Renault's abject failure and Tesla's success in the same period holds an important lesson about the electric car market: strong demand for Tesla's status-conferring premium EVs does not translate into strong demand for more modest pure electric transportation appliances. The Model S tapped into the prestige market that had once put Priuses next to Ferraris in affluent driveways from Hollywood to Palo Alto, but without the massive battery that gave the Model S its range and performance, electric cars lost their appeal. Saving the planet is great if you look cool in the process, but it becomes a lot less appealing when it means driving a pokey hatchback with modest range.

This helps explain why Tesla has all but abandoned Musk's master-plan strategy of selling ever-cheaper electric vehicles. Demand for the 40 kWh Model S, which followed through on Tesla's promise of cutting the Roadster's price in half with its second-generation vehicles, was ostensibly so slow that the first-ever "more affordable" Tesla was discontinued. Rather than making the Model X either more affordable or more profitable, Tesla doubled down on flashy high-tech prestige with its supercar-style falcon-wing doors and higher price point.

Though the huge number of reservations for the Model 3 suggests that there is indeed demand for a mass-market EV, weak demand for other affordable EVs suggests that another factor is at play. Whenever premium brands move downmarket, initial demand for their new products is almost always strong because consumers imagine that the new product will be fundamentally the same as the brand's high-end products. If Bentley or Ferrari announced a $20,000 family sedan, people would assume that it would be fundamentally better than (say) a comparably priced Honda or Toyota simply because their perception of the brand is defined by vehicles costing ten times more.

What these buyers fail to realize is that there is no free lunch: the same intense cost pressures that made the Leaf what it is will necessarily apply to any other affordable EV. Especially with electric cars, which concentrate a huge percentage of overall vehicle cost in a battery, affordable models demand major compromises in every other aspect of the design, materials, and features. If buyers weren't tempted by the Leaf, whose roughly one-hundred-mile range covers the majority of daily commutes, any comparably priced vehicle will either offer similar range or have even more spartan appointments.

What Model 3 buyers are signing up for, then, is their chance to own a (relatively) affordable car with a prestigious brand. This is confirmed by the fact that the vast majority of owners knew almost nothing about the car when they put down their refundable reservation for one. There was no cross shopping for comparison, just an opportunity to buy a piece of a brand that they love and aspire to but thus far were priced out of.

The lesson of the Model 3, then, is not that Tesla has been able to translate its success at designing and selling high-end cars into the mass market, but that its high-end vehicles were incredibly successful at establishing a desirable brand. Rather than an endorsement of Musk's entire master plan, Tesla's success has thus far only validated its first step: selling expensive, desirable vehicles that alter perceptions of electric cars. There was an underappreciated level of demand for futuristic electric vehicles among wealthy, high-end car buyers, and Tesla's slick products and relentless hype built a powerful brand that came to define this new market space.

As the power of Tesla's brand became increasingly clear, high-end automakers began looking closely at their opportunities to tap into the intense excitement the upstart had discovered. Though small, the market for high-end EVs had the potential to be quite lucrative for any automaker that could crack the code behind Tesla's success, while laying the groundwork for a longer-term transition toward EV technology. More important than even the potential profits to be won by taking on Tesla, the premium car brands saw an opportunity to regain the futurism and prestige that made Tesla the most talked-about automaker. Tesla's ability to capture "mindshare," rather than its modest market share and minimal operating profit margins, inspired the auto industry empire to strike back.

One by one, the premium automakers began to announce the products that they hoped would prove they could do anything that Tesla could. With powerful, long-range electric drivetrains, sleek styling, and high-tech details, this new generation of high-end EVs made no bones about who their target was. And unlike Tesla, which was under increasing pressure to show that it could make money with its small lineup, this new competition could afford to be loss leaders subsidized by booming sales of high-margin premium cars, trucks, and SUVs.

Smaller premium brands saw their so-called "Tesla Killers" as a way to gain an edge in the highly competitive luxury market, and they raced to beat their better-established competitors to the showroom. Jaguar was one of the most aggressive, rushing an electric crossover called the I-PACE into production by 2018 in hopes of taking advantage of Tesla's relatively weak Model X and carving out a niche. Designed as an EV from the ground up on a "skateboard"-style platform, the I-PACE merged the organic curves of Jaguar's design language with Tesla-like details such as self-presenting door handles, large interior displays, and a drivetrain that paired brisk acceleration with a 220-mile range. To bring the car to market without investing in new production facilities or running the risk of the manufacturing and quality issues that plagued Tesla, Jaguar enlisted the famed contract manufacturer Magna Steyr to build the new I-PACE for them.

Also joining the battle in 2018 would be the first "Tesla Killer" from the massive Volkswagen Group, an electric Audi crossover also aimed directly at the Model X. Called the e-tron quattro, this fastback midsized ute (SUV) would leverage Audi's famed all-wheel-drive expertise with either two motors driving all four wheels in the base version or three motors (one each on the back two wheels and one driving the front two) to deliver torque-vectoring in the top-level spec, for relentless grip. With over three hundred miles of range, a 4.6-second zero-to-sixty acceleration time, and fast-charge capabilities that claim to rival the speeds of Tesla's Superchargers, the e-tron quattro is the tip of the spear for Germany's largest automaker.

And Volkswagen wouldn't stop there. Hard on the heels of Audi's Model X fighter, a pair of sedans was planned to take on the Model S: an e-tron GT sedan from Audi and a sister model from its fellow VW Group brand Porsche, initially codenamed "Mission E" and later named "Taycan." Sharing a new dedicated EV platform, the two sedans would bracket Tesla's most famous model by offering more luxury in the case of the Audi and better real-world driving capabilities in the case of the Porsche. Though neither was likely to match the raw acceleration of Tesla's quickest Model S P100D, Porsche aimed to outdo Tesla by developing a sports sedan that could lap punishing tracks like the famed Nürburgring without overheating and going into a power-limiting "limp mode" to protect the battery, as Teslas invariably do after short amounts of spirited driving. Porsche also joined with BMW to one-up Tesla on charging speed, rolling out fast chargers capable of 450 kilowatts in Europe and 350 kW in the US, which are considerably faster than Tesla's 145 kW Superchargers. (Tesla plans on upgrading its chargers to 250 kW.)

By developing a single highly capable platform for multiple premium high-performance electric cars, VW Group not only spread the development cost between Audi and Porsche but also opened up the possibility of adding high-end versions even for its other brands. In 2017, Bentley showed its first pure electric concept car, which hinted at the possibility of a luxuriously appointed boulevard cruiser based on the same underpinnings. There were even rumors of a super-high-performance Lamborghini version of the platform, which might compete directly with Tesla's drag-racing chops while bringing Italian design flair into the segment. With just one electric platform, VW Group could bracket Tesla's premium products from every side, potentially splitting Tesla's market into buyers who prefer Audi's high-tech minimalism, Porsche's real-world performance, Bentley's bespoke luxury, and Lamborghini's over-the-top performance and design.

Nor is Volkswagen the only automaker remaking itself in the image of Tesla. Daimler has committed $23 billion for EV batteries through 2023, is converting its Smart city car lineup to 100 percent electric power, and is launching ten new pure electric vehicles under a new "EQ" brand, all based off its own recently introduced modular electric platform. BMW rounds out the major German automakers with twelve fully electric vehicles—from a subcompact MINI Cooper to a massive Rolls-Royce—planned by 2025. Volvo also plans to take on Tesla directly with a range of high-end pure electric performance vehicles from its Polestar sub-brand.

This flood of high-end electric vehicles will be joined by models from nearly every luxury car maker on the planet, including Hyundai's new Genesis brand, which plans to sell a pure electric sedan by 2021. A limited-production Aston Martin electric performance sedan demonstrates that even the smaller premium brands will pile into the upscale electric segment. Toyota's Lexus says that it too will compete with pure electric vehicles, and Infiniti will release an electric sedan by 2019. In Detroit, Ford has committed to building sixteen full electric vehicles by 2022 while GM says its Cadillac brand will lead its electric vehicle offensive in 2022.

Among the luxury brands planning electric vehicles, there's little doubt that Tesla's success has served as an inspiration, but ultimately, tougher regulations in China and Europe are motivating much of the new investment. And, in what may be a somewhat ironic twist, the most ambitious electric vehicle plans are largely the product of the worst environmental scandal to hit the industry in decades: Volkswagen's so-called "Dieselgate" emissions scandal.

In response to the global excoriation from regulators and the public alike over its emissions regulation cheating, VW has skipped ahead to Elon Musk's mass-market electric car endgame even as its luxury brands prepare to take the fight to Tesla. A new compact modular electric platform will provide a variety of more affordable VW Group long-range EVs targeting Tesla's third-generation Model 3 and Model Y. Following VW's broader strategy of flexible modular architectures, this "MEB" platform will underpin three new electric Volkswagens to start: a compact hatchback, a compact crossover, and a van with styling that harkens back to the iconic VW bus. By 2025, the VW Group plans to offer at least twenty-seven models based on the MEB platform across four of its makes, with prices as low as 20,000 euros and generating three million in sales per year.

With 150 kW fast-charging batteries and a new simplified ordering process that will leverage Tesla-like showrooms in shopping malls, the MEB-based electric assault represents the first step in the complete Tesla-fication of one of the world's largest automakers. It isn't just talk, either: VW has committed over $90 billion to its electric vehicle strategy, $48 billion for long-term battery supply contracts, assigned sixteen manufacturing sites to electric vehicle production, and is reportedly in discussions to license its MEB platform to other automakers.

As the global majors and established premium brands pile into the high-end EV market Tesla pioneered, demand for affordable EVs seem to be increasing fastest where Tesla has been relegated to a bit player: China. China's government has been trying to develop a local auto industry for decades, requiring foreign majors to partner with domestic automakers in joint ventures to enjoy access to China's large and growing car market. With its cities choked by air pollution, the nation has provided extra incentives for plug-in vehicles while also creating additional rules that would ensure that its domestic industry maintained control of the new electrified car business.

These partnerships have accelerated the development of China's automakers, transferring technology and know-how from established players to the local newcomers, but they've also effectively marginalized Tesla in what could be one of its most promising markets. Tesla's fiercely independent streak, which has made so many of its partnerships challenging, kept it away from any joint venture that might dilute its brand or technological advantage. To produce a plug-in vehicle in China, Tesla would have not only needed to form a joint venture with a Chinese partner, it would also have needed to sell it under a new Chinese brand and power it using Chinese-produced batteries.

For years, Tesla had to endure stiff tariffs on the American-made vehicles it exported from its Fremont factory rather than submitting to China's rules, limiting its sales to tiny volumes purchased by younger scions of China's wealthiest classes. By 2018, with China's plug-in vehicle market growing to roughly triple the size of that of the United States, Tesla's marginal role in the world's largest EV (and passenger car) market was becoming untenable. Then, suddenly an opportunity presented itself: China relaxed its rules, allowing foreign automakers to build wholly owned factories in its free-trade zones without a joint-venture partner.

Rumors that Tesla was trying to build a factory in a free-trade zone near Shanghai had been circulating for years, and with the rule change it announced plans to build a plant capable of manufacturing half a million vehicles each year. But with Tesla struggling to bring down the price of its US-made Model 3 to the promised $35,000 price point in the US, its China-made vehicles would face even tougher pricing challenges in a market where the top-selling EV (a modest 125-mile-range hatchback made by Beijing Auto called the EC series) costs less than $25,000.

Though Chinese firms built a wide variety of plug-in passenger vehicles that would compete with traditional cars (ranging from basic affordable compacts to Tesla-challenging high-tech premium vehicles), the real explosion in zero-emission transportation in China came from much smaller, cheaper vehicles that weren't even categorized as cars. Whereas China bought some 770,000 plug-in cars in 2017, its market for these micro-EVs boomed to 1.75 million in the same year. Exempt from crash-test standards and even driving license requirements, these tiny electric vehicles could cost less than $1,000 while providing better safety and weather protection than the scooters and motorcycles that they typically replaced.

The dramatic impact of these micro-EVs present a radical challenge to the entire premise underpinning Tesla's success in the US. Tesla was created to explicitly overturn the assumption that all EVs had to be tiny, unsafe "golf carts." In the car-centric US, Tesla's success at designing safe, powerful, status-conferring long-range EVs kick-started the premium plug-in segment. However, established premium brands are now starting to pour into that market. And the Nissan-Renault Alliance is even moving to fill the gap between micro-EVs and more affordable electric cars, building an electric version of its $5,000 India-market Renault Kwid in China that could bring real car luxuries and about eighty miles of electric range closer to the $10,000 price point. Announced in 2018, this double down on affordable electric cars is a bet that more global markets will be opened by lowering the cost of EVs with Leaf-like range rather than increasing the range of vehicles at the Leaf's once-revolutionary $30,000 price point.

From a US perspective, it made sense that Tesla's approach of fitting EVs into the existing automotive paradigm would lead the transition to sustainable transportation. Outside the US, however, where the built landscape doesn't so strongly reinforce American automotive values and where developing economies put $30,000 vehicles beyond the reach of the masses, small, cheap, low-speed, short-range EVs—the very antithesis of Tesla's cars—have become the foundation of an electric revolution. And even within the US, electric "micromobility" is becoming a hot trend driven by dockless scooters and electric-assist bicycles that reduce electric mobility to its minimalist essence. After two waves of innovation that sought to fit electric drivetrains and autonomous-drive technology into the existing mental model of the large, powerful, long-range American automobile, electric vehicles seem to be gravitating to a number of smaller form factors.

Though Tesla played a vital role in driving awareness and excitement to electric mobility, the momentum it created seems to be leaving it behind. Having defined itself at the cutting edge of the mobility technology revolution, Tesla's mission is to engineer electric vehicles that are rooted in the traditional car values of private ownership, long-range capability, power, and status. The vision behind Tesla was to replace a monoculture of privately owned, gas-powered cars with a monoculture of privately owned, electric-powered vehicles. Instead, history seems to have a very different vision of progress.

Rather than simply shifting from gas to electric, the automobile's monopoly is giving way to a great flowering of diversity. A "cambrian explosion" of new mobility modes enabled by smartphone-based access is exploding the entire notion that people need to own large, expensive, vehicles capable of driving across the country at a moment's notice. We can now open an app and choose whether to catch a ride in someone else's car, on a bus or shuttle, grab a scooter or e-bike, or temporarily rent a truck, SUV, or long-range touring car. This new mobility paradigm is replacing car ownership by default; we're now more conscious about how we choose to get around. Most Americans drive less than fifty miles per day, with the vast majority of trips going only a handful of miles; it seems all but inevitable that many privately owned vehicles will be replaced by on-demand mobility. Those who do still buy cars will choose vehicles that are far more optimized for their typical daily use patterns than Tesla's expensive long-range vehicles, which trade efficiency for the ability to take rare road trips.

This transition to smartphone-based markets for on-demand micromobility and shared vehicles is the true disruptive innovation in mobility technology. It seems obvious to say it, but it's worth thinking about the fact that a one-dollar electric scooter ride can take you across downtown San Francisco far more cheaply, quickly, and efficiently than a $100,000 Model S. Rather than building a better car, as Tesla has done, new mobility technology companies are building vehicles and platforms that subvert the entire need for privately owned cars. The benefits of this disruption, in terms of economics, the environment, and even urban development and congestion, are going to dramatically outstrip any shift from gas cars to electric cars.

Tesla has played an important role in bringing the technology sector's focus to bear on mobility. It has inspired many of the entrepreneurs now developing the vehicles and platforms that are beginning to make Tesla look almost antiquated. Without pioneers like Tesla, it's impossible to say if we'd be seeing the radical explosion of new mobility concepts and technologies we see today. Moreover, there will likely be consumer interest in high-end privately owned electric vehicles like Tesla's for decades as these new technologies and consumer behavior patterns steadily take hold.

Like Citroën, Tesla created ultra-inspiring products that allowed the masses to glimpse the future . . . while simultaneously unleashing innovation that would ultimately leave it behind. Citroën's technological advantages became "table stakes" for everyone who followed it, and the true competitive advantages went to companies like Toyota, whose pragmatism took Citroën's vision and refined it into less exciting but more useful mobility appliances.

That Citroën does not dominate the car market of the early twenty-first century takes nothing away from the influence, innovation, and beauty of its landmark vehicles. But it does illustrate an important point: the innovator is often a transitional figure. Once the impact of its vision is understood, it often falls to less fanciful and risk-tolerant players to translate the vision into more accessible and prosaic forms.

This seems likely to become Tesla's fate: its place in the history books is secure, but its present is coming under direct assault from more experienced, pragmatic automakers. At the same time, its future is being disrupted by a fresh crop of innovators who are leaving the entire idea of the car behind.

CHAPTER 16

LUDICROUS MODE

The most you could say is that Solyndra executives were too optimistic. They presented a better face to the situation than should have been presented in the final few months, but then, if they didn't do that, it would have become a self-fulfilling prophecy of—as soon as a CEO says 'I'm not sure if we'll survive,' you're dead. You know, I think people are making too much of this Solyndra thing.
Elon Musk, September 29, 2011

The crowd went nuts as Elon Musk emerged from a giant silver semitruck, walked to the center of the stage, and spread his arms in greeting. "I want to give the trucks a moment," he said, stepping aside to show off the two prototype tractor trailers as the shouts of triumph rose above the ocean of upraised smartphones capturing the moment.

Despite their working-class form factor, the trucks looked every bit as sleek and futuristic as any other Tesla vehicle, and they bristled with Muskian ambition. From the futuristic exterior to its minimalistic, touchscreen-dominated interior, from the blistering acceleration to the planned dedicated 100 percent solar-powered "megacharger" network, the Tesla "Semi" was built around the assumption that long-haul trucking was ready for its own Model S. It would even have its own version of Tesla's Autopilot, which Musk claimed would make it impossible to jackknife, along with a windshield made of glass that Musk said could withstand a nuclear explosion.

After announcing that production of the Semi would start within two years, Musk thanked the crowd and waved his farewell. There was an awkward pause as one of the drivers appeared to struggle to put his truck in gear, eventually turning to drive away as Musk walked past the front of the crowd, shaking hands. Then, suddenly, the lights and music changed, and it became clear that the presentation was not in fact over. In the tradition of Steve Jobs, Tesla had "one more thing" to show fans, and the air positively crackled with anticipation.

A ramp dropped out of the back of one of the stopped trucks, and a low-slung red sports car emerged as the music built to a thunderous crescendo. Tesla's chief designer, Franz von Holzhausen, pumped his fist out of the open roof of what turned out to be the firm's next-generation Roadster. A gigantic four-seat coupe in contrast with the lithe Lotus-based original Roadster, Tesla's latest flagship had a zero-to-sixty time of under two seconds, a top speed above 250 miles per hour, over six hundred miles of range, and a base price of $200,000. Clearly soaking up the enthusiasm, Musk admitted the new car's numbers "sound nutty . . . but they're real."

If the crowd had been fired up by the Semi, the surprise unveiling of the new Roadster blew the roof off the place. Faces were contorted by full-throated screams as onlookers shook with excitement. "The point of this is to deliver a hard-core smackdown to gasoline cars," Musk explained as onlookers melted down into a frenzy. As the presentation ended, Musk urged the crowd to jump the barriers and come see his latest creation up close. "Thank you for coming," he shouted as he and the Roadster were swarmed by frantic fans.

It had been a performance unlike any other in the company's history. Though Musk's showmanship had become an increasingly important ingredient in Tesla's success, the company had never surprised its fans so completely before. The Roadster hadn't even been referenced in Musk's second master plan, nor had anyone anticipated the firm's return to extreme echelons of price and performance. Musk's barrage of dramatic claims about the Semi and the Roadster had wiped away every preconception about where Tesla was headed as a company, temporarily incapacitating rational analysis with a wave of pure hype.

The brain-scrambling tsunami of excitement that Musk had unleashed could hardly have been better timed. Since announcing the start of production for Model 3 four months earlier, Tesla had made fewer than one thousand of its first mass-market car. Stories citing sources at Tesla and its suppliers were bubbling up around the media, revealing that the Model 3 production ramp had been plagued by chaos, confusion, and unrealistic expectations.

This disconnect between Tesla's mass-market struggles and its pricey next-gen hype left its latest spectacle feeling oddly hollow. Having largely subsisted on prototypes and promotion for much of the past decade, Model 3 was the company's chance to prove that it could deliver the affordable electric car it had been promising since 2006. But when it found itself mired in "production hell," its answer was to double down on even flashier but farther off prototypes. It was as if Tesla was becoming a parody of itself.

The gargantuan semitruck embodied the company's lack of focus, branching out into a product class that had nothing to do with the vehicles Tesla made or the markets it served. If Tesla's cars had to make up for their shortcomings in reliability and affordability with style and performance, how were they supposed to sell an unproven semi to trucking companies that live and die on cost and uptime? A sexy drag-racing tractor-trailer truck may have fit in with the goofy, overgrown kid aspect of Musk's personal brand, but it clashed badly with the perception that Tesla was finally growing up and becoming a real car company.

Worse still, an electric semi was simply not a particularly promising concept. The limited range, long recharge times, heavy batteries, and high cost of an electric vehicle are a fundamentally poor match to the long-range, weight-hauling, moneymaking mission of a tractor-trailer truck. Meanwhile, Tesla was missing out on a far more suitable commercial use for its technology: short-range delivery vehicles that could enhance a business's brand while ensuring that deliveries would continue even in cities that were moving toward bans and restrictions on diesel and gas cars. Eliminating the pollution caused by trucks crawling through urban gridlock could have profound environmental and public health benefits without requiring the absurdly optimistic costs, specifications, and unique charging network needed to make an electric semi seem like a viable proposition.

Unexpected though it was, the new Roadster at least fit in with Tesla's established brand and technical competencies, bringing the company full circle to its high-performance roots. The new Roadster's eye-popping performance claims instantly inspired a new meme format, in which each specification is presented alongside increasingly absurd points of comparison. Beginning with an image comparing the Roadster to a Bugatti Chiron, the meme quickly devolved to iterations like "Tesla Roadster vs. 1996 Toyota Previa," "Tesla Roadster vs. Lightning McQueen [from Disney's *Cars*]," and "Tesla Roadster vs. Banana." To achieve these astounding numbers, Tesla had sandwiched two of its 100 kWh battery packs on top of each other, creating a gigantic and somewhat oddly proportioned beast of a muscle car compared to the svelte original Roadster.

Had the Model 3 ramp been going smoothly, the new Roadster would have been a stunning statement of Tesla's intention to never stop pushing the limits of electric car technology even as it churned out hundreds of thousands of practical, affordable vehicles. But because of the circumstances in which it was revealed, it seemed more like a reflection of Tesla's ambivalence toward becoming a mass-market automaker and desire to maintain its high-end positioning. Musk radiated joy as he rattled off the new performance benchmarks the Roadster would set, but a question lingered over the entire exercise: Why? Hadn't Tesla already repeatedly proven that electric cars could "smack down" any gas car in a drag race?

One potential answer came when Musk announced pricing. The new Roadster started at $200,000, it cost $50,000 to secure a reservation, and if you gave Tesla $5,000 of it that night, you could be among the first to get a ride in the prototype. But that was just the base model. As usual there was a Founders Edition as well, but to reserve one of the one thousand limited-run versions, Tesla required the entire $250,000 price be paid within ten days of placing an order. If, or when, Tesla sells out of Founders Edition Roadsters, it will have brought more cash into the company than it raised in its IPO.

Despite bringing in tens of millions of dollars in interest-free loans, reinvigorating the fan community that was impatiently waiting for Model 3s, and generally putting on a hell of a show, the Semi and Roadster spectacle didn't boost Tesla's stock price the way other events had. The stock did briefly take off several weeks later when Musk revealed that Tesla was developing custom processing chips for artificial intelligence, suggesting that investors saw more potential in autonomous-drive technology than the cash Tesla raised from Semi and Roadster deposits.

Despite its weakening stock market performance, Tesla's board proposed a new ten-year compensation plan for Musk in January 2018 that put more emphasis than ever on the firm's share price. To vest its twelve tranches of shares, each of which was worth 1 percent of Tesla's outstanding equity, Musk had to lead Tesla to massive new stock price gains. Starting at the company's then current valuation of $59 billion, Musk's first target was a $100 billion market cap with another tranche vesting with every $50 billion of market cap growth until the company was worth an eye-watering $650 billion. In spite of persistent criticism of Tesla's lack of profits, the "operational milestones" Musk also had to hit were tied only to growth in the company's revenue and EBITDA (earnings before interest, tax, depreciation, and amortization), both of which excluded significant costs that could keep a company from true profitability or positive cash flow.

This compensation plan effectively took Musk's biggest financial incentive, namely growing the value of stock that he was the largest owner of, and turbocharged it. If fully achieved, Musk will have made Tesla worth more than any company is today, save Apple, Amazon, and Alphabet (as of Q2 2018). In that scenario, Musk's personal wealth would grow by as much as $55 billion, only slightly less than Tesla's total valuation at the time the award was proposed and more than four times his then current $13 billion stake.

As staggering as the numbers are, the truly astonishing part of the plan is that it puts so much emphasis on growing the stock price as a primary goal. Musk had already proved that he is incredibly good at boosting the company's stock with bold visions and big promises, but he'd fallen short when it came to execution and building a sustainably profitable business. Given that Tesla was still dependent on markets for the regular capital infusions it needed to survive, and was thus in a fundamentally precarious position, the board might have nudged Musk to focus more on building a sound operational foundation.

Tesla's board seemed to be overlooking the most fundamental truth of the modern car business: Growth in the good times is only as good as the ability to survive the bad times. As Musk often liked to point out, Tesla and Ford were the only two American automakers to never have gone bankrupt. What kept Ford in that club through the most recent downturns was not maximizing growth or the stock price but knowing to make the tough decisions before recession hit. These decisions, like Ford's dramatic restructuring in 2006, are almost always unpopular with investors due to the ugly short-term house-cleaning charges (Ford lost $12 billion in 2006), but they allow automakers to endure, rebuild on a strong foundation, and grow again when times improve.

Musk's new compensation package reflected the impression left by the Semi and Roadster event: that Tesla was playing up unfocused hype while execution challenges mounted. Musk's own original master plan had made the Model 3 the culmination of the company's mission, but while "production hell" dragged on, he had prioritized an event selling advance deposits for a car that wasn't even part of his second master plan. Musk was leading Tesla as if it were a startup looking for a seed round and not a 35,000 employee automaker with hundreds of thousands of deposits for an affordable electric car that was falling ever further behind schedule.

Of course, hitching Tesla's fortunes to the belief that Musk could deliver on seemingly impossible promises had been undeniably good for the company so far. Its valuation rivaled established automakers with decades of experience and vastly greater scale and profits, largely based on belief in Musk's personal abilities. But as time went on, Musk's lengthening record of missed deadlines was being exacerbated by unforced errors that had nothing to do with Tesla or the car business.

Musk's wild ambitions and goofy jokes had always been part of his appeal, so it's difficult to say when his behavior started to cross the line between lighthearted joking and something more serious. By 2017, however, there had been several unmistakable red flags: claiming that he tweets under the influence of a dangerous cocktail of Ambien and alcohol and admitting he might be bipolar certainly raised eyebrows in some corners. Combined with his ever-growing collection of ambitious ventures—including the Boring Company's plan to revolutionize tunneling, the Hyperloop tunnel-based transport concept, Neuralink's "implantable brain-computer interface," and OpenAI's effort to promote "friendly artificial intelligence"—it seemed that Musk was beginning to lose himself in an endless quest for more hype.

His increasingly erratic behavior burst into the spotlight in 2018, when an escalating series of Twitter conflicts with journalists, analysts, and critics led to a full-scale assault on stock analysts and the media. Musk cut short questions about Tesla's reservations and capital requirements during the company's first-quarter earnings call, saying "boring bonehead questions are not cool," and snubbing respected analysts to field questions from a YouTuber representing "retail investors." Just weeks later, stung by reports about workplace injuries at Tesla's Fremont factory, he claimed to be launching a website for rating the accuracy of journalists and their stories to battle "the holier-than-thou hypocrisy of big media companies who lay claim to the truth, but publish only enough to sugarcoat the lie."

These outbursts generated considerable furor in the media, but even they were just a prelude to what was still to come. Later that summer, Musk developed a miniature submarine to help with the rescue of a youth soccer team stuck in a flooded cave in Thailand. One of the lead rescue divers dismissed Musk's involvement as a PR stunt that did nothing to contribute to the ultimately successful mission. Musk responded with a series of tweets calling the diver a "pedo," and suggesting that as an expat living in Thailand, he was somehow "sus," or suspicious.

Musk eventually apologized, but within weeks he repeated the accusation in an angry, profanity-laced email sent to BuzzFeed reporter Ryan Mac, prompting the diver to file defamation lawsuits in both the UK and the United States. Tesla's share price fell, and even Musk's most loyal investors expressed concern about his Twitter presence, which not long before had been held up as one of Tesla's unique marketing capabilities. With all of his companies struggling to deliver on colossal promises, Musk's long and escalating pattern of defamatory attacks on critics increasingly made him seem less like an altruistic visionary and more like a thin-skinned, egotistical hype man lashing out at encroaching accountability.

Even after months of open antagonism with the media, the low point of Musk's summer meltdown came from his own tweet on August 7, 2018: "Am considering taking Tesla private at $420. Funding secured." Increasingly fixated on short sellers, whom he saw as waging a war of misinformation on Tesla in hopes of driving down its heady stock price, Musk had held limited discussions with the Saudi Arabian Public Investment Fund about taking Tesla private and building a Gigafactory in the gulf kingdom that was increasingly looking to technology and renewable energy as a hedge on the uncertain future of its oil-dependent economy.

Coming on the same day as news of the Saudi PIF taking a 5 percent stake in Tesla, Musk's tweet gave Tesla's stock a double pump that inflicted massive losses on the hated shorts.

But euphoria about the possibility of a private Tesla, free from the disclosures and controversy that come with being a public company, soon turned to doubt as hard details of the deal failed to materialize. As confidence crumbled, so too did the chances of a "short squeeze" that Musk had been promising all summer, and Tesla's share price began to erode as quickly as it had been pumped up. Within a week of Musk's tweet, the *New York Times* reported that the Securities and Exchange Commission had subpoenaed Tesla in connection with an investigation into the possibility that Musk's tweet constituted securities manipulation.

Always the focus of inordinate media attention, Tesla and Musk were becoming a feeding frenzy of increasingly negative press. The rapper Azealia Banks (who had been invited to Musk's home by his then girlfriend, the electronic music star Grimes) began posting outlandish and attention-grabbing claims about Musk tweeting under the influence of LSD, his wild search for investors for his go-private deal, and bizarre personal details. The media circus hit high gear a month after his tweet, when he punctuated a lengthy and rambling appearance on the popular Joe Rogan podcast by drinking whiskey and taking a puff from a joint.

By the last week of September, the SEC was ready to bring charges against Musk, offering him a settlement that would have removed him as chairman of Tesla for two years and cost him $10 million in civil penalties. Though initially open to the deal, Musk abruptly rejected the offer and threatened to leave the company entirely if the board didn't back his decision and "extol his integrity," according to the *New York Times*. The board then issued a joint statement with Musk crediting him with leading Tesla to become "the most successful U.S. auto company in over a century." The next day the SEC publicly filed suit against Musk, accusing him of making false and misleading statements and seeking to bar him from serving as an officer or director of any public company.

After a day of watching Tesla's stock price plummet and receiving a phone call from Mark Cuban urging him to reconsider his defiance, Musk gave in and settled with the SEC for slightly worse terms than it had previously offered. Musk would be barred from serving as Tesla's chairman for three years, both he and Tesla would pay $20 million each in fines, two new independent directors would be added to Tesla's board, and a committee would be established to supervise Musk's communications with investors and the public. The penalties were hardly earth-shattering, but Musk's erratic handling of the matter—as well as a subsequent tweet taunting the SEC for being the "Shortseller Enrichment Commission"—shook confidence in his leadership.

Musk's unsupervised Twitter presence, once a major asset for Tesla, had become a liability. The trolling, spin, and diatribes against critical coverage and the Big Oil and short seller conspiracies against Tesla that used to regularly boost Tesla's image and share price were now having the opposite effect. Controversies surrounding Musk himself were eclipsing Tesla and its mission, forcing fans to explain and apologize for his behavior rather than basking in the glow of his heroically altruistic aura.

Musk's volatile behavior had been creating problems inside Tesla long before it spilled out into the open. Turnover had long been high by auto industry standards at Tesla, but the exodus accelerated with forty-one top-level executives leaving the company in the first nine months of 2018, according to one count. Significant portions of critical teams were hired away wholesale by competitors, as lower-ranking employees followed the executives who had insulated them from Musk's growing control.

Once Musk settled with the SEC and the media circus that had surrounded him for months started to die down, Tesla seemed to emerge from the controversy as strong as ever. With the Model 3's year of "production hell" finally in the rearview mirror, Tesla recorded a blockbuster third quarter profit of $312 million and Musk projected positive profits and cashflow "for all quarters going forward." He kept that promise in the fourth quarter, delivering another $139 million in profit and closing out 2018 on a positive note.

Tesla delivered 245,240 vehicles over the course of the tumultuous year, nearly as many as it had sold in its history up to that point. It had taken $4.5 billion in new cash raised in debt and equity since the reveal of the Model 3. It was still not even halfway to the five hundred thousand–unit annual volume Musk's accelerated production plans had called for, but this was still an impressive accomplishment for any automaker. The fact that Tesla was turning consecutive quarterly profits and projecting profitability to continue suggested that the company might finally be on sustainable footing.

This perception didn't last long, as it quickly became clear that Tesla would struggle to maintain the level of financial performance it had demonstrated during the second half of 2018. The company had been in the sweet spot of its Model 3 order book, delivering the higher-priced versions to customers on its extensive waiting list. As the new year dawned, it brought fresh questions about the sustainability of Tesla's demand. These questions were fueled by the sundowning of Tesla's $7,500 federal tax credit at the end of the year, which was cut in half starting in January and would be cut in half again six months later.

Musk continued to forecast strong demand for the company's products, but the company's actions told a different story as Tesla slashed Model 3 prices by $2,000 in January and another $1,100 in February in hopes of maintaining sales volume while slashing thousands of jobs. "This is a strong indication that demand in the U.S. for both the mid-range and long-range Model 3 versions has largely been exhausted, and the company is still working through the estimated ~6.8k of unsold Model 3 inventory," Cowen's analysts stated in a note circulated at the end of January. In addition to lowering prices in North America, Tesla began delivering Model 3 to Europe and China.

Then, at the end of February, Tesla announced in a call with select members of the media that it was taking the final step culminating

Musk's master plan: it would start taking orders for the long-awaited $35,000 base-model version of the Model 3. This should have been a huge accomplishment, the culmination of the dream laid out in Musk's original master plan. But rather than the triumphant announcement one might expect, the news was overshadowed by the steps Musk said would have to be taken to deliver on the $35,000 promise. To achieve that price point, Tesla would shut down "many" of its more than three hundred store locations and shift its entire sales operation online, making up for the lack of test drives with a seven-day return policy.

This stunning news came just one month after Tesla tweeted about new store openings, and it was promptly reported that once again many employees had no idea about this major strategic pivot until Musk announced it on the media call. The abruptness of the move suggested that Tesla needed the base version of the Model 3 to keep demand flowing, and that cost reductions on the manufacturing and supply chain side weren't coming fast enough. Walking away from a large part of its retail footprint could deliver the needed savings, but only if the company was able to get out of its leases.

Then, just as unexpectedly as the store cuts were announced, Tesla walked them back days later saying just ten percent would be closed and another twenty percent were being evaluated. That news was in turn followed by reports that planned deliveries of the Standard Range Model 3 were canceled by Tesla at the last minute, and that the company was calling customers who had waited three years for the $35,000 Tesla, trying to upsell them to higher-spec versions. The cheapest version was then pulled from the company's website, ostensibly due to weak demand, apparently dooming it to the same fate that had claimed the $50,000 Model S.

Consecutive quarterly profits had engendered a sense of optimism, but it evaporated in a matter of months as Tesla's frantic price cuts, layoffs, and store closing plans once again painted a picture of a company in crisis. If Tesla wasn't able to sustain demand at the higher Model 3 price points or build the $35,000 version profitably, it was caught between two tough choices: either keep prices high, let sales slide, and risk the "hypergrowth" narrative that underpinned its stock valuation, or deliver the affordable cars it had promised and return to regular quarterly losses until it could cut enough costs from manufacturing and the supply chain.

This is precisely the kind of dilemma that automakers anticipate and plan for years in advance, doing detailed market research to match production of each trim level and specification of a new vehicle as closely as possible with demand. Producing vehicles beyond what the market will bear is the most dreaded outcome in the business. It forces a company to lower prices, which in turn forces the company to cut its own costs, which can further reduce demand. The ensuing negative feedback loop has marked the end of the road for many automakers, including GM and Chrysler in 2008. The Model 3's massive preorders had goaded Musk into the wildly ambitious manufacturing plans that created "production hell." Now it seemed that the same preorders had led him to overestimate ongoing demand.

With billions needed to develop the Roadster, Semi, and Model Y crossover, as well as to build the Shanghai factory it needed to reach a half-million units of annual production, Tesla's projected return to quarterly losses ratcheted up the pressure. In the past, Tesla might have returned to debt or equity markets to fund these projects, but the company insisted that it had no plans to do so. With the projected 2020 start of production for all three of its new products drawing steadily closer, unanswered questions about where they would be built and how Tesla planned to pay for those manufacturing investments absent strong profits or another Wall Street capital raise loomed.

Meanwhile, the repeated price cuts, layoffs, and back-and-forth decisions about the store closures (not to mention the sales referral program that Tesla canceled in January and brought back in March plus a series of changes to Autopilot pricing) all contributed to questions about Musk's leadership. In spite of his reputation as a far-sighted futurist visionary, Musk seemed to be running Tesla on a week-by-week basis and impulsively announcing decisions that had to be promptly walked back once their full implications were understood. With the SEC hauling Musk back to court over allegations that he wasn't complying with the settlement agreement they had reached, and the sudden departure of the general counsel Tesla had hired in the wake of the "funding secured" debacle, the sense of chaos and crisis surrounding Tesla once again seemed to be emanating from its mercurial CEO.

On Twitter, the war between Tesla's believers and the $TSLAQ skeptics raged on, with each new twist prompting another battle between interpretations and neither side budging from their preexisting perspectives. The only thing it seemed the two sides could agree on was poignantly summarized by the prominent $TSLAQ account @TeslaCharts: "Elon Musk is willing to do anything to win. Anything."

In fact, much of the company's history comes down to this pattern: Tesla runs into one of the auto industry's brutally tough challenges and Musk coming up with a rescue that looks heroic to his fans and desperate to his critics. Musk's ability to find a way through the toughest situations has kept the company going despite challenges that could have spelled the end for another automaker. And yet, these exploits have never yet gotten the company to a truly sustainable state, no matter how many times Musk finds a way to raise more cash or engineer surprising quarterly results.

CHAPTER 17

WHERE THE RUBBER MEETS THE ROAD

nside every Tesla, dominating the otherwise spartan dashboard and defining the car's interior, is a screen. Specifically, a projected capacitive touchscreen that spans seventeen inches in the Model S and X and fifteen inches in the Model 3. When Tesla first debuted the Model S, nobody had ever seen a display that size in a production car dashboard before, and it was instrumental in establishing Tesla as a technology brand, rather than just another green car brand.

As Tesla has evolved into a unique cultural phenomenon, these enormous screens can be seen as more than just screens. They are a symbol that crystalizes the strengths and weaknesses of Tesla's entire approach to cars, and they help explain why opinions on the company are so polarized.

At first glance, Tesla's giant screen communicates the brand's values on an aesthetic level. It tells the customer that this is as much a device as a car, and that Tesla is as much a high-tech company as it is an automaker. Though the screen is what catches the eye, the full aesthetic impact comes from what you don't see: buttons and knobs. When compared to the interior of any other car, a Tesla's clean, button-free touch-screen interface looks like an iPhone in a world of BlackBerrys.

Even the layout of the user interface recalls a smartphone or tablet, with menus and functions arrayed like apps on the periphery of the screen. It's as fast and graphically rich as many smartphones, and you can use the same multitouch gestures you would with a smartphone or tablet, including swipes and pinch to zoom. After you've spent some time in a Tesla, the small size, clunky performance, and modest visuals of other vehicles' more typical in-car touchscreens make you feel like you've traveled back in time.

The all-digital interface also reflects the centrality of software in Tesla's vehicle design, something else it has picked up from modern consumer electronics. Without the constraints of a hardware interface, Tesla has far more scope to adjust and improve the user experience in its cars. Using over-the-air updates, Tesla can tweak the user interface and add new features without worrying about how it will be controlled. The infinite digital space of a screen and software opens new horizons of possibility that Tesla is still only just beginning to explore.

This flexibility enables one of the things that gives Tesla an entirely different character than other any car or car company: in-car "Easter eggs." These digital tchotchkes are purposefully frivolous, turning the navigation screen into the surface of Mars or making the car displayed on the instrument cluster look like Santa's sleigh. A "sketch pad" mode allows users to draw pictures using the central screen and "TeslAtari" mode turns the display into a classic arcade with playable old-school games like Lunar Lander and Missile Command. For all their absurdity, these Easter eggs push the boundaries of what a car can do and what a customer's relationship with a car company can be.

All of these screen-enabled features are fundamental to Tesla's deep appeal, if not to the actual usability of the vehicle itself. For a lot of fans (particularly the youngest), the quirky frivolity of the Easter eggs is the first thing they've ever cared about in a car, signaling that this inanimate object is as playful as they are and fostering a deep affinity with the brand. For serious techies, on the other hand, the fact that a Tesla is more software-centric and computer-like than other cars makes it intrinsically more relatable and appealing than any other vehicle.

At a time when uniqueness is harder than ever to come by in an auto market full of century-old companies and brands, these are distinct advantages. Once upon a time, consumers would have to do extensive research to make sure that they bought a car that was appealing, afford-able, and reliable. Now that all cars are competitively benchmarked to the point of homogeneity, the hardest task car buyers face is not avoid-ing a lemon but picking a car that stands out from the crowd. Tesla's gigantic screens, the brand image it projects, and the things it enables easily solve that problem for anyone who can afford it.

The uniqueness of Tesla's screens also presents a rarely consid-ered question: If intense competition has led automakers to make sure their cars have the same features as everyone else's, and Tesla's screen is a standout, where is the competition for Tesla's screen? Why haven't other car companies offered seventeen-inch touchscreens, either before the Model S or since?

One trite answer is that Tesla is a Silicon Valley disruptor, and as such, it is simply more technologically advanced than the lumbering auto-industry dinosaurs. But for anyone who looks beyond this mean-ingless tautology, a totally different perspective on Tesla awaits.

The key to answering this question comes from Elon Musk him-self, when he told Ashlee Vance about the seventeen-inch screen that made the Model S so distinctive. "When we first talked about the touchscreen, the guys came back and said 'there's nothing like that in the automotive supply chain,'" he explains in Vance's book. "I said 'I know. That's because it's never been put in a fucking car before.'" But, the story goes, Musk figured that since laptops are robust enough to endure drops, heat, and other abuse, it wouldn't be too hard to make one stand up to the conditions it would see in a car.

However, Vance writes:

After contacting the laptop suppliers, Tesla's engineers came back and said that the temperature and vibration loads for the computers did not appear to be up to automotive standards. Tesla's supplier in Asia also kept pointing the carmaker to its automotive division instead of its computing division. As Musk dug into the situation more, he discovered that the laptop screens simply had not been tested before under tougher automotive conditions, which included large temperature fluctuations. When Tesla performed the tests, the electronics ended up working just fine.

It's not clear what tests Tesla subjected its screens to when qualifying them for use in their cars, but we do know that the Innolux G170J1-LE1 they use in Model S and X is an industrial screen whose initial specs were not up to basic "automotive grade" standards. Located under a large glass roof, and with multiple processors and a heater core packed behind it in the dash, Tesla put the G170J1-LE1 in a thermal sandwich it wasn't designed for. A car's dashboard can reach the screen's 80 degrees Celsius (176 degrees Fahrenheit) maximum operating temperature, even without help from the processors needed to power the infotainment and Autopilot or extra solar radiation from a glass roof.

Sure enough, Tesla owners have reported problems with their seventeen-inch displays that strongly suggest chronic thermal overload. In 2012–2015 Teslas, an adhesive in the screens would soften in high heat, forming bubbles around the edge of the display and eventually leaking out into the cabin. As soon as that problem was addressed in production, owners reported yellow bands forming around the edge of screens in 2016 and later Teslas, another issue that is almost certainly tied to high heat. By December 2018, Tesla owners were reporting that the company would not replace screens until it developed a new version, sometime during the summer of 2019.

Ironically, this yellow banding/border issue is just another way in which Tesla's vehicles are like smartphones and tablets. Yellow border problems of various kinds have been reported on devices like Apple iPhones and Microsoft Surface Books and others, but they're a bigger deal on a six-figure car than a three-figure device. Not only are quality expectations higher for cars, with repair costs ranging from about $1,000 for the screen alone and about $3,000 for the entire infotainment module, the out-of-warranty costs are much higher. For Tesla, these problems not only hurt customer satisfaction, but they hurt the company's thin (at best) operating margins as well.

Once you start to look beyond the gee-whiz factor of a car that resembles a smartphone and start thinking about the kinds of problems that smartphones have, the whole idea becomes less appealing. On one hand, the steady flow of new features and software updates seems like such an obvious improvement of cars. Yet on the other, this can also make cars as unstable and finicky as smartphones, which are prone to bugs and glitches. Rebooting your phone because a website made it crash is no big deal, but what if a website or a software update made your car computer crash or reboot while you're driving? What if a website made your odometer fail to properly record mileage, effectively causing you to commit inadvertent odometer fraud? (Tesla drivers have reported both things on forums.)

Launching a "minimum viable product" and then updating it after you've started selling it works for software and even smartphones, provided they are not relied upon in safety-critical situations. But the reason automakers choose to use proven technology and automotive-grade components, and then spend years validating them before selling to customers, is that cars are fundamentally safety-critical systems. When you start to think about the numbers—about 1.25 million people die on roads around the world every year, nearly forty thousand of them in the United States alone—it becomes easier to understand why automakers don't "beta test" on their customers.

The inherent danger of driving is also why other automakers haven't fully eliminated buttons and knobs to make their cars look more like smartphones. Unlike a phone, the ability to operate a car's controls without looking at them can be a matter of life and death. If BlackBerry's physical keyboard offered an advantage for users (an equivalent of the knobs and buttons in our cars that let us turn down the heat or turn up a song while still watching the road), it would almost certainly still be around. Even though eliminating buttons and knobs could save automakers massive amounts of money and give their cars a dash of smartphone cool, for most automakers those advantages aren't worth the risk of an interface that requires drivers to take their eyes off the road.

Besides, even Teslas still don't have the feature that helped smartphones become indispensable: apps. At the reveal of the Model S prototype, Elon Musk told Tesla investor and board member Steve Jurvetson that "we've got people, like, writing apps for the car," but currently there's no sign of a Tesla app store. Without independent developers coming up with unique software applications for Tesla's cars, cars will never have the creative and financial engine that made the smartphone what it is today. Even for Tesla, the risks of opening up vehicle code to third parties is just too high.

Making cars more like smartphones is one of those ideas that sounds appealing in theory, but it keeps running into the same inconvenient reality: cars are not smartphones. Now, most people would probably agree that they don't need or want their car to do the same things their phone does. So if making cars into smartphones doesn't make much sense, why has Tesla been so successful doing just that?

History holds the answer. People today respond to Tesla's smartphone-inspired looks for the same reason that cars in the 1920s borrowed cues from streamliner trains, or cars in the 1950s were slathered with tail fins, fake intakes, and other references to jet aircraft. By aligning the look and feel of its products with the symbology and logic of the high-tech sector, Tesla has associated itself with the transformative change that smartphones have wrought on nearly every aspect of our lives.

The question that these trends always pose is: How far do we let the automotive cosplay take us? Are we so obsessed with the newest technology that we will go beyond cosmetic elements like tail fins and

waste fortunes trying to develop actual jet-powered cars before we con-
cede they are too loud, polluting, and pavement-melting to actually be
a good idea? (Absurd as it sounds, Chrysler spent a quarter century
and $100 million on precisely that, and the Environmental Protection
Agency kicked in an extra $19 million in taxpayer money.)

There's no doubt that the technologies that gave us smartphones
are changing cars and will continue to do so, even creating a diverse
range of new alternatives to cars. But there's also a significant difference between technology for the sake of technology and technology
that is applied to real problems. Is Tesla really solving a problem, or is
the entire company like the giant screen in its cars: a shiny object that's
perfectly designed to tap into the hopes and anxieties of our particular
historical moment and not much else?

The answer depends entirely on your view of Elon Musk who, like
Tesla's screens, inspires profoundly different perspectives. To his fans,
Musk is a rare example of a truly altruistic genius in public life, a hero
at a time when heroes seem less common than ever. To his detractors,
Musk cynically uses environmentalism to sell cars, secure subsidies,
and deflect criticism. If you believe one of these things or the other, the
chances of you changing your mind are not good.

It is possible, however, to fairly objectively assess Tesla's environmental impact. The company claims that its cars have collectively offset
about four million tons of carbon. That figure is on the generous side,
considering that it is based on the assumption that every Tesla vehicle
is always powered by zero carbon power when even the company's own
Superchargers aren't all zero-emission. That's a drop in the bucket, considering that the world emitted some 37 billion tons of carbon in 2018
alone.

But the real problem with Tesla's image as an environmental cause
is the cost of that impact. To hit that four-million-ton carbon reduction,
Tesla has had to raise no less than $19 billion in capital from private and
public markets. That puts the price of its environmental contribution
at $4,750 per ton of carbon, or an order of magnitude higher than the

$417 per ton recently calculated as the "social cost of carbon." It also makes almost every other form of carbon reduction look like a screaming deal, including carbon capture for fossil-fuel power plants (up to $600 per ton), building advanced nuclear plants ($59 per ton), and a home weatherization assistance program ($350 per ton).

In short, if Tesla were a government carbon-reduction program, it would be indefensible on a cost-benefit basis. And unless it eventually generates enough profits to repay that $19 billion plus a reasonable return, the traditional private market justifications don't really work out either. Investing in Tesla might be reasonably seen as a long-shot bet on its autonomous-drive technology proving to be a moneymaker, but even that doesn't fully explain the deep financial and emotional support that Tesla enjoys.

As the evidence propping up Tesla's mythology fades under increasing scrutiny, many of its fans have simply dug in, reinforcing their emotional attachment to the company and its controversial leader. Their love of their car, their faith in the technological progress it represents, their need for a hero to look up to, and the generally low bar set for public figures all protect their deep faith in Tesla and Musk. Since the core of Musk's appeal is his willingness to take on any and all odds, it's not surprising that even the most warranted adversity and criticism only makes his fans love him all the more.

At the same time, as the number of Teslas on the road has grown, the company has increasingly had to contend with customers who aren't true believers but simply want the coolest car out there. As their high expectations and high monthly payments collide with Tesla's poor quality and worse service, they aren't making the excuses or demonstrating the forbearance of Tesla's hard-core early adopter fan base. Tesla's base of support might be solid as a rock, but that base doesn't seem to be growing like it once did.

These customers represent the market force that has shaped the auto industry into what it is today. They may want tail fins or a huge smartphone-like touchscreen when it's cool, but not at the expense of a vehicle that reliably gets them from point A to point B and a customer experience that doesn't require an almost religious faith in the company or its CEO. The aesthetics, performance, and image that Tesla brings to cars are appealing, but the boring reliability and ubiquitous dealerships of the established players are necessary beyond a small, premium niche.

For a certain segment, Tesla has a deep, unwavering appeal. But the company struggles to broaden that appeal to a more pragmatic mass market. At this point, the major looming threat to Tesla as a company is the thing that killed most of the hundreds of defunct car companies: an economic recession. Tesla didn't have a significant manufacturing operation in 2008, and even so it only survived by the skin of its teeth. Another downturn would not only do to Tesla what it does to every car company, cutting demand and turning its operational footprint into a financial anchor, but it would also put immense pressure on those who have been investing in the company's altruistic mission rather than hard financial results.

If Tesla survives the next downturn, it will have passed the fundamental test of an automaker. If it doesn't, it might be bought, where the brand would live on as part of one of the major automakers. The company's future increasingly comes down to its bold bet on "Full Self-Driving" technology, which could theoretically create massive demand for its cars if they deliver on the promise to earn a healthy cashflow for owners (and Tesla) as robotaxis. As ambivalent as ever about the traditionally low-margin business of manufacturing and selling cars, Tesla's ongoing commitment to self-driving technology seems like a last-ditch bid to achieve profits that match its heady valuation.

Having built such a powerful brand, one way that Tesla could survive is by abandoning Musk's original master plan and committing to a small-volume, high-margin luxury strategy. Failing that, it could sell itself or partner with an established player to improve its manufacturing quality and service footprint. Neither of these things would take away from the fact that Tesla has already accomplished its mission of accelerating the adoption of electric vehicles, but both of them would be admissions that Musk's vision and leadership has limits.

The fact that this hasn't happened yet adds to the growing evidence that Tesla exists to serve Musk above all else. Ever since he first complained about being left out of a *New York Times* story back in 2006, his centrality to the company's identity has grown deeper. When the board of directors bowed to his threat to leave the company if they didn't "extol his integrity" in the wake of the SEC charging him with fraud, it seemed that Tesla had reached the point of no return.

Given Musk's increasing unpredictability, it's impossible to say what he will do next. Only one thing is certain: Tesla no longer has a sense of identity independent of Musk, and it will be dragged along on any adventure he finds himself drawn into. Once you select Ludicrous Mode, it seems there is no going back.

ACKNOWLEDGMENTS

This book would not have been possible without the current and former Tesla insiders at all levels of the company, from the boardroom to maintenance, who took personal and professional risks to speak with me about their experiences. I would also like to recognize the friends and colleagues who helped introduce me to these sources. I won't name any of these people here so as to prevent even the chance of retribution, but they know who they are. You have my eternal thanks.

The humbling experience of writing my first book could easily have been far more humbling without the expertise, dedication, and patience of my agent, Jane Dystel, my publisher, Glenn Yeffeth, my editor, Claire Schulz, and the whole team at BenBella books.

This book is the culmination of a career that I wasn't even smart enough to choose for myself, and I would never have made it this far without the people who have helped and guided me along the way. Bertel Schmitt has been my mentor and collaborator for my entire career, and he has always been a deep well of experience, insight, and guidance. My father, Paul Niedermeyer, helped get me into automotive writing in the first place, and his high standards, encyclopedic knowledge of automotive history, and frank feedback have always challenged me to make the most of my potential. Robert Farago gave me my start at *TTAC*, and put immense trust in me early on. Tobin Harshaw gave me my first big break at the *New York Times*, brought me in at Bloomberg View, and has generally done as much for my career as anyone. Finally, my cohosts at the *Autonocast*, Alex Roy and Kirsten Korosec, have always been stalwart sources of wisdom and support, and our conversations are one of the strongest influences on my thinking.

This book builds on the excellent work, performed under relentlessly tough conditions, of the journalists who have covered Tesla with integrity and tenacity. These include, in no particular order: Dana Hull of Bloomberg; Lora Kolodny of CNBC; Kirsten Korosec of *Fortune/TechCrunch*; Mike Ramsey, Tim Higgins, and Charley Grant of the *Wall Street Journal*; Ryan Felton of Jalopnik/*Consumer Reports*; Russ Mitchell and Jerry Hirsch of the *Los Angeles Times*; Jonathan Gitlin, Tim Lee, and Cyrus Farivar of Ars Technica; Amir Efrati of The Information; Peter Campbell of the *Financial Times*; Caroline O'Donovan and Ryan Mac of BuzzFeed; John Voelcker of Green Car Reports; and Drake Baer and Linette Lopez of Business Insider.

Owen Thomas's tenacious and insightful coverage of Tesla and Musk at *Valleywag*, VentureBeat, and elsewhere deserves special recognition. Ashlee Vance's book and reporting at Bloomberg was also an especially helpful resource while working on this project.

A special thanks is due to some of the people whose Twitter accounts made that platform such a dynamic and valuable source of news, analysis, rumors, insight, opinion, and humor: Bozi Tatarevic (@hoonable), John Rosevear (@john_rosevear), Horace Dediu (@asymco), Bonnie Norman (@bonnienorman), Matthew Klippenstein (@ElectronComm), Ken Tindell (@kentindell), Sam Abuelsamid (@samabuelsamid), Paul Huettner (@Paul_M_Huettner), @Smack_Check, @eriz35, @TeslaCharts, @skabooshka, @Ex_Tesla, @temp_worker, and @ElonBachman. I have almost certainly forgotten at least a few great Tesla Twitter accounts, whom I expect will savage my mentions when they note my shameful omission.

Last but far from least, my deepest thanks go to my partner, Andrea. Her patience during the countless weekend and evening hours I spent at the computer, her love and support when things got overwhelming, and her excellent feedback on early drafts were instrumental to the creation of this book.

NOTES

Chapter 1

8   *"You did it!" . . . as Musk beamed down at them from the stage:* https://youtu.be/LBuTElFMOvA

10   *it is being produced at a rate of more than five thousand units per week:* Tom Randall and Dean Halford. "Tesla Model 3 Tracker." Bloomberg, latest update February 14, 2019. https://www.bloomberg .com/graphics/2018-tesla-tracker/

10   *Yet, it's taken about $4.5 billion in fresh capital:* Alexandria Sage. "Tesla raises $1.46 billion in stock sale." Reuters, May 19, 2016. https://www.reuters.com/article/us-tesla-offering/tesla-raises-1-46 -billion-in-stock-sale-ifr-idUSKCN0YB08W; Rishika Sadam. "Tesla raises $1.2 billion, 20 percent more than planned." Reuters, March 17, 2017. https://www.reuters.com/article/us-tesla-offering -idUSKBN16O1NH; Evelyn Chang. "Tesla's first junk bond offering is a hit, but now Elon Musk must deliver." CNBC, August 11, 2017. https://www.cnbc.com/2017/08/11/tesla-debt-offering -raised-to-1-point-8-billion-300-million-more-than-planned-on-high-demand.html

10   *demand for all but the cheapest versions:* Alexandria Sage. "Exclusive: Tesla's delivery team gutted in recent job cuts – sources." Reuters, February 8, 2019. https://www.reuters.com/article /us-tesla-demand/teslas-delivery-team-gutted-in-recent-job-cuts-sources-idUSKCN1PY00J

10   *deliveries were down by more than thirty percent:* Tesla Motors press release. "Tesla Q1 2019 Vehicle Production & Deliveries." April 3, 2019. https://ir.tesla.com/news-releases/news-release-details /tesla-q1-2019-vehicle-production-deliveries

11   *an automaker needed to produce on the order of five million units per year just to survive:* Edward Niedermeyer. "Sergio Marchionne Is Insane." *The Truth About Cars,* May 4, 2009. https://www .thetruthaboutcars.com/2009/05/sergio-marchionne-is-insane/

12   *Eight other states have adopted CARB's ZEV mandate:* "California applauds multi-state coalition's releases new Zero-Emission Vehicle Action Plan." California Air Resources Board, June 20, 2018. https://ww2.arb.ca.gov/index.php/news/california-applauds-multi-state-coalitions-releases-new -zero-emission-vehicle-action-plan

19   *as the company's PR department has claimed:* Charles Duhigg. "Dr. Elon & Mr. Musk: Life Inside Tesla's Production Hell." *Wired,* December 13, 2018. https://www.wired.com/story/elon-musk -tesla-life-inside-gigafactory/

Chapter 2

21   *The post, titled "The Secret Tesla Motors Master Plan (just between you and me)":* https://www.tesla.com/blog/secret-tesla-motors-master-plan-just-between-you-and-me

22   *Eberhard and Tarpenning's initial business plan:* Drake Baer. "Tesla: The Origin Story." Business Insider, November 11, 2014. https://www.businessinsider.com/tesla-the-origin-story-2014-10

24   *which had dropped its lead-acid battery pack for an array of small cylindrical lithium-ion battery cells:* Michael Shnayerson. "Quiet Thunder." *Vanity Fair,* May 2007. https://www.vanityfair.com/news/2007/05/tesla200705

24   *Cocconi's bitter experience with the EV1 program:* Michael Shnayerson. *The Car That Could: The Inside Story of GM's Revolutionary Electric Vehicle* New York: Random House, 1996

25   *According to Elon Musk, electric cars were what had first brought him to Silicon Valley:* Elon Musk. "In the Beginning." *Tesla Motors Blog* (since deleted, accessed via web.archive.org). https://web.archive.org/web/20090624221445/http://www.teslamotors.com/blog2/?p=73

25   *Errol, owned a 50 percent stake in a Zambian emerald mine:* Phillip De Wet. "'We had so much money we couldn't even close our safe': Elon Musk's Dad tells BI about the family's insanely casual attitude to wealth." Business Insider, February 23, 2018. https://www.businessinsider.com/elon-musks-dad-tells-bi-about-the-familys-casual-attitude-to-wealth-2018-2

25   *having sold his first computer game at age twelve:* Ashlee Vance. *Elon Musk: Tesla, SpaceX, and the Quest for a Fantastic Future.* New York: Ecco (HarperCollins), 2015.

26   *"It's a million-dollar car":* Elon Musk best videos. "Young Elon Musk featured in documentary about millionaires (1999)." YouTube video, October 24, 2015. https://youtu.be/eb3pmifEZ44

26   *Musk would say that his first meeting with Straubel "was really what ultimately led to Tesla as it is today":* Darren Bryant. "Elon Musk recounts Tesla's history at 2016 shareholders meeting." YouTube video, January 10, 2017. https://youtu.be/AKfiKvbqbQw

26   *Afterward, Straubel emailed Musk:* Elon Musk. "In the Beginning." *Tesla Motors Blog* (since deleted, accessed via web.archive.org). https://web.archive.org/web/20090624221445/http://www.teslamotors.com/blog2/?p=73

27   *"AC Propulsion shares your view":* Ibid.

29   *The fragile prototypes:* Darren Bryant. "Elon Musk recounts Tesla's history at 2016 shareholders meeting." YouTube video, January 10, 2017. https://youtu.be/AKfiKvbqbQw

30   *he had sent an email (since published at Business Insider) to Tesla's de facto PR man, Mike Harrigan, saying that "the portrayal of my role to date has been incredibly insulting":* Drake Baer. "The Making of Tesla: Invention, Betrayal, and the Birth of the Roadster." Business Insider, November 11, 2014. https://www.businessinsider.com/tesla-the-origin-story-2014-10

Chapter 3

33   *"We had no idea what we were doing," Elon Musk told the crowd:* Darren Bryant. "Elon Musk recounts Tesla's history at 2016 shareholders meeting." YouTube video, January 10, 2017. https://youtu.be/AKfiKvbqbQw

34   *hundreds of automakers had gone bankrupt:* "List of defunct automobile manufacturers of the United States." Wikipedia. https://en.wikipedia.org/wiki/List_of_defunct_automobile_manufacturers_of_the_United_States

35   *"Tesla will build high-performance electric sports cars"*: Drake Baer. "The Making of Tesla: Invention, Betrayal, and the Birth of the Roadster." Business Insider, November 11, 2014. https://www .businessinsider.com/tesla-the-origin-story-2014-10

37   *To Eberhard and Tarpenning, who, in their initial feasibility study*: Ashlee Vance. *Elon Musk: Tesla, SpaceX, and the Quest for a Fantastic Future*. New York: Ecco (HarperCollins), 2015.

37   *Tesla would have to license the Elise's aluminum chassis and then reengineer it*: Martin Eberhard. "Lotus Position." *Tesla Motors Blog*, July 25, 2006. https://www.tesla.com/blog/lotus-position

38   *either out of concern for his wife*: Ashlee Vance. *Elon Musk: Tesla, SpaceX, and the Quest for a Fantastic Future*. New York: Ecco, 2015.

38   *or for taller customers*: Martin Eberhard. "Lotus Position." *Tesla Motors Blog*, July 25, 2006. https:// www.tesla.com/blog/lotus-position

38   *the resulting car shared only 7 percent of its parts*: Darryl Siry. "Mythbusters Part 2: The Tesla Roadster Is Not a Converted Lotus Elise." *Tesla Motors Blog*, March 3, 2008. https://www.tesla.com/blog /mythbusters-part-2-tesla-roadster-not-converted-lotus-elise

39   *according to Drake Baer, he was the only leading figure at Tesla not invited to Eberhard's final design Bake -Off*: Drake Baer. "The Making of Tesla: Invention, Betrayal, and the Birth of the Roadster," Business Insider. November 11, 2014. https://www.businessinsider.com/tesla-the-origin-story-2014-10

39   *He would later take credit*: Elon Musk. "In the Beginning." *Tesla Motors Blog* (since deleted, accessed via web.archive.org). https://web.archive.org/web/20090624221445/http://www.teslamotors .com/blog2/?p=73

Chapter 4

41   *"How to Be Silicon Valley"*: Paul Graham. "How to Be Silicon Valley." PaulGraham.com, May 2006. http://paulgraham.com/siliconvalley.html

43   *As Tarpenning explained in Charles Morris's history of the company*: Charles Morris. *Tesla Motors: How Elon Musk and Company Made Electric Cars Cool and Sparked the Next Tech Revolution*, excerpted in *Charged Electric Vehicles Magazine*, September 7, 2014. https://chargedevs.com/features /new-book-excerpt-the-early-days-of-tesla/

44   *This process started with the development of a digital motor controller*: Darren Bryant. "Elon Musk recounts Tesla's history at 2016 shareholders meeting." YouTube video, January 10, 2017. https:// youtu.be/AKfiKvbqbQw

44   *Eberhard's original plan for Tesla*: Drake Baer. "The Making of Tesla: Invention, Betrayal, and the Birth of the Roadster." Business Insider, November 11, 2014. https://www.businessinsider.com /tesla-the-origin-story-2014-10

44   *Even when the car failed to work properly*: Darren Bryant. "Elon Musk recounts Tesla's history at 2016 shareholders meeting." YouTube video, January 10, 2017. https://youtu.be/AKfiKvbqbQw

45   *By October he was pushing Eberhard*: Drake Baer. "The Making of Tesla: Invention, Betrayal, and the Birth of the Roadster." Business Insider, November 11, 2014. https://www.businessinsider.com /tesla-the-origin-story-2014-10

46   *a presentation to CARB*: Martin Eberhard. "California ARB ZEV Symposium presentation." September 26, 2006. https://www.arb.ca.gov/msprog/zevprog/2006symposium/presentations /eberhard.pdf

46   *fundamental to Tesla's Series D funding pitch:* "Tesla Motors Secures $45 Million Series D Investment
Round Led by Technology Partners and Elon Musk." Tesla Motors press release, May 11, 2007.
http://www.marketwired.com/press-release/tesla-motors-secures-45-million-series-d-investment
-round-led-technology-partners-elon-734724.htm

47   *Eberhard had told Tesla's new investors:* Elon Musk. "In the Beginning." *Tesla Motors Blog* (since
deleted, accessed via web.archive.org). https://web.archive.org/web/20090624221445/http://
www.teslamotors.com/blog2/?p=73

47   *On the day he took over as CEO:* Ibid.

49   *prompting Magna to sue for breach of contract:* Craig Rubens. "Tesla's Other Lawsuit: Transmission
Troubles." GigaOm, April 15, 2008. https://gigaom.com/2008/04/15/teslas-other-lawsuit
-transmission-troubles/#more-1887

49   *Straubel and his team would have to completely redesign the remaining AC Propulsion technology:* Darren
Bryant. "Elon Musk recounts Tesla's history at 2016 shareholders meeting." YouTube video, January
10, 2017. https://youtu.be/AKfiKvbqbQw

49   *Moore's Law came to Tesla's rescue:* Brian McCullough. "Transcript of interview with
co-founder of Tesla, Marc Tarpenning." *Internet History Podcast*, May 15, 2016. http://www
.internethistorypodcast.com/2016/05/co-founder-of-tesla-marc-tarpenning/

49   *33 percent higher:* JB Straubel. "An Engineering Update on Powertrain 1.5." *Tesla Motors Blog*, May
27, 2008. https://www.tesla.com/blog/engineering-update-powertrain-15

50   *Musk's ouster of Eberhard had badly shaken morale:* Martin Eberhard. "Stealth Bloodbath." *Tesla
Founders Blog* (since deleted, accessed via web.archive.org), January 10, 2008. https://web.archive
.org/web/20080115134414/http://teslafounders.wordpress.com/2008/01/10
/stealth-bloodbath/

Chapter 5

56   *technology analyst Horace Dediu points out:* Horace Dediu. "The Entrant's Guide To The Automobile
Industry." Asymco.com, February 23, 2015. http://www.asymco.com/2015/02/23 /the-entrants
-guide-to-the-automobile-industry/

57   *Ohno began combining Deming's ideas:* Takahiro Fujimoto. *The Evolution of a Manufacturing System at
Toyota.* New York: Oxford University Press, 1999.

58   *According to longtime VP of Powertrain Technology Jim Dunlay:* Charles Fine, Loredana Padurean,
and Milo Werner. "The Tesla Roadster (A): Accelerated Supply Chain Learning." *MIT Sloan
Management Review,* 14–157, July 24, 2014. Accessed via Studylib.net.
https://studylib.net/doc/8714121/the-tesla-roadster--a---accelerated-supply-chain-learning

59   *The build quality of a contemporary Lotus Evora:* Dan Neil. "Ecstasy-to-drive Lotus Evora leaves one
question: Take a check?" *Los Angeles Times,* January 22, 2010. https://www.latimes.com/archives
/la-xpm-2010-jan-22-la-fi-neil22-2010jan22-story.html

59   *the emphasis on speed—which would . . . won out:* Mark Donovan and James P. Womack. "The Tesla
Way vs. The Toyota Way." The Lean Post, June 2, 2016. https://www.lean.org/LeanPost/Posting
.cfm?LeanPostId=581

60   *Musk extolling eighty-hour work weeks:* Olivia Rudgard. "Elon Musk: Workers Should Put In 100
Hours a Week to Change the World." The Telegraph, November 27, 2018. https://www.telegraph
.co.uk/technology/2018/11/27/elon-musk-workers-should-put-80-hours-week-change-world/

60   *workers reporting twelve- to sixteen-hour shifts:* Tom Randall, Josh Eidelson, Dana Hull, and John Lippert. "Hell for Elon Musk Is a Midsize Sedan." Bloomberg Businessweek, July 12, 2018. https://www.bloomberg.com/news/features/2018-07-12/how-tesla-s-model-3-became-elon-musk -s-version-of-hell

60   *employees sleeping in the factory:* Caroline O'Donovan. "At Tesla's Factory, Building the Car of the Future Has Painful and Permanent Consequences for Some Workers." BuzzFeed News, February 4, 2018. https://www.buzzfeednews.com/article/carolineodonovan/tesla-fremont-factory-injuries

60   *exhaustion- and Red Bull-fueled "Tesla stare":* Tom Randall, Josh Eidelson, Dana Hull, and John Lippert. "Hell for Elon Musk Is a Midsize Sedan." Bloomberg Businessweek, July 12, 2018. https://www.bloomberg.com/news/features/2018-07-12/how-tesla-s-model-3-became-elon-musk -s-version-of-hell

60   *Luxury and premium car brands like Ferrari and Land Rover:* "2018 What Car? Reliability Survey." What Car? November 30, 2018. https://www.whatcar.com/news/2018-what-car-reliability-survey /n17826

61   *the actor gave a less than glowing review:* Tom Junod. "George Clooney's Rules for Living." *Esquire,* November 11, 2013. https://www.esquire.com/news-politics/a25952/george-clooney-interview -1213/

61   *Musk struck back, sardonically tweeting:* Elon Musk. Twitter, November 12, 2013. https://twitter .com/elonmusk/status/400411503742164992

62   *would continue to trade off with the principles of successful manufacturing culture throughout the company's history:* Jeffrey Liker. "Tesla vs. TPS: Seeking the Soul in the New Machine." *Industry Week,* March 7, 2018. https://www.industryweek.com/operations/tesla-vs-tps-seeking-soul-new -machine

Chapter 6

64   *We need to get the company to cash flow–positive:* Chris Paine. *Revenge of the Electric Car,* 2011.

65   *leading to the departure of Tesla's VP of marketing:* Owen Thomas. "Tesla's Motormouth Marketer Dodged Deposit Dilemma." *Valleywag,* February 26, 2009. https://gawker.com/5160624%2Fteslas -motormouth-marketer-dodged-deposit-dilemma

65   *Tesla had just $9 million in its bank accounts:* Nichola Groom, Kevin Krolicki. "Tesla sees new financing, founder offers support." Reuters, October 30, 2009. https://www.reuters.com/article /autos-tesla/tesla-sees-new-financing-founder-offers-support-idUSN3130815920081031

66   *Musk told the* New York Times: Claire Cain Miller. "Musk Unplugged: Tesla C.E.O. Discusses Car Troubles." *New York Times,* October 24, 2008. https://bits.blogs.nytimes.com/2008/10/24 /musk-unplugged-tesla-ceo-discusses-car-troubles/

66   *when it put out a press release:* Tesla Motors press release. "Tesla Motors Receives $40 Million Financing Commitment." November 3, 2008 http://ir.tesla.com/static-files/633611b0-e8d8-44da -83de-ebfd860ca7ea

66   *and Reuters reported that the funding was "secured":* Kevin Krolicki. "Tesla secures $40 million in convertible financing." Reuters, November 3, 2008. https://www.reuters.com/article/tesla-funding /tesla-secures-40-million-in-convertible-financing-idUSN0331410320081103

66   *repeating the Christmas Eve story:* "Tesla and SpaceX—Elon Musk's industrial empire." *60 Minutes,* original air date March 30, 2014. YouTube video. https://youtu.be/52x0ukhE2Vo; Sebastian

Blanco. "Full text of Elon Musk's Paris COP21 speech." Autoblog.com. December 5, 2015. https://www.autoblog.com/2015/12/05/full-text-of-elon-musks-paris-cop21-speech/

67   *Eberhard had testified:* "Testimony of Martin Eberhard CEO and Cofounder of Tesla Motors Inc." Finance Committee of the United States Senate, May, 1, 2007. https://www.finance.senate.gov/imo /media/doc/050107testme.pdf

67   *Tesla had obtained a contract to supply battery packs:* Sam Abuelsamid. "Tesla offers up more details on TH!NK battery deal." *Autoblog,* May 23rd, 2007. https://www.autoblog.com/2007/05/23 /tesla-offers-up-more-details-on-th-nk-battery-deal/

67   *establish a new division for this business called "Tesla Energy Group":* Martin Eberhard. "Introducing Tesla Energy Group." *Tesla Motors Blog,* May 22, 2007. https://web.archive.org/web/20090814225 814/http://www.teslamotors.com/blog2/?p=50

68   *A third version, published in* Wired *in 2010:* Joshua Davis. "How Elon Musk Turned Tesla into the Car Company of the Future." *Wired,* September 27, 2010. https://www.wired.com/2010/09 /ff-tesla/

68   *Musk would later call Daimler's investment:* Darren Bryant. "Elon Musk recounts Tesla's history at 2016 shareholders meeting." YouTube video, January 10, 2017. https://youtu.be/AKfiKvbqbQw

69   *In one of the first emails to customers:* Jason Calacanis. "Tesla Customer update . . ." Calacanis.com, January 17, 2009. https://calacanis.com/2009/01/17/tesla-customer-update/

69   *predictably fueled confusion and suspicion:* Tesla Motors Club. "Tesla Increases Prices for Existing 2008 Orders." Teslamotorsclub.com, January 15, 2009. https://teslamotorsclub.com/tmc/threads /tesla-increases-prices-for-existing-2008-orders.2199/

69   *Musk wrote another email:* Tom Saxton. "Elon Musk Explains the Roadster Price Increase." Saxton .org, January 22, 2009. https://saxton.org/tom_saxton/2009/01/price-increase-explanation.html

70   *or pony up $6,700 to $9,350 more:* Tom Saxton. "The New Tesla Prices." Saxton.org, January 17, 2009. https://saxton.org/tom_saxton/2009/01/new-tesla-prices.html

71   *In a February 11, 2009, email to customers:* Matt Hardigree. "Tesla Model S Coming March 26, But Where's the DOE Funding?" Jalopnik, February 11, 2009. https://jalopnik.com/tesla-model-s -coming-march-26-but-wheres-the-doe-fundi-5151712

71   *the DOE did announce that Tesla was among the companies:* "Obama Administration Awards First Three Auto Loans for Advanced Technologies to Ford Motor Company, Nissan Motors and Tesla Motors." US Department of Energy, June 23, 2009. https://www.energy.gov/articles /obama-administration-awards-first-three-auto-loans-advanced-technologies-ford-motor-company

71   *wouldn't be signed for nearly another year:* "Secretary Chu Announces Closing of $465 Million Loan to Tesla Motors." US Department of Energy, January 21, 2010. https://www.energy.gov/articles /secretary-chu-announces-closing-465-million-loan-tesla-motors

71   *the Department of Energy confirmed:* Dan Strumpf. "Tesla expects to get $350M in government funds." *San Mateo Daily Journal,* February 12, 2009. https://www.smdailyjournal.com/news/local /tesla-expects-to-get-m-in-government-funds/article_4cf14333-1e53-5351-a1bb-8f47ffff4b08 .html

72   *posted the email to its blog:* Elon Musk. "Tesla Motors Update." *Tesla Motors Blog,* via web.archive.org. https://web.archive.org/web/20090215045336/http://www.teslamotors.com/blog2/?p=70

72   *in August 2009, Tesla proudly announced:* Chuck Squatriglia. "Tesla Finally Turns a Profit." *Wired,* August 7, 2009. https://www.wired.com/2009/08/tesla-profit/

72 *in the company's official press release:* "Tesla Motors Attains Profitability Milestone." Business Wire, August 7, 2009. https://www.businesswire.com/news/home/20090807005516/en /Tesla-Motors-Attains-Profitability-Milestone

72 *the company filed paperwork to go public:* Tesla Motors. "Form S1 Registration Statement." US Securities and Trade Commission, January 29, 2010. https://www.sec.gov/Archives/edgar /data/1318605/000119312510017054/ds1.htm

72 *in fact:* Tesla Motors. "IPO Prospectus." US Securities and Trade Commission, June 28, 2010. https://www.sec.gov/Archives/edgar/data/1318605/000119312510149105/d424b4.htm

72 *telling Bloomberg that Tesla:* Ronald Frover. "To the Moon: Elon Musk's High-Powered Visions." *Bloomberg Businessweek,* September 11, 2009. www.bloomberg.com/news/articles/2009-09-11 /to-the-moon-elon-musks-high-powered-visionsbusinessweek-business-news-stock-market-and -financial-advice

73 *Darryl Siry reported in* Wired: "Tesla Subsidy Vanishing Amid Electric Car Boom." *Wired,* August 2, 2010. https://www.wired.com/2010/08/tesla-subsidy-vanishing-amid-electric-vehicle-boom/

73 *according to Vance:* Ashlee Vance. *Elon Musk: Tesla, SpaceX, and the Quest for a Fantastic Future.* New York: Ecco (HarperCollins), 2015.

73 *Musk drove a sleek, fastback silver-gray sedan:* dougdirac. "Tesla Model S unveiling party – Part1." YouTube video, March 29, 2009. https://youtu.be/OFugGJZcFoE

74 *During a test ride in the prototype that evening:* dougdirac. "Ride in the Tesla Model S sedan." YouTube video, March 27, 2009. https://youtu.be/6-GSWzsTtts

74 *Musk emphasized the car's affordability:* Tesla Motors. "Tesla unveils world's first mass-produced, highway-capable EV." *Tesla Motors Blog,* April 20, 2010. https://www.tesla.com/blog /tesla-unveils-world%E2%80%99s-first-mass-produced-highway-capable-ev

75 *leading to tentative headlines like:* John Voelcker. "The Tesla Model S Won't Be Real Unless Elon Musk Has a Few Hundred Million to Spare." Green Car Reports, March 26, 2009. https://www .greencarreports.com/news/1019686_the-tesla-model-s-wont-be-real-unless-elon-musk-has-a-few- hundred-million-to-spare

75 *by using borrowed control stalks:* Bozi Tatarevic. "The Parts the Tesla Model S Shares With Other Cars." *Road & Track,* February 6, 2018. https://www.roadandtrack.com/car-culture/a16570798 /tesla-model-s-parts-other-cars-have/

76 *the mayor of Downey told the media:* Michael Graham Richard. "Mayor of Downey, CA: Deal with Tesla for Model S Factory '99.9% done.'" Treehugger, November 25, 2009. https://www.treehugger .com/corporate-responsibility/mayor-of-downey-ca-deal-with-tesla-for-model-s-factory-999-done .html

76 *was deeply worried that "big company disease" was eroding the automaker's competitive edge:* Alex Taylor III. "Toyota's new man at the wheel." *Fortune,* June 26, 2009. http://archive.fortune .com/2009/06/23/autos/akio_toyoda_toyota_new_president.fortune/index.htm

76 *in May of 2010:* Poornima Gupta and Chang-Ran Kim. "Toyota gets Tesla stake, Tesla gets Toyota factory." Reuters, May 20, 2010. https://www.reuters.com/article/us-tesla-toyota /toyota-gets-tesla-stake-tesla-gets-toyota-factory-idUSTRE64J70O20100521

77 *Panasonic invested $30 million in Tesla:* "Panasonic Invests $30M in Tesla." New Statesman America, November 5, 2010. https://www.newstatesman.com/energy-and-clean-tech/2010/11 /panasonic-battery-tesla

77   *the two firms began to partner on the next generation of EV batteries:* Poornima Gupta. "Tesla, Panasonic partner on electric car batteries." Reuters, January 7, 2010. https://www.reuters.com /article/tesla-panasonic/tesla-panasonic-partner-on-electric-car-batteries-idUSN0721766720100 107

77   *culminating in a 2014 commitment to build a massive joint plant:* Tesla Motors Press Release. "Panasonic and Tesla Sign Agreement for the Gigafactory." July 31, 2014. https://ir.teslamotors .com/news-releases/news-release-details/panasonic-and-tesla-sign-agreement-gigafactory

78   *Musk would repeatedly blame Eberhard.* "In the Beginning." *Tesla Motors Blog* (since deleted, accessed via web.archive.org). https://web.archive.org/web/20090624221445/http://www.teslamotors .com/blog2/?p=73; Claire Cain Miller, "Musk Unplugged: Tesla C.E.O. Discusses Car Troubles." *New York Times,* October 24, 2008. https://bits.blogs.nytimes.com/2008/10/24/musk-unplugged -tesla-ceo-discusses-car-troubles/

79   *Musk told a conference:* Eliot Van Buskirk. "Tesla Motors' Musk: Let Me Run Detroit." *Wired,* June 15, 2009. https://www.wired.com/2009/06/elon-musk-on-the-inevitability-of-the-ev-running -detroit-and-firing-a-certain-someone/

Chapter 7

80   *Musk fired back at the entire financial establishment:* sunnydays020388. "Elon Musk Disses Jim Cramer Live on CNBC." Youtube video, June 29, 2010. https://youtu.be/OJ40QRTC0RA

81   *the high-tech investors that Tesla had targeted:* Ben Wojdyla. "Inside the Secret $178 Million Tesla IPO Presentation." Jalopnik, June 22, 2010. https://jalopnik.com/inside-the-secret-178-million -tesla-ipo-presentation-5569882

81   *By presenting Tesla as a "frickin' technology velociraptor":* Lindsay Riddell. "Beware the Tesla velociraptor." *San Francisco Business Times,* June 23, 2010. https://www.bizjournals.com /sanfrancisco/blog/2010/06/beware_the_tesla_velociraptor.html

81   *Revenue from the Roadster:* Tesla Motors. "Form 10-K." US Securities and Exchange Commission, February 28, 2011. https://www.sec.gov/Archives/edgar/data/1318605/000119312511054847 /d10k.htm

82   *the loan agreement included a number of conditions:* "Loan Arrangement and Reimbursement Agreement between Tesla Motors, Inc and United States Department of Energy." US Securities and Exchange Commission, January 20, 2010. https://www.sec.gov/Archives/edgar/ data/1318605/000119312510129878/dex1037.htm; "First Amendment to Loan Arrangement and Reimbursement Agreement." US Securities and Exchange Commission, June 15, 2011. https://www.sec.gov/Archives/edgar/data/1318605/000119312512081990/d279413dex1037a .htm; "Limited Waiver to the Loan Arrangement and Reimbursement Agreement." US Securities and Exchange Commission, February 22, 2012. https://www.sec.gov/Archives/edgar /data/1318605/000119312512081990/d279413dex1037b.htm; "Second Amendment to the Loan Arrangement and Reimbursement Agreement." US Securities and Exchange Commission, June 20, 2012. https://www.sec.gov/Archives/edgar/data/1318605/000119312512332138 /d364775dex102.htm; "Second Limited Waiver to the Loan Arrangement and Reimbursement Agreement." US Securities and Exchange Commission, September 24, 2012. https://www.sec.gov /Archives/edgar/data/1318605/000119312512402293/d413621dex101.htm; "Third Amendment to the Loan Arrangement and Reimbursement Agreement." US Securities and

Exchange Commission, December 20, 2012. https://www.sec.gov/Archives/edgar
/data/1318605/000119312513096241/d452995dex1037d.htm; "Fourth Amendment to the Loan
Arrangement and Reimbursement Agreement." US Securities and Exchange Commission, March 1,
2013. https://www.sec.gov/Archives/edgar/data/1318605/000119312513096241
/d452995dex1037f.htm

83   *officially delivered the first customer Model S:* Tesla Model S "Customer Delivery Event." YouTube
video, July 31, 2012. https://youtu.be/SLio4A13Ric

83   *reservations were not converting into sales as fast as Tesla needed them to:* Ashlee Vance. *Elon Musk:
Tesla, SpaceX, and the Quest for a Fantastic Future.* Ecco, 2015.

83   *the company's annual automotive sales revenue:* Tesla "Form 10-K." US Securities and Exchange
Commission, January 31, 2013. https://www.sec.gov/Archives/edgar/data/1318605/0001193125
13096241/d452995d10k.htm

84   *Tesla hiked the prices by $2,500:* George Blankenship. "2013 Model S Price Increase." *Tesla Motors
Blog,* November 29, 2012. https://www.tesla.com/blog/2013-model-s-price-increase

84   *Tesla told reservation holders:* Jay Cole. "Tesla 60 kWh Model S Deliveries Delayed to
January-February, Entry Level Until March-April." InsideEVs, December 4, 2012. https://insideevs.
com/tesla-60-kwh-model-s-deliveries-delayed-january-february-entry-level-until-march-april/

84   *In quarterly calls with Wall Street analysts:* "Q3 2012 Tesla Motors Inc Earnings Conference Call" via
Bamsec (paid service). https://www.bamsec.com/transcripts/4928460; "Q4 2012 Tesla Motors
Inc Earnings Conference Call" via Bamsec (paid service). https://www.bamsec.com
/transcripts/5010443

84   *poor body panel fit:* Tesla Motors Club. "Body Panel Gap and Alignment Issues." Teslamotorsclub
.com, December 29, 2012. https://teslamotorsclub.com/tmc/threads/body-panel-gap-and
-alignment-issues.12255/

84   *creaks and rattles:* Tesla Motors Club. "Model S Squeaks, Creaks, and Rattles." Teslamotorsclub.com,
November 26, 2012. https://teslamotorsclub.com/tmc/threads/model-s-squeaks-creaks-and
-rattles.12221/

84   *missing software features:* Tesla Motors Club. "Tesla Needs an Army of Developers!"
Teslamotorsclub.com, December 12, 2012. https://teslamotorsclub.com/tmc/threads/tesla-needs
-an-army-of-developers.11829/

85   *Earlier in the year, Musk had said:* John Voelcker. "Tesla Motors Won't Need More Money, Says CEO
Musk." Green Car Reports, February 15, 2012. https://www.greencarreports.com/news/1073019
_tesla-motors-wont-need-more-money-says-ceo-musk

85   *Musk published a blog post:* Elon Musk. "An Update From Elon Musk" *Tesla Motors Blog,* October 3,
2012. https://www.tesla.com/blog/update-elon-musk

85   *contacting reservation holders and asking them to take delivery as soon as possible:* Jay Cole. "Tesla
Works the System To Give $7,500 Federal Credit Christmas Present to Future Model S Owners
. . . And Maybe Themselves." InsideEVs, December 17, 2012. https://insideevs.com/tesla-works-the
-system-to-give-7500-federal-credit-christmas-present-to-model-s-owners-and-maybe-themselves/

85   *the fact that the IRS clearly states:* Internal Revenue Service. About Form 8936, Qualified Plug-in
Electric Drive Motor Vehicle Credit. https://www.irs.gov/forms-pubs/about-form-8936

87   *Tesla sent an email to reservation holders in March:* Alex Davies. "Tesla Asked Buyers to Pay for
Cars Early to Make It Profitable for the Quarter." Business Insider, April 3, 2013. https://www
.businessinsider.com/tesla-urged-buyers-to-pay-for-cars-early-make-it-profitable-2013-4

87   *Musk claimed to not have been aware of this "overzealous" effort:* Alex Davies. "Elon Musk: Asking Buyers to Pay for Cars Early to Make Tesla Profitable Was 'Overzealous.'" Business Insider, April 5, 2013. https://www.businessinsider.com/elon-musk-email-to-buyers-was-overzealous-2013-4

87   *On the Q1 call:* "Q1 2013 Tesla Motors Inc Earnings Conference Call" via Bamsec (paid service). https://www.bamsec.com/transcripts/5067540

87   *completely changed its reservation system:* Tesla. "Form 10-Q." US Securities and Exchange Commission, April 30, 2013. https://www.sec.gov/Archives/edgar/data/1318605/000119312513 212354/d511008d10q.htm

87   *contemporary forum posts:* Tesla Motors Club. "Cancelled My Reservation – Refund Timeline is Rediculous." Teslamotorsclub.com, March 7, 2013. https://teslamotorsclub.com/tmc/threads /cancelled-my-reservation-refund-timeline-is-rediculous.14587/

88   *Musk told Tesla's PR staff:* Ashlee Vance. *Elon Musk: Tesla, SpaceX, and the Quest for a Fantastic Future.* New York: Ecco (HarperCollins), 2015.

88   *an asterisk-laden lease plan:* Adi Robertson. "New Tesla sales plan offers the Model S for $500 a month, but only after some extremely creative math (update)."The Verge, April 2, 2013. https://www.theverge.com/2013/4/2/4175196/new-tesla-sales-plan-knocks-down-model-s-price -with-creative-math

88   *the goal of making its Superchargers "zombie apocalypse-proof":* Todd Woody. "Elon Musk: Buy a Tesla electric car and you'll survive the zombie apocalypse." Quartz, May 30, 2013. https://qz.com/8951 9/elon-musk-buy-a-tesla-electric-car-and-youll-survive-the-zombie-apocalypse/

88   *battery-swap system that would automatically recharge:* Lance Whitney. "Tesla demos electric battery swap in just 90 seconds." CNET, June 21, 2013. https://www.cnet.com/news/tesla-demos-electric -battery-swap-in-just-90-seconds/

88   *an "Autopilot" system that would be able to drive itself:* Richard Waters and Henry Foy. "Tesla moves ahead of Google in race to build self-driving cars." *Financial Times,* September 17, 2013. https://www.ft.com/content/70d26288-1faf-11e3-8861-00144feab7de

88   *prompting a statement from the regulator warning it not to overstate its ratings:* Sean Hollister. "NHTSA tells Tesla there's no such thing as a 5.4-star crash rating." The Verge, November 23, 2013. https://www.theverge.com/2013/11/23/5135258/nhtsa-tesla-star-safety-advertising-guidelines

89   Chart: *Tesla's stock price and trading volume from IPO through 2014:* "Tesla Inc." Morningstar. https://www.morningstar.com/stocks/xnas/tsla/quote.html

89   Chart: *Tesla's monthly operating profit and loss from 2010 through 2014:* Tesla Motors. DOE Compliance Certificates delivered pursuant to Loan Arrangement and Reimbursement Agreement of January 2010; financial statements April 16, 2010, through May 15, 2013. Obtained by FOIA request; Tesla Motors. "Tesla Motors, Inc. – First Quarter 2012 Shareholder Letter." Tesla.com, May 9, 2012. https://ir.tesla.com/static-files/417d6054-dcf5-405c-84eb-cb90036cbacc; Tesla Motors. "Tesla Motors, Inc. – Second Quarter 2012 Shareholder Letter." Tesla.com, July 25, 2012. https://ir.tesla.com/static-files/f262168e-0398-49fa-8f33-48f60ed70422; Tesla Motors. "Tesla Motors, Inc. – Third Quarter 2012 Shareholder Letter." Tesla.com, November 5, 2012. https:// ir.tesla.com/static-files/3ca8964c-c4e2-4274-b792-241436083431; Tesla Motors. "Tesla Motors, Inc. – Fourth Quarter & Full Year 2012 Shareholder Letter." Tesla.com, February 20, 2013. https:// ir.tesla.com/static-files/6c8b6893-0564-4ffe-a2ac-30049f5bb248; Tesla Motors. "Tesla Motors, Inc. – First Quarter 2013 Shareholder Letter." Tesla.com, May 8, 2013. https://ir.tesla.com /static-files/26b677b6-a22c-4222-a3c6-4bb516bfdac8; Tesla Motors. "Tesla Motors, Inc. – Second

Quarter 2013 Shareholder Letter." Tesla.com. August 7, 2013. https://ir.tesla.com/index.php
/static-files/8a80aee7-ca20-4ff2-9d5b-e25aae776331; Tesla. "Tesla Motors, Inc. – Third Quarter
2013 Shareholder Letter." Tesla.com. November 5, 2013. https://ir.tesla.com/index.php/static
-files/6496fc94-630f-41c7-96c6-94d4cafe4e86; Tesla. "Tesla Motors, Inc. – Fourth Quarter & Full
Year 2013 Shareholder Letter." Tesla.com, February 19, 2014. https://ir.tesla.com/index.php/static
-files/dcbd65a8-c7aa-4538-8a81-49b1b1971a14. Tesla Motors. "Tesla Motors, Inc. – First Quarter
2014 Shareholder Letter." Tesla.com, May 7, 2014. https://ir.tesla.com/static-files/a6276682-8422
-4150-bb10-c9d701220537; Tesla Motors. "Tesla Motors, Inc. – Second Quarter 2014 Shareholder
Letter." Tesla.com, July 31, 2014. https://ir.tesla.com/static-files/b818e6ca-a8ba-4189-8b5d
-a64b90307917; Tesla Motors. "Tesla Motors, Inc. – Third Quarter 2014 Shareholder Letter." Tesla
.com, November 5, 2014. https://ir.tesla.com/static-files/53e161cf-e04f-495c-9fa5-60dcd79231fd;
Tesla Motors. "Tesla Motors, Inc. – Fourth Quarter & Full Year 2014 Shareholder Letter." Tesla
.com, February 11, 2015. https://ir.tesla.com/static-files/be63b49e-c7ff-4c02-a5ea-2545f60e5b79

90   *Musk's share of Tesla had already exceeded a billion dollars:* "How Elon Musk Became a Billionaire
Twice Over." *Forbes,* March 12, 2012. https://www.forbes.com/sites/calebmelby/2012/03/12
/how-elon-musk-became-a-billionaire-twice-over/

90   *he was named* Fortune's *businessman of the year:* Marylin Adamo and Colleen Leahey. "2013's Top
People in Business." *Fortune,* November 21, 2013. http://fortune.com/2013/11/21/2013s-top
-people-in-business/

90   *the upside could have exceeded a billion dollars:* Scott Woolley. "Tesla Is Worse Than Solyndra." *Slate,*
May 29, 2013. https://slate.com/business/2013/05/tesla-is-worse-than-solyndra-how-the-u-s
-government-bungled-its-investment-in-the-car-company-and-cost-taxpayers-at-least-1-billion.html

90   *In an end-of-quarter announcement:* Tesla. "Tesla Mode S Sales Exceed Target." US Securities and
Exchange Commission, March 31, 2013. https://www.sec.gov/Archives/edgar
/data/1318605/000119312513135229/d514482dex991.htm

Chapter 8

93   *even a drive-in restaurant:* Fred Lambert. "Elon Musk talks about building retro drive-in restaurant at
Tesla Supercharger with in-car digital menu." Electrek, January 7, 2018. https://electrek.co/2018
/01/07/elon-musk-tesla-retro-drive-in-restaurant-supercharger/

93   *a music streaming service:* Fred Lambert. "A first look at Tesla's own music streaming service in the
works." Electrek, August 31, 2017. https://electrek.co/2017/08/31/tesla-music-streaming-service/

95   *an object lesson in the dangers of such hyperbull online echo chambers:* Joshua Kennon. "Case Study:
Read a Group of Stockholders Realize in Real Time They've Lost Their Entire Life Savings When
GT Advanced Technologies Declares Bankruptcy." joshuakennon.com, October 19, 2014.
https://www.joshuakennon.com/gt-advanced-technologies-bankruptcy/

95   *a thread on GTAT quickly developed a consensus:* The Contrarian Investor Forum. "GT Advanced
Technologies Inc. (GTAT)" forum. thecontrarianinvestor.com, via web.archive.org, March 4, 2014.
https://web.archive.org/web/20180325034632/http://forum.thecontrarianinvestor.com/index
.php?threads/gt-advanced-technologies-inc-gtat.69/

98   *Electrek's distinct editorial focus on promoting Tesla and defending it from criticism:* Edward
Niedermeyer. "The Truth Behind Electrek's Shady Alliance with Tesla." The Drive, June 29, 2018.
http://www.thedrive.com/tech/21838/the-truth-behind-electreks-dark-alliance-with-tesla

98   *promoted Tesla stock via StockTwits:* Jon Jivan's StockTwits profile. https://stocktwits.com/jonjiv

98   *written about Tesla's potential as an investment*: Fred Lambert's Motley Fool profile. https://boards
.fool.com/profile/FredericLambert/activity.aspx

98   *in 2015, he was sued*: Michael Balaban. "Saleen Is Suing a Guy On Reddit for Calling Them a Scam."
Jalopnik, July 22, 2015. https://jalopnik.com/saleen-is-suing-a-guy-on-reddit-for-calling-them-a
-scam-1719508130

99   *Lambert eventually settled*: Patrick George. "Saleen Settles Lawsuit With Redditor Who Called Them
a Scam." Jalopnik, July 29, 2015. https://jalopnik.com/saleen-settles-case-with-reddit-user-they
-sued-for-call-1720904330

99   *but not before soliciting financial support*: Zach Shahan. "Help FredTesla." Gas2, July 22, 2015. http://
gas2.org/2015/07/22/help-fredtesla/

99   *Lambert wrote an Electrek piece defending the company*: Fred Lambert. "AutoNation CEO goes after
Tesla, compares company to a 'Ponzi scheme' and lies about cost." Electrek, April 11, 2017. https://
electrek.co/2017/04/11/tesla-autonation-ceo-ponzi-scheme/

100   *reported that Tesla's Investor Relations team was recommending that investors get their news*: Charley
Grant. "Investors who have met with IR in private told me they said to go to Reddit and Electrek for
news instead of the mainstream media." Twitter, March 27, 2018. https://twitter.com/CGrantWSJ
/status/978730569109594112

101   *according to the California New Car Dealers Association*: Katie Burke. "Tesla referral programs draw
new round of complaints from Calif. dealers." *Automotive News*, September 8, 2017. https://www
.autonews.com/article/20170908/OEM/170909790/tesla-referral-programs-draw-new-round-of
-complaints-from-calif-dealers

101   *criticism from other automotive media outlets*: Katie Burke. "Electrek faces criticism for giving readers
Tesla discount codes." *Automotive News*, October 4, 2017. https://www.autonews.com/article
/20171004/MOBILITY/171009878/electrek-faces-criticism-for-giving-readers-tesla-
discount-codes

101   *Tesla did attempt to limit full-time referral shilling*: Gene. "Tesla Referral Program crackdown: Musk to
'shut down' referral code abuse." Teslarati, May 24, 2017. https://www.teslarati.com/musk
-shutdown-tesla-referral-program-misuse/

107   *Musk taunted him by posting an image of Miley Cyrus*: Mike Brown. "Elon Musk Responds to
Controversy Over Tesla Critic 'Montana Skeptic.'" Inverse, July 26, 2018. https://www.inverse
.com/article/47461-elon-musk-responds-to-controversy-over-tesla-critic-montana-skeptic

Chapter 9

109   *"If you travel less than 350 miles per week"*: Elon Musk. "The Secret Tesla Motors Master Plan (just
between you and me)." *Tesla Motors Blog*. August 2, 2006. https://www.tesla.com/blog/secret-tesla
-motors-master-plan-just-between-you-and-me

110   *It was June of 2013, and Musk was sharing the stage with a giant obelisk*: Tesla. "Tesla Motors
Supercharger Event." YouTube video, September 25, 2012. https://youtu.be/wgk5-eB9oTY

110   *In a company press release, Musk called the Supercharger network "a game changer for electric vehicles"*:
Tesla. "Tesla Motors Launches Revolutionary Supercharger Enabling Convenient Long Distance
Driving." Tesla.com, September 24, 2012. http://ir.tesla.com/news-releases/news-release-details
/tesla-motors-launches-revolutionary-supercharger-enabling

112   *not a single station had solar panels until 2015, when one was opened in Rocklin, CA:* George Parrott. "UPDATE: Tesla's First Solar-Powered Supercharger-Store-Service Center Now Open." Green Car Reports, March 2, 2015. https://www.greencarreports.com/news/1096926_teslas-first-solar -powered-supercharger-store-service-center-is-almost-ready

112   *This hadn't stopped Musk from grabbing headlines in 2013:* Kevin Bullis. "Tesla Is Prepared for the Zombie Apocalypse." *MIT Technology Review,* May 30, 2013. https://www.technologyreview .com/s/515561/tesla-is-prepared-for-the-zombie-apocalypse/

112   *Only "a half-dozen or so" of the firm's eight hundred charging stations:* Fred Lambert. "Tesla plans to disconnect 'almost all' Superchargers from the grid and go solar+battery, says Elon Musk." Electrek, June 19, 2017. https://electrek.co/2017/06/09/tesla-superchargers-solar-battery-grid-elon-musk/

113   *When he was told on Twitter that a coal plant:* Ibid.

114   *when it held yet another event in Hawthorne to unveil a battery-swapping system:* Tesla. "Battery Swap Event." Tesla.com, June 21, 2013. https://www.tesla.com/videos/battery-swap-event

115   *a company blog post announced that the first Tesla swap station:* The Tesla Team. "Battery Swap Pilot Program." Tesla.com, December 19, 2014. https://www.tesla.com/blog/battery-swap-pilot -program

115   *By Memorial Day weekend, there was only one report:* Edward Niedermeyer. "Tesla Battery Swap Unused Over Busy Holiday Weekend." *Daily Kanban,* May 27, 2015. https://dailykanban.com /2015/05/tesla-battery-swap-unused-over-busy-holiday-weekend/

116   *suddenly forum reports flooded in of Tesla owners receiving invitations:* Tesla Motors Club. "Tesla Battery Swap Program Invite – Pros and Cons?" Teslamotorsclub.com, April 18, 2015. https://teslamotorsclub.com/tmc/threadstesla-battery-swap-program-invite-pros-and-cons.46083/

116   *At the 2015 Tesla shareholder meeting in mid-June:* Bob Sorokanich. "Musk: Tesla ", unlikely," to pursue battery swapping stations." *Road and Track,* June 10, 2015. https://www.roadandtrack.com /new-cars/car-technology/news/a25872/elon-musk-tesla-battery-swap/

117   *In 2013, California revised its Zero Emissions Vehicle credit system:* Edward Niedermeyer. "Tesla Battery Swap: CARB's Bridge to Nowhere." *Daily Kanban,* June 23, 2015. https://dailykanban .com/2015/06/tesla-battery-swap-carbs-bridge-to-nowhere/

117   *By demonstrating battery swap on just one vehicle:* Ibid.

118   *As it turned out, the California Air Resources Board staff:* Edward Niedermeyer. "Tesla Battery Swap: CARB's Bridge to Nowhere." *Daily Kanban,* June 23, 2015. https://dailykanban.com/2015/06 /tesla-battery-swap-carbs-bridge-to-nowhere/

118   *the company earned some $217 million from ZEV credits in 2014:* John Lippert.."Will Tesla Ever Make Money?" *Bloomberg Markets Magazine,* March 3, 2015. https://www.bloomberg.com/news /articles/2015-03-04/as-tesla-gears-up-for-suv-investors-ask-where-the-profits-are

118   *Tesla's pivotal Q1 2013 (non-GAAP) profit of $11 million:* James R. Healey and Fred Meier. "Tesla earns first profit—$11 million in Q1." *USA Today,* May 8, 2013. https://www.usatoday.com/story /money/cars/2013/05/08/tesla-first-profit/2145065/

118   *Tesla's only other quarterly profit, which brought in $22 million during the third quarter of 2016, was similarly made possible by $139 million in ZEV credit revenue:* Tesla. "Tesla Third Quarter 2016 Update." Tesla.com. http://ir.tesla.com/static-files/cf3629e2-4ecd-4299-a550-2d2d2d125acb

118   *By exploiting CARB's fast-refueling rules, Tesla appears to have earned as much as $100 million in additional revenue:* Tesla Motors Club. "Blogger Claims Tesla's Battery Swap a Scam."

Teslamotorsclub.com, June 2, 2015. https://teslamotorsclub.com/tmc/threads
/blogger-claims-teslas-battery-swap-a-scam.48158/page-2#post-1027921

119   *Tesla regularly releases updates on the amount of carbon:* Fred Lambert. "Tesla claims its owners saved
~2.5 million tons of CO2 – releases new map of its fleet's impact." Electrek, September 29, 2017.
https://electrek.co/2017/09/29/tesla-global-fleet-carbon-emission-saved-map/

119   *and yet new promises of off-grid Superchargers were still coming:* Fred Lambert. "Tesla plans to
disconnect 'almost all' Superchargers from the grid and go solar+battery, says Elon Musk." Electrek,
June 9, 2017. https://electrek.co/2017/06/09/tesla-superchargers-solar-battery-grid-elon-musk/

Chapter 10

120   *As Ashlee Vance tells it:* Ashlee Vance. *Elon Musk: Tesla, SpaceX, and the Quest for a Fantastic Future.*
New York: Ecco, 2015.

121   *and Musk himself disputes that there was a formal offer:* Mike Ramsey. "Elon Musk Takes
Uncustomary Humble Tone for Tesla's Sales." *Wall Street Journal,* May 4, 2015. https://blogs.wsj
.com/corporate-intelligence/2015/05/04/elon-musk-takes-uncustomary-humble-tone-for-teslas
-sales/

122   *I think Tesla will most likely develop its own autopilot system for the car:* Alan Ohsnman. "Tesla
CEO Talking With Google About 'Autopilot' Systems." Bloomberg, May 7, 2013. https://www
.bloomberg.com/news/articles/2013-05-07/tesla-ceo-talking-with-google-about-autopilot-systems

123   *"Intense effort underway at Tesla to develop a practical autopilot system for Model S":* Elon Musk.
Twitter, September 18, 2013. https://twitter.com/elonmusk/status/380451200782462976

123   *"We should be able to do 90 percent of miles driven within three years":* Richard Waters and Henry Foy.
"Tesla moves ahead of Google in race to build self-driving cars." *Financial Times,* September 17,
2013. https://www.ft.com/content/70d26288-1faf-11e3-8861-00144feab7de

123   *Marc Tarpenning would later say the technology:* Startup Grind. "The Story of Building Tesla."
YouTube video, June 2, 2018. https://youtu.be/pGf1tyPXBpA

124   *arguing that Google's full self-driving strategy was unnecessary:* Alan Ohsnman. "Tesla CEO Talking
With Google About 'Autopilot' Systems." Bloomberg, May 7, 2013. https://www.bloomberg.com
/news/articles/2013-05-07/tesla-ceo-talking-with-google-about-autopilot-systems

125   *"In one year we will have a car that drives on auto-pilot from freeway on ramp to freeway off ramp":* Dana
Hull. "Five takeaways from Tesla's shareholder meeting." *Silicon Beat,* June 3, 2014. http://www
.siliconbeat.com/2014/06/03/five-takeaways-from-teslas-shareholder-meeting/

126   *"It's $2,500 to activate the autonomous features forever":* Electrek. "Tesla press conference for the
Autopilot v7.0 software." YouTube video, May 14, 2015. https://www.youtube.com
/watch?v=73_Qjez1MbI

126   *In the Tesla blog post announcing the release of Autopilot:* The Tesla Team. "Your Autopilot has
arrived." *Tesla Motors Blog,* October 14, 2015. https://www.tesla.com/blog/your-autopilot-has
-arrived

126   *Musk echoed the warning at a press event announcing the new feature:* Electrek. "Tesla press conference
for the Autopilot v7.0 software." YouTube video, May 14, 2015. https://www.youtube.com
/watch?v=73_Qjez1MbI

126   *"I went hands-free in Tesla's Model S on Autopilot, even though I wasn't supposed to":* Nick Jaynes. "I
went hands-free in Tesla's Model S on Autopilot, even though I wasn't supposed to." Mashable,
October 14, 2015. https://mashable.com/2015/10/14/tesla-auotpilot-hands-on/

126   *"Tesla's Cars Now Drive Themselves, Kinda":* Molly McHugh. "Tesla's Cars Now Drive Themselves, Kinda." *Wired*, October 14, 2015. https://www.wired.com/2015/10/tesla-self-driving-over-air-update-live/

126   *From Slate:* Will Oremus. "The Paradox of the Self-Driving Car." Slate, November 12, 2015. https://slate.com/technology/2015/11/teslas-autopilot-is-a-safety-feature-that-could-be-dangerous.html

126   *to Car and Driver:* Don Sherman. "Elon, Take the Wheel! We Test Tesla's New Autopilot Feature." *Car and Driver*, October 14, 2015. https://www.caranddriver.com/news/a15352468/elon-take-the-wheel-we-test-teslas-new-autopilot-feature/

127   *concerns resurfaced with a vengeance when Tesla published a blog post:* The Tesla Team. "A Tragic Loss." *Tesla Motors Blog*, June 30, 2016. https://www.tesla.com/blog/tragic-loss

128   *just months earlier had tweeted a video:* Elon Musk. Twitter, April 17, 2016. https://twitter.com/elonmusk/status/721829237741621248?lang=en

128   *it was revealed that a twenty-three-year-old Tesla owner named Gao Yaning had died:* Neal E. Boudette. "Autopilot Cited in Death of Chinese Tesla Driver." *New York Times,* September 14, 2016. https://www.nytimes.com/2016/09/15/business/fatal-tesla-crash-in-china-involved-autopilot-government-tv-says.html

128   *When* Fortune *magazine questioned why Tesla had not disclosed the Brown crash:* Carol J. Loomis. "Elon Musk Says Autopilot Death 'Not Material' to Tesla Shareholders." *Fortune*, July 15, 2016. http://fortune.com/2016/07/05/elon-musk-tesla-autopilot-stock-sale/

129   *Autonomous car experts derided Musk's safety statistic comparisons:* Tom Simonite. "Tesla's Dubious Claims About Autopilot's Safety Record." *MIT Technology Review*, July 6, 2016. https://www.technologyreview.com/s/601849/teslas-dubious-claims-about-autopilots-safety-record/

129   *Because Tesla's data-recording capabilities did not fit the precise definition:* Bozi Tatarevic. "Who Owns Your Vehicle's Crash Data?" *The Truth About Cars*, June 30, 2016. https://www.thetruthaboutcars.com/2016/06/owns-vehicles-crash-data/

129   *finally released a data-reading tool:* Tesla. Tesla.com. https://edr.tesla.com/

129   *in the wake of a lawsuit:* Edward Niedermeyer. "Tesla's EDR About-Face Raises More Questions." *Daily Kanban*, March 6, 2018. https://dailykanban.com/2018/03/teslas-edr-face-raises-questions/

129   *One such owner, profiled in the* Wall Street Journal: Mike Spector, Jack Nicas, and Mike Ramsey. "Tesla's Autopilot Vexes Some Drivers, Even Its Fans." *Wall Street Journal*, July 6, 2016. https://www.wsj.com/articles/teslas-autopilot-vexes-some-drivers-even-its-fans-1467827084

130   *Musk's frustration boiled over in an October conference call:* "Elon Musk Autopilot 2.0 Conference Call Transcript." Xautoworld, October 19, 2016. http://www.xautoworld.com/tesla/transcript-elon-musk-autopilot-2-conference-call/

131   *Not only did NHTSA's final report exonerate Autopilot:* Kareem Habib. "ODI Resume PE-16-007." National Highway Traffic Safety Administration, January 19, 2017. https://static.nhtsa.gov/odi/inv/2016/INCLA-PE16007-7876.PDF

131   *Shortly after the report came out, a company called Quality Control Systems:* Safety Research & Strategies, Inc. "Quality Control Systems Corp. Sues DOT for Tesla Data." Safetyresearch.net, June 28, 2017. http://www.safetyresearch.net/blog/articles/quality-control-systems-corp-sues-dot-tesla-data

131   *In May 2018, NHTSA finally admitted:* David Shepardson. "U.S. safety agency says 'did not assess' Tesla Autopilot effectiveness." Reuters, May 2, 2018. https://www.reuters.com/article/us-tesla-autopilot/us-safety-agency-says-did-not-assess-tesla-autopilot-effectiveness-idUSKBN1I334A

131   *after two years of Tesla and NHTSA fighting QCS's calls for transparency:* Safety Research & Strategies, Inc. "New Analysis Challenges Bold Tesla Claims." Safetyresearch.net, February 8, 2019. http://www.safetyresearch.net/blog/articles/new-analysis-challenges-bold-tesla-claims

131   *when yet another Tesla crashed while on Autopilot, killing its driver:* The Tesla Team. "An Update on Last Week's Accident." *Tesla Motors Blog,* March 30, 2018. https://www.tesla.com/blog/update -last-week's-accident

132   *but the fact that Tesla and NHTSA had argued:* United States District Court for the District of Columbia Memorandum Opinion and Order, September 30, 2018. http://www.safetyresearch.net/ Library/Memorandum_Opinion_and_Order.pdf

132   *the National Transportation Safety Board had conducted a thorough investigation:* NTSB News Release. "Driver Errors, Overreliance on Automation, Lack of Safeguards, Led to Fatal Tesla Crash." National Transportation Safety Board, September 12, 2017. https://www.ntsb.gov/news/press-releases /Pages/PR20170912.aspx

132   *Autopilot engineers would tell the* Wall Street Journal: Tim Higgins. "Tesla Considered Adding Eye Tracking and Steering-Wheel Sensors to Autopilot System." *Wall Street Journal,* May 14, 2018. https://www.wsj.com/articles/tesla-considered-adding-eye-tracking-and-steering-wheel-sensors-to -autopilot-system-1526302921

132   *a claim Musk called "false" in a tweet:* Elon Musk. Twitter, May 14, 2018. https://twitter.com /elonmusk/status/996102919811350528

Chapter 11

137   *According to Ashlee Vance, Musk and Tesla's design boss Franz von Holzhausen:* Ashlee Vance. *Elon Musk: Tesla, SpaceX, and the Quest for a Fantastic Future.* New York: Ecco, 2015.

138   *"Everyone tried to come up with an excuse as to why we couldn't do it," one engineer told Vance:* Ibid.

138   *Tesla filed a lawsuit against the US division of a Swiss automotive supplier:* "Tesla Motors, Inc. v Hoerbiger Automotive Comfort Systems, LLC and Hoerbiger America Holding, Inc." Scribd, January 19, 2016. https://www.scribd.com/document/296081396/Tesla-Complaint

138   *Media reports implying HOERBIGER was responsible:* Ibid.

140   *door and window seal problems:* Tesla Motors Club. "Seal issues?" Teslamotorsclub.com, March 15, 2016. https://teslamotorsclub.com/tmc/threads/seal-issues.65746/

141   *interior squeaks and rattles:* Tesla Motors Club. "Anyone else have door rattles in their Model X?" Teslamotorsclub.com, April 1, 2016. https://teslamotorsclub.com/tmc/threads/anyone-else-have -door-rattles-in-their-model-x.67081/

141   *doors didn't align properly:* Tesla Motors Club. "Driver side window hitting the frame when closing." Teslamotorsclub.com, March 23, 2016. https://teslamotorsclub.com/tmc/threads /driver-side-window-hitting-the-frame-when-closing.66339/

141   *refused to open:* Tesla Motors Club. "Driver door won't open or close completely." Teslamotorsclub .com, March 17, 2016. https://teslamotorsclub.com/tmc/threads/driver-door-wont-open-or-close -completely.65928/

141   *stopped self-presenting:* Tesla Motors Club. "Model X Self-presenting front door." Teslamotorsclub .com, August 31, 2016. https://teslamotorsclub.com/tmc/threads/model-x-self-presenting-front -door.76495/page-2

141 *even opened themselves randomly:* Tesla Motors Club. "Passenger rear door popping open and screen going black." Teslamotorsclub.com, March 24, 2016. https://teslamotorsclub.com/tmc/threads /passenger-rear-door-popping-open-and-screen-going-black.66392/#post-1434707

141 *owners would share the latest suggestions from their local service center:* Tesla Motors Club. "Model X Auto Opening and Closing Door Issues." Teslamotorsclub.com, February 19, 2016. https://teslamotorsclub.com/tmc/threads/model-x-auto-opening-and-closing-door-issues.62975 /#post-1390791

141 *Eventually Tesla issued a firmware update:* Richard Truett. "Updated Tesla Model X falcon wing door frustrates owners." *Automotive News,* August 31, 2016. https://www.autonews.com/article/201608 31/OEM11/160839968/updated-tesla-model-x-falcon-wing-door-frustrates-owners

141 *popularly illustrated with YouTube videos showing the doors chopping:* Jason Torchinsky. "Did Tesla Quietly Remove a Safety Feature From the Model X's Falcon Doors?" Jalopnik, August 31, 2016. https://jalopnik.com/did-tesla-quietly-remove-a-safety-feature-from-the-mode-1786000681

141 *panels to be within specification, a mismatch was easy to see:* Tesla Motors Club. "How far will Tesla go to fix alignment issues (doors, chrome trim, etc.)." Teslamotorsclub.com, April 30, 2016. https:// teslamotorsclub.com/tmc/threads/how-far-will-tesla-go-to-fix-alignment-issues-doors-chrome -trim-etc.69311/page-9#post-1568260

142 *on the first quarterly earnings call of 2016:* Cadie Thompson. "Elon Musk keeps a sleeping bag next to Tesla's production line so that he can personally inspect vehicles." Business Insider, May 4, 2016. https://www.businessinsider.com/elon-musk-sleeps-at-the-tesla-factory-2016-5

143 *When the X was rated "much worse than average" in the 2018* Consumer Reports *survey:* Peter Valdes-Dapena. "Tesla sinks in Consumer Reports reliability rankings." CNN Business, October 24, 2018. https://www.cnn.com/2018/10/24/cars/consumer-reports-reliability-tesla/index.html

144 *problems with both the self-presenting:* Tesla Motors Club. "Auto-Presenting Doors not working." Teslamotorsclub.com, October 3, 2017. https://teslamotorsclub.com/tmc/threads /auto-presenting-doors-not-working.99302/

144 *and falcon-wing doors:* Tesla Motors Club. "Falcon doors (randomly) only open part-way." Teslamotorsclub.com, October 5, 2018. https://teslamotorsclub.com/tmc/threads/falcon-doors -randomly-only-open-part-way.130949/

144 *seals:* Tesla Motors Club. "Falcon door flaw." Teslamotorsclub.com, December 20, 2018. https://teslamotorsclub.com/tmc/threads/falcon-door-flaw.138475/

144 *windows:* Tesla Motors Club. "Cold weather – doors won't close." Teslamotorsclub.com, January 30, 2019. https://teslamotorsclub.com/tmc/threads/cold-weather-doors-won%E2%80%99t-close .141739/

144 *panel fit:* Tesla Motors Club. "Painting and Doors aligment issues." Teslamotorsclub.com, February 5, 2019. https://teslamotorsclub.com/tmc/threads/painting-and-doors-aligment-issues.142178/

144 *half-shaft consumption:* Tesla Motors Club. "Acceleration Shudder." Teslamotorsclub.com, July 23, 2016. https://teslamotorsclub.com/tmc/threads/acceleration-shudder.74184/page-21

144 *squeaks:* Tesla Motors Club. "MX 7 seater squeaky second row." Teslamotorsclub.com, November 28, 2018. https://teslamotorsclub.com/tmc/threads/mx-7-seater-squeaky-second-row.136515/

144 *whistles:* Tesla Motors Club. "Wind whistle behind dash . . ." Teslamotorsclub.com, January 13, 2019. https://teslamotorsclub.com/tmc/threads/wind-whistle-behind-dash.140289/

144   *forums remain stubbornly well-stocked with complaints:* Tesla Motors Club. "Tesla is losing me."
       Teslamotorsclub.com, December 19, 2018. https://teslamotorsclub.com/tmc/threads
       /tesla-is-losing-me.138369/
       Tesla Motors Club. "Auto-Presenting Doors not working." Teslamotorsclub.com, October 3, 2017.
       https://teslamotorsclub.com/tmc/threads/auto-presenting-doors-not-working.99302/
       Tesla Motors Club. "Acceleration Shudder." Teslamotorsclub.com, July 23, 2016.
       https://teslamotorsclub.com/tmc/threads/acceleration-shudder.74184/page-21
       Tesla Motors Club. "Wind whistle behind dash . . ." Teslamotorsclub.com, January 13, 2019.
       https://teslamotorsclub.com/tmc/threads/wind-whistle-behind-dash.140289/

144   *maybe 30 percent of the parts are in common between the S and the X":* Jerry Hirsch. "Tesla's Musk:
       New 'ludicrous' mode shoots Model S to 60 mph in 2.8 seconds." *Los Angeles Times,* July 17, 2015.
       https://www.latimes.com/business/autos/la-fi-hy-elon-musk-tesla-ludicrous-20150716-story.html

144   *There was way too much complexity right at the beginning":* Alistair Charlton. "Elon Musk admits the
       'very foolish' mistakes he made with the Tesla Model X." *International Business Times,* June 7, 2017.
       https://www.ibtimes.co.uk/elon-musk-admits-very-foolish-mistakes-he-made-tesla-model-x
       -1625151

145   *The Model X "is like a Fabergé egg of cars," he said at the 2017 shareholders meeting:* Sean O'Kane. "7
       things we learned from Elon Musk's Tesla shareholder meeting." The Verge, June 6, 2017.
       https://www.theverge.com/2017/6/6/15750228elon-musk-tesla-model-3-model-y-twitter-red
       -wine

Chapter 12

147   *collapsed into bankruptcy and infamy:* Frank Pangallo. "Sun Cube Saga." *Today Tonight Adelaide,*
       November 18, 2013. https://www.todaytonightadelaide.com.au/stories/sun-cube-saga

147   *his Flickr folder of images of Model S vehicles with broken suspensions:* Keef Wivaneef. "Tesla -Whompy
       Wheels." *Flickr.* https://www.flickr.com/photos/136377865@N05/sets/72157658490111523/

148   *a Tesla owner named Peter Cordaro posted a thread at the Tesla Motors Club forum:* Tesla Motors Club.
       "Suspension Problem on Model S." Teslamotorsclub.com, April 28, 2016. https://teslamotorsclub
       .com/tmc/threads/suspension-problem-on-model-s.69204/

151   *Not only was Tesla covering up its quality problems, it was covering up the fact that it was covering up
       its quality problems:* Edward Niedermeyer. "Tesla Suspension Breakage: It's Not the Crime, It's the
       Coverup." *Daily Kanban,* June 8, 2016. https://dailykanban.com/2016/06/tesla-suspension
       -breakage-not-crime-coverup/

152   *the company blog post twisted my story:* The Tesla Team. "A Grain of Salt." *Tesla Motors Blog,* June 9,
       2016. https://www.tesla.com/blog/grain-of-salt

153   *NHTSA confirmed to other sources that it was still collecting data:* Jeff Cobb. "Contrary to Musk's
       Suggestion, NHTSA Did Not Call Tesla Suspension Complaints 'Fraudulent.'" HybridCars.com,
       June 14, 2016. https://www.hybridcars.com/contrary-to-musks-suggestion-nhtsa-did-not-call-tesla
       -suspension-complaints-fraudulent/

154   *I took the unusual step of writing a blog post:* Edward Niedermeyer and Bertel Schmitt. "Declarations
       Under Penalty of Perjury Re Tesla Motors." *Daily Kanban,* June 13, 2016. https://dailykanban
       .com/2016/06/declarations-penalty-perjury-re-tesla-motors/

155 *A separate TMC thread:* Tesla Motors Club. "When to report NHTSA issues?" Teslamotorsclub
.com, September 18, 2013. https://teslamotorsclub.com/tmc/threads/when-to-report-nhtsa-issues
.21682/

157 *vividly illustrated by its handling of an earlier problem that caused its vehicles to suddenly lose power:*
Edward Niedermeyer. "With Misleading Messages and Customer NDAs, Tesla Performs Stealth
Recall." *Combustion,* April 2017. http://newcartographer.com/combustion/teslarecall.html

159 *Tesla's motivation for concealing real or potential defects or safety problems can be found:* Tesla. "Form
10-Q." US Securities and Exchange Commission, April 29, 2016. https://www.sec.gov/Archives
/edgar/data/1318605/000156459016018886/tsla-10q_20160331.htm

Chapter 13

163 *when an Elon Musk tweet suddenly blew them away:* Elon Musk. Twitter, July 10, 2016. https://twitter
.com/elonmusk/status/752182992982843392

163 *The company's stock jumped 4 percent:* BBC. "Tesla stock rises after Elon Musk's masterplan tweet."
BBC, July 11, 2016. https://www.bbc.com/news/technology-36765823

164 *Six days later, Musk tweeted:* Elon Musk. Twitter, July 16, 2016. https://twitter.com/elonmusk
/status/754272832440250368

164 *The next day he delayed again:* Elon Musk. Twitter, July 17, 2016. https://twitter.com/elonmusk
/status/754772663365664768

164 *Musk finally delivered:* Elon Musk. "Master Plan, Part Deux." *Tesla Motors Blog,* July 20, 2016.
https://www.tesla.com/blog/master-plan-part-deux

168 *Musk fired back:* Mike Ramsey. "Mobileye Ends Partnership With Tesla." *Wall Street Journal,* July 26,
2016. https://www.wsj.com/articles/mobileye-ends-partnership-with-tesla-1469544028

168 *The war of words continued into September:* Eric Auchard and Tova Cohen. "Mobileye says Tesla was
'pushing the envelope in terms of safety.'" Reuters, September 14, 2016. https://www.reuters.com
/article/us-mobileye-tesla/mobileye-says-tesla-was-pushing-the-envelope-in-terms-of-safety-idUS
KCN11K2T8

168 *and Musk contending that Mobileye:* Alexandria Sage. "Tesla says Mobileye balked after learning
carmaker to make own cameras." Reuters, September 15, 2016. https://www.reuters.com/article
/us-mobileye-tesla/tesla-says-mobileye-balked-after-learning-carmaker-to-make-own-cameras
-idUSKCN11L2XI

168 *Mobileye responded with a press release:* Mobileye. "Mobileye Responds to False Allegations."
PRNewswire, September 16, 2016. https://www.prnewswire.com/news-releases/mobileye
-responds-to-false-allegations-300329427.html

169 *Tesla announced that its new post-Mobileye Autopilot hardware was complete:* The Tesla Team. "All
Tesla Cars Being Produced Now Have Full Self-Driving Hardware." *Tesla Motors Blog,* October 19,
2016. https://www.tesla.com/blog/all-tesla-cars-being-produced-now-have-full-self-driving
-hardware

169 *In a conference call with reporters:* "Elon Musk Autopilot 2.0 Conference Call Transcript."
Xautoworld, October 19, 2016. http://www.xautoworld.com/tesla/transcript-elon-musk-autopilot
-2-conference-call/

170 *Tesla released a video:* Tesla, Inc. "Full Self-Driving Hardware on All Teslas." Vimeo video, October
19, 2016. https://vimeo.com/188105076

170 *Tesla filmed the car driving the route multiple times:* Edward Niedermeyer. "CA DMV Report Sheds New Light on Misleading Tesla Autonomous Drive Video." *Daily Kanban*, February 3, 2017. https://dailykanban.com/2017/02/ca-dmv-report-sheds-new-light-misleading-tesla-autonomous -drive-video/

170 *Several months later, when the state of California released:* California Department of Motor Vehicles. "Autonomous Vehicle Disengagement Reports 2016." https://www.dmv.ca.gov/portal/dmv/detail /vr/autonomous/disengagement_report_2016

171 *to which he replied, "3 months maybe, 6 months definitely":* Elon Musk. Twitter, January 23, 2017. https://twitter.com/elonmusk/status/823727035088416768

171 *at least in part due to the belief:* Ianthe Jeanne Dugan and Mike Spector. "Tesla's Push to Build a Self-Driving Car Sparked Dissent Among Its Engineers." *Wall Street Journal*, August 24, 2017. https://www.wsj.com/articles/teslas-push-to-build-a-self-driving-car-sparks-dissent-among-its -engineers-1503593742

171 *so Musk promised that the next update:* Elon Musk. Twitter, May 21, 2017. https://twitter.com /elonmusk/status/866470387248316416

172 *By August, Tesla fan site Electrek was reporting:* Fred Lambert. "Tesla has a new Autopilot '2.5' hardware suite with more computing power for autonomous driving." Electrek, August 9, 2017. https://electrek.co/2017/08/09/tesla-autopilot-2-5-hardware-computer-autonomous-driving/

172 *By the summer of 2018, Tesla was hyping:* Greg Kumparak. "Tesla is building its own AI chips for self-driving cars." TechCrunch, August 1, 2018. https://techcrunch.com/2018/08/01/tesla-is -building-its-own-ai-chips-for-self-driving-cars/

172 *Morgan Stanley analyst Adam Jonas predicted:* Michelle Jones. "Tesla Motors Inc Up After Morgan Stanley Raises Price Target." Valuewalk, August 17, 2015. https://www.valuewalk.com/2015/08 /tesla-motors-morgan-stanley-raises-price-target/

173 *the on-demand mobility market could be worth $2 trillion:* Arjun Kharpal. "Tesla could be worth 'multiples' of current $50 billion market cap by 2020, fund manager says." CNBC, May 19, 2017. https://www.cnbc.com/2017/05/19/tesla-stock-valuation-driverless-taxi.html

175 *Gartner released its latest "hype cycle" analysis:* Mike Ramsey. "Autonomous Vehicles Fall Into the Trough of Disillusionment . . . But That's Good." *Forbes*, August 14, 2018. https://www.forbes.com/ sites/enroute/2018/08/14/autonomous-vehicles-fall-into-the-trough-of-disillusionment-but-thats -good/#3b5a3c6e7b5a

176 *John Krafcik publicly admitted that autonomous vehicles might never work in all locations:* Sam Abuelsamid. "Transition to Autonomous Cars Will Take Longer Than You Think, Waymo CEO Tells Governors." *Forbes*, July 20, 2018. https://www.forbes.com/sites/samabuelsamid/2018/07 /20/waymo-ceo-tells-governors-av-time-will-be-longer-than-you-think/#277b432cd7da

178 *reports of heavy discounts during the third quarter of 2016:* Liane Yvkoff. "Tesla Confirms—And Ends —Discounts, But Why Were They Offered in the First Place?" *Forbes*, September 29, 2016. https://www.forbes.com/sites/lianeyvkoff/2016/09/29/tesla-confirms-and-ends-discounts-but -why-were-they-offered-in-the-first-place/

Chapter 14

180 *Tesla's earnings call for the first quarter of 2016:* Thomson Reuters. "Q1 2016 Tesla Motors Inc Earnings Call Transcript." Bamsec, May 10, 2016. https://www.bamsec.com/transcripts/5986830

182 *Musk cited line speed and volumetric density as the major areas for improvement:* "This is why we're long Tesla." *Teslamondo,* June 2, 2016. https://teslamondo.com/2016/06/02/this-is-why-were-long-tesla/

182 *he mocked the slow speed of the industry's assembly lines:* Sean O'Kane. "Tesla faces a critical year, but Elon Musk is obsessed with the future." The Verge, February 8, 2018. https://www.theverge.com/2018/2/8/16990730/tesla-earnings-2017-elon-musk

184 *straining the local road infrastructure and labor and housing markets:* Benjamin Spillman. "Musk plunges Tesla into Nevada's housing crisis." *Reno Gazette Journal,* October 12, 2018. https://www.rgj.com/story/news/2018/10/12/elon-musk-tesla-gigafactory-nevada-housing-crisis/1619609002/

184 *were already pointing the way to the trouble ahead:* Jeff Cobb. "Model 3 'Bottleneck' Blamed on Chaos and Incompetence at Tesla Gigafactory." HybridCars.com, October 31, 2017. https://www.hybridcars.com/model-3-bottleneck-blamed-on-chaos-and-incompetence-at-tesla-gigafactory/

186 *one of its trademark extravaganza events at the Fremont factory:* Model 3 Owners Club. "Model 3 Delivery event live stream." YouTube video, July 28, 2017. https://youtu.be/NO9q0Rq44uc

186 *he had recently broken up with the actress Amber Heard:* Neil Strauss. "Elon Musk: The Architect of Tomorrow." *Rolling Stone,* November 15, 2017. https://www.rollingstone.com/culture/culture-features/elon-musk-the-architect-of-tomorrow-120850/

186 *At the beginning of 2017:* Thomson Reuters. "Q1 2017 Tesla Motors Inc Earnings Call Transcript." Bamsec, May 7, 2017. https://www.bamsec.com/transcripts/10231043

186 *Tesla dialed those targets back:* Elon Musk and Deepak Ahuja. "Tesla Second Quarter 2017 Update." Tesla.com. http://ir.tesla.com/static-files/967ca2fa-9f4c-415c-856d-ee19c184331b

187 *Tesla revealed that it had built a total of just 260 Model 3s:* Angelica LaVita and Phil LeBeau. "Tesla Model 3 deliveries lower than expected because of, "production bottlenecks.'" CNBC, October 2, 2017. https://www.cnbc.com/2017/10/02/tesla-q3-deliveries.html

187 *the situation was worse than anyone had imagined:* Tim Higgins. "Behind Tesla's Production Delays: Parts of Model 3 Were Being Made by Hand." *Wall Street Journal,* October 6, 2017. https://www.wsj.com/articles/behind-teslas-production-delays-parts-of-model-3-were-being-made-by-hand-1507321057

188 *Musk told analysts that the initial production run:* Thomson Reuters. "Q2 2017 Tesla Motors Inc Earnings Call Transcript." Bamsec, August 31, 2017. https://www.bamsec.com/transcripts/10723104

188 *Tesla released a technical service bulletin:* Tesla, Inc. "Replace Rear Drive Unit." National Highway Traffic Safety Administration, January 23, 2018. https://static.nhtsa.gov/odi/tsbs/2018/MC-10142979-9999.pdf

188 *multiple reports saying that a stunningly high percentage of its cars needed to be reworked:* Lora Kolodny. "Tesla employees say automaker is churning out a high volume of flawed parts requiring costly rework." CNBC, March 14, 2018. https://www.cnbc.com/2018/03/14/tesla-manufacturing-high-volume-of-flawed-parts-employees.html; Alexandria Sage. "Build fast, fix later: speed hurts quality at Tesla, some workers say." Reuters, November 29, 2017. https://www.reuters.com/article/us-tesla-quality-insight/build-fast-fix-later-speed-hurts-quality-at-tesla-some-workers-say-idUSKBN1DT0N3

189 *reports published at BusinessInsider, CNBC, and Bloomberg, alleging . . . problems at the sprawling Nevada plant:* Linette Lopez. "Tesla employees describe what it's like to work in the gigantic

Gigafactory." Business Insider, September 4, 2018. https://www.businessinsider.com/tesla
-workers-describe-working-in-gigafactory-2018-8; Linette Lopez. "Insiders describe a world of
chaos and waste at Panasonic's massive battery-making operation for Tesla." Business Insider, April
16, 2019. https://www.businessinsider.com/panasonic-battery-cell-operations-tesla-gigafactory
-chaotic-2019-4; Lora Kolodny. "Tesla employees say to expect more Model 3 delays, citing
inexperienced workers, manual assembly of batteries." CNBC, January 28, 2018. https://www
.cnbc.com/2018/01/25/tesla-employees-say-gigafactory-problems-worse-than-known.html; Matt
Robinson and Zeke Faux. "When Elon Musk Tried to Destroy a Tesla Whistleblower." Bloomberg
Businessweek, March 13, 2019. https://www.bloomberg.com/news/features/2019-03-13
/when-elon-musk-tried-to-destroy-tesla-whistleblower-martin-tripp

189   *Cuts in maintenance hit the paint shop especially hard:* Edward Niedermeyer. "Tesla Veterans Reveal
Fires, Accidents, and Delays Inside Elon Musk's Company." The Daily Beast, June 5, 2018. https://
www.thedailybeast.com/tesla-veterans-reveal-fires-accidents-and-delays-inside-elon-musks
-company

190   *Tesla eventually hit its goal of producing five thousand Model 3s per week:* Drew Harwell. "Tesla hits
5,000-a-week Model 3 production goal." *Washington Post,* July 2, 2018. https://www.
washingtonpost.com/business/economy/tesla-hits-5000-a-week-model-3-production-goal/2018
/07/02/a3306ca0-7e48-11e8-b660-4d0f9f0351f1_story.html?utm_term=.595a5d3f189f

191   *20 percent of reservations canceled by the end of the third quarter:* Elon Musk and Deepak Ahuja. "Tesla
Third Quarter 2018 Update." Tesla.com. http://ir.tesla.com/static-files/725970e6-eda5-47ab-96e1
-422d4045f799

Chapter 15

195   *Again and again, automotive innovations quickly shift:* Horace Dediu. Twitter, April 9, 2014.
https://twitter.com/asymco/status/453920989098045441

196   *"Innovation Killers: How Financial Tools Destroy Your Capacity to Do New Things":* Clayton M.
Christensen, Stephen P. Kaufman, and Willy C. Shih. "Innovation Killers: How Financial Tools
Destroy Your Capacity to Do New Things." *Harvard Business Review,* January 2008. https://hbr
.org/2008/01/innovation-killers-how-financial-tools-destroy-your-capacity-to-do-new-things

198   *as Ghosn explained it to* Wired *magazine:* Chuck Squatriglia. "Q&A: Renault-Nissan CEO Pledges
$5.6 Billion for EVs." *Wired,* June 16, 2011. https://www.wired.com/2011/06/qa-with-carlos
-ghosn/

199   Wired *said he was "either a brilliant visionary or crazy as a loon":* Chuck Squatriglia. "Q&A:
Renault-Nissan CEO Pledges $5.6 Billion for EVs." *Wired,* June 16, 2011. https://www.wired
.com/2011/06/qa-with-carlos-ghosn/

203   *Porsche also joined with BMW to one-up Tesla on charging speed, rolling out fast chargers capable of 450
kilowatts in Europe:* Jon Porter. "Porsche and BMW unveil EV charger that's three times faster than
Tesla's." The Verge, December 14, 2018. https://www.theverge.com/2018/12/14/18140868
/fastcharge-porsche-bmw-450kw-electric-vehicle-charging-station

205   *with prices as low as 20,000 euros, and generating three million sales per year:* Edward Taylor and Jan
Schwartz. "Bet everything on electric: Inside Volkswagen's radical strategy shift." Reuters, February
5, 2019. https://www.reuters.com/article/us-volkswagen-electric-insight/bet-everything-on
-electric-inside-volkswagens-radical-strategy-shift-idUSKCN1PV0K4

205 *It isn't just talk, either: VW has committed over $90 billion to its electric vehicle strategy:* Andreas Franke. "Volkswagen Group doubles electric vehicle battery contract volume to Eur40 billion" S&P Global Platts, May 8, 2018. https://www.spglobal.com/platts/en/market-insights/latest-news/metals /050818-volkswagen-group-doubles-electric-vehicle-battery-contract-volume-to-eur40-billion

206 *By 2018, with China's plug-in vehicle market growing to roughly triple the size of that of the United States:* Roland Irle. "China Plug-in Vehicle Sales for the 1st Half of 2018." EV-volumes.com. http://www .ev-volumes.com/country/china/

206 *Then, suddenly an opportunity presented itself: China relaxed its rules:* Bloomberg News, with assistance by Ying Tian, Yan Zhang, Christoph Rauwald, Elisabeth Behrmann, Kevin Buckland, Jeanny Yu, and Jamie Butters. "Tesla Gets Edge Under China's Relaxed Rules for Foreign Automakers." Bloomberg, April 17, 2018. https://www.bloomberg.com/news /articles/2018-04-17/china-to-remove-auto-ventures-foreign-ownership-limit-by-2022

206 *its China-made vehicles would face even tougher pricing challenges in a market where the top-selling EV:* Mark Kane. "Nearly 1 in Every 25 Cars Sold in China Plugged in This July." InsideEVs, August 23, 2018. https://insideevs.com/1-in-25-cars-sold-china-plug-in/

207 *its market for these micro-EVs boomed to 1.75 million in the same year:* Trefor Moss. "China's Giant Market for Really Tiny Cars." *Wall Street Journal*, September 21, 2018. https://www.wsj.com /articles/chinas-giant-market-for-tiny-cars-1537538585

Chapter 16

211 *The crowd went nuts as Elon Musk emerged:* Tesla. "Tesla Semi & Roadster Unveil." YouTube video, December 14, 2017. https://youtu.be/5RRmepp7i5g

212 *when Musk announced pricing:* Claudia Assis. "Want the new Tesla Roadster in 2020? Prepare to pay Tesla $250,000 now." MarketWatch, November 22, 2017. https://www.marketwatch.com/story /want-the-new-tesla-roadster-in-2020-prepare-to-pay-tesla-250000-now-2017-11-17

214 *the new Roadster instantly inspired a meme:* "Tesla Roadster Comparisons." KnowYourMeme.com, November 21, 2017. https://knowyourmeme.com/memes/tesla-roadster-comparisons

215 *Tesla's board proposed a new ten-year compensation plan for Musk:* Tesla. "Tesla Announces New Long -Term Performance Award for Elon Musk." Tesla.com, January 23, 2018. http://ir.tesla.com/news -releases/news-release-details/tesla-announces-new-long-term-performance-award-elon-musk

217 *claiming that he tweets under the influence:* Elon Musk. Twitter, June 6, 2017. https://twitter.com /elonmusk/status/872260000491593728

217 *admitting he might be bipolar:* Katie Collins. "Elon Musk tweets about 'terrible lows and unrelenting stress.'" CNET, July 31, 2017. https://www.cnet.com/news/elon-musk-tweets-about-terrible-lows -and-unrelenting-stress/

217 *Musk cut short questions about Tesla's reservations and capital requirements:* Thomson Reuters. "Q1 2018 Tesla Motors Inc Earnings Call Transcript." Bamsec, June 1, 2018. https://www.bamsec.com /transcripts/11482485

217 *he claimed to be launching a website:* Matt Stevens. "Why Is Elon Musk Attacking the Media? We Explain. (Also, Give Us a Good Rating!)" *New York Times*, May 24, 2018. https://www.nytimes .com/2018/05/24/business/elon-musk-tesla-twitter-media.html

218 *he repeated the accusation in an angry, profanity-laced email:* Ryan Mac, Mark DiStefano, and John Paczkowski. "In a New Email, Elon Musk Accused a Cave Rescuer of Being a 'Child Rapist' and

Said He 'Hopes' There's a Lawsuit." Buzzfeed, September 4, 2018. https://www.buzzfeednews.com/article/ryanmac/elon-musk-thai-cave-rescuer-accusations-buzzfeed-email

218 *even Musk's most loyal investors expressed concern:* Sam Levin. "Tesla investors demand Elon Musk apologize for calling Thailand diver 'pedo.'" The *Guardian*, July 17, 2018. https://www.theguardian.com/technology/2018/jul/17/tesla-elon-musk-thailand-diver-pedo

218 *his own tweet on August 7, 2018:* Elon Musk. Twitter, August 7, 2018. https://twitter.com/elonmusk/status/1026872652290379776

219 *Coming on the same day as news:* Arash Massoudi. "Saudi Arabia's sovereign fund builds $2bn Tesla stake." *Financial Times*, August 7, 2018. https://www.ft.com/content/42ca6c42-a79e-11e8-926a-7342fe5e173f

219 *Within a week of Musk's tweet:* Matthew Goldstein, Jessica Silver-Greenberg, and Kate Kelly. "Tesla Is Said to Be Subpoenaed by S.E.C. Over Elon Musk Tweet." *New York Times*, August 15, 2018. https://www.nytimes.com/2018/08/15/business/tesla-musk-sec-subpoena-goldman.html

219 *began posting outlandish and attention-grabbing claims:* Constance Grady. "Banks, Elon Musk, and Grimes, explained." Vox, August 16, 2018. https://www.vox.com/2018/8/16/17692700/azealia-banks-elon-musk-grimes-explained

219 *a lengthy and rambling appearance on the popular Joe Rogan podcast:* PowerfulJRE. "Joe Rogan Experience #1169 - Elon Musk." Youtube video, September 6, 2018. https://youtu.be/ycPr5-27vSI

219 *Musk abruptly rejected the offer and threatened to leave the company:* James B. Stewart. "Elon Musk's Ultimatum to Tesla: Fight the S.E.C., or I Quit." *New York Times*, October 2, 2018. https://www.nytimes.com/2018/10/02/business/tesla-elon-musk-sec.html

219 *The next day the SEC publicly filed suit:* Matthew Goldstein and Emily Flitter. "Tesla Chief Elon Musk Is Sued by S.E.C. in Move That Could Oust Him." *New York Times*, September 27, 2018. https://www.nytimes.com/2018/09/27/business/elon-musk-sec-lawsuit-tesla.html

220 *receiving a phone call from Mark Cuban:* Susan Pulliam, Dave Michaels, and Tim Higgins. "Mark Cuban Prodded Tesla's Elon Musk to Settle SEC Charges." *Wall Street Journal*, October 4, 2018. https://www.wsj.com/articles/mark-cuban-prodded-teslas-elon-musk-to-settle-sec-charges-1538678655

220 *a subsequent tweet taunting the SEC:* Elon Musk. Twitter, October 4, 2018. https://twitter.com/elonmusk/status/1047943670350020608?lang=en

220 *forty-one top-level executives . . . according to one count:* Sara Salinas. "Tesla keeps losing senior leadership—here are some of the key departures this year." CNBC, September 8, 2018. https://www.cnbc.com/2018/09/07/tesla-executive-departures-in-2018.html

221 *Tesla slashed Model 3 prices by $2,000:* Clifford Atiyeh. "Tesla cuts prices on Model 3, Model S, and Model X by $2000." Car and Driver, January 2, 2019. https://www.caranddriver.com/news/a25725993/tesla-price-cut-model-3/

221 *another $1,100 in February:* "Tesla cuts Model 3 price for second time this year." CNBC, February 5, 2019. https://www.cnbc.com/2019/02/06/tesla-cuts-model-3-price-for-second-time-this-year.html

221 *slashing thousands of jobs:* The Tesla Team. "Company Update." *Tesla Motors Blog.* January 18, 2019. https://www.tesla.com/blog/tesla-company-update

221 *"There is a strong indication that . . . note circulated at the end of January:* Sonam Rai and Jasmine I.S., "Musk not worried about Tesla Model 3 demand, Wall Street thinks otherwise." Reuters. January

31, 2019. https://www.reuters.com/article/us-tesla-results-stocks/musk-not-worried-about-tesla-model-3-demand-wall-street-thinks-otherwise-idUSKCN1PP1TO

222   *Tesla tweeted about new store openings:* Tesla. Twitter, December 10, 2018. https://twitter.com/Tesla/status/1072297925957554176

222   *it was promptly reported that once again many employees had no idea:* Dana Hull. "Tesla Sell-Off Worsens After Elon Musk's Surprise Store Closings." Bloomberg, March 4, 2019. https://www.bloomberg.com/news/articles/2019-03-05/musk-is-said-to-blindside-tesla-staff-with-store-closing-plans

222   *Tesla walked them back days later:* Tom Krisher. "Tesla walks back its plan to close most showrooms." March 11, 2019. https://www.foxnews.com/us/tesla-walks-back-its-plan-to-close-most-showrooms

222   *reports that planned deliveries of the Standard Range Model 3 were canceled by Tesla at the last minute:* Edward Niedermeyer. "Tesla Delaying Deliveries of Standard Range Model 3." The Drive, March 25, 2019. https://www.thedrive.com/tech/27150/tesla-delaying-deliveries-of-standard-range-model-3

222   *The cheapest version was then pulled:* Tim Higgins. "Tesla Halts Online Sales of $35,000 Version of Model 3." Wall Street Journal, April 12, 2019. https://www.wsj.com/articles/tesla-halts-online-sales-of-35-000-version-of-model-3-weeks-after-introducing-it-11555050405

223   *and brought back in March:* Sean Hollister. "Tesla brings back its customer referral program – with fewer free cars." The Verge, March 21, 2019. https://www.theverge.com/2019/3/21/18276559/tesla-brings-back-its-customer-referral-program-with-fewer-free-cars

223   *a series of changes to Autopilot pricing:* Rob Stumpf. "Musk Says Lowering Price Was a Mistake, Tesla to Also Increase Autopilot Cost." The Drive, March 12, 2019. https://www.thedrive.com/news/26902/musk-says-lowering-price-was-a-mistake-tesla-to-also-increase-autopilot-cost

224   *sales referral program that Tesla canceled in January:* Andrew J. Hawkins. "Tesla to end customer referral program, Elon Musk says." The Verge. January 17, 2019. https://www.theverge.com/2019/1/17/18186753/tesla-end-customer-referral-program-elon-musk

224   *the SEC hauling Musk back to court:* Ahiza Garcia. "SEC: Elon Musk's failure to comply with court order over his tweets is 'stunning.'" CNN Business, March 19, 2019. https://www.cnn.com/2019/03/18/tech/elon-musk-sec-contempt-of-court/index.html

224   *sudden departure of the general counsel Tesla had hired:* Ryan Lovelace. "Tesla GC Butswinkas Makes Hasty Return to Williams & Connolly." National Law Journal, February 20, 2019. https://www.law.com/nationallawjournal/2019/02/20/tesla-gc-butswinkas-makes-hasty-return-to-williams-connolly/

224   *summarized by the prominent $TSLAQ account @TeslaCharts:* TeslaCharts. "The $TSLA bull thesis is the same as the bear thesis: Elon Musk is willing to do anything to win. Anything. We saw that in spades last night." Twitter, October 25, 2018. https://twitter.com/TeslaCharts/status/1055420713253982208

Chapter 17

225   *a projected capacitive touchscreen:* Andrew Rassweiler, Mark Boyadjis, and Stephanie Brinley. "Tesla Motors: A case study in disruptive innovation." IHS Markit, October 7, 2014. https://ihsmarkit.com/research-analysis/q14-tesla-motors-a-case-study-in-disruptive-innovation.html

228   *a dashboard can reach:* Hussain H. Al-Kayiem. "Study on the Thermal Accumulation and Distribution Inside a Parked Car Cabin." *American Journal of Applied Sciences,* January 2010. https://

www.researchgate.net/publication/46179184_Study_on_the_Thermal_Accumulation_and_
Distribution_Inside_a_Parked_Car_Cabin

228 *even without help from:* Cristian Sorin Popescu. "Thermal and fluid simulation of the environment
under the dashboard, compared with measurement data." IOP Conference Series: Material
Science and Engineering, October 2017. https://www.researchgate.net/publication/320579641_
Thermal_and_fluid_simulation_of_the_environment_under_the_dashboard_compared_with_
measurement_data

228 *In 2012–2015 Teslas:* Tesla Motors Club. "bubbles on touchscreen." Teslamotorsclub.com, October
18, 2015. https://teslamotorsclub.com/tmc/threads/bubbles-on-touchscreen.55868/

228 *In 2012–2015 Teslas:* Tesla Motors Club. "Touchscreen: Mositure/Leak?" Teslamotorsclub.com,
August 16, 2015. https://teslamotorsclub.com/tmc/threads/touchscreen-mositure-leak.51679/

228 *In 2012–2015 Teslas:* Tesla Motors Club. "Bubbles on Display." Teslamotorsclub.com, March 31,
2017. https://teslamotorsclub.com/tmc/threads/bubbles-on-display.88412/

228 *In 2012–2015 Teslas:* "Gel Leaking from Touchscreen." Forums.tesla.com, November 12, 2015.
https://forums.tesla.com/forum/forums/gel-leaking-touchscreen

228 *In 2012–2015 Teslas:* "Touch screen bubbles/leakage." Forums.tesla.com, August 12, 2017. https://
forums.tesla.com/forum/forums/touch-screen-bubbles-leakage

228 *yellow bands forming around the edge of screens in 2016 and later Teslas:* Tesla Motors Club. "The
yellow screen fringe, seems to be a bigger issue for them." Teslamotorsclub.com, August 21, 2018.
https://teslamotorsclub.com/tmc/threads/the-yellow-screen-fringe-seems-to-be-a-bigger-issue-for
-them.126429/

228 *yellow bands forming around the edge of screens in 2016 and later Teslas:* Tesla Motors Club. "Yellow
ring around Main Display?" Teslamotorsclub.com, August 22, 2018. https://teslamotorsclub.com
/tmc/threads/yellow-ring-around-main-display.106017/

228 *yellow bands forming around the edge of screens in 2016 and later Teslas:* Tesla Motors Club. "screen
discoloration." Teslamotorsclub.com, August 10, 2017. https://teslamotorsclub.com/tmc/threads
/screen-discoloration.96016/

228 *yellow bands forming around the edge of screens in 2016 and later Teslas:* "Yellow band along borders of
touchscreen." Forums.tesla.com, September 21, 2017. https://forums.tesla.com/forum/forums
/yellow-band-along-borders-touchscreen

228 *yellow bands forming around the edge of screens in 2016 and later Teslas:* "MCU Touch Screen Yellow
Border: Dealer Update." Forums.tesla.com, December 5, 2018. https://forums.tesla.com/forum
/forums/mcu-touch-screen-yellow-border-dealer-update

228 *almost certainly tied to high heat:* Silvia Cruz et al. "Analysis of the bonding process and materials
optimization for mitigating the Yellow Border defect on optically bonded automotive display
panels." *Displays*, February 2017. https://www.researchgate.net/publication/314125064_Analysis
_of_the_bonding_process_and_materials_optimization_for_mitigating_the_Yellow_Border
_defect_on_optically_bonded_automotive_display_panels

228 *the company would not replace screens:* Tesla Motors Club. "Tesla halts center screen replacements."
Teslamotorsclub.com, November 30, 2018. https://teslamotorsclub.com/tmc/threads/tesla-halts-
center-screen-replacements.136674/

228 *Apple iPhones:* MacRumors. "iPhone 5 edge of screen turning yellow?" MacRumors, March 25,
2014. https://forums.macrumors.com/threads/iphone-5-edge-of-screen-turning-yellow.1719879/

229   *Microsoft Surface Books:* iFixIt. "Yellow streak around edge of screen." iFixit, July 26, 2017. https://www.ifixit.com/Answers/View/414634/Yellow+streak+around+edge+of+screen

229   *what if a website:* Tesla Motors Club. "Tesla blames MCU resets on Tesla Waze Website." Teslamotorsclub.com, May 24, 2018. https://teslamotorsclub.com/tmc/threads/tesla-blames-mcu-resets-on-tesla-waze-website.116126/

229   *or a software update:* Tesla Motors Club. "48.12.1 = Daily MCU Crash." Teslamotorsclub.com, January 2, 2019. https://teslamotorsclub.com/tmc/threads/48-12-1-daily-mcu-crash.139405/

229   *a website made your odometer fail:* Tesla Motors Club. "Advice on ICU / MCU issues (S90D 2017)." Teslamotorsclub.com, May 16, 2018. https://teslamotorsclub.com/tmc/threads/advice-on-icu-mcu-issues-s90d-2017.115458/

230   *"we've got people, like, writing apps for the car":* Sival Teokal. "Elon Musk takes first Model S buyer for a spin (2009)." YouTube video, June 30, 2015. https://youtu.be/1llEcjAIDjY

INDEX

ABOUT THE AUTHOR

Edward Niedermeyer has been investigating and analyzing the auto industry since 2008, and he is currently building a new online vertical for mobility technology coverage called Merge. His work has been published in the *New York Times, Wall Street Journal,* Bloomberg View, The Daily Beast, Quartz, The Verge, and elsewhere. With Alex Roy and Kirsten Korosec, Edward cohosts *The Autonocast,* a podcast about autonomous cars, automated driving, and the future of mobility. He lives in Portland with his partner and two cats, and spends what little free time he has hiking, camping, and ski touring.